The Genealogist's Internet

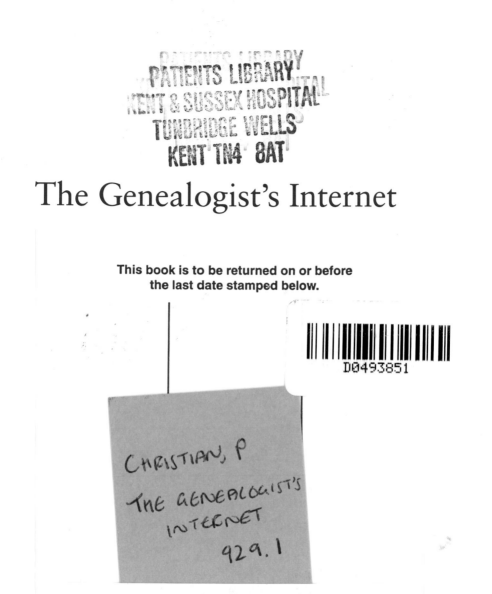

The Genealogist's Internet

Peter Christian

PUBLIC RECORD OFFICE

Public Record Office
Kew
Richmond
Surrey TW9 4DU

First published 2001
Reprinted with corrections 2002

ISBN 1 903365 16 3

British Library Cataloguing-in-Publication Data
A catalogue record for this book is available from the British Library

Front cover, from top: the Reverend John Eliot, 1990 (PRO COPY 1/402; photographer Richard Michael Latham, Stroud); 1891 cenus return for West Newton, Norfolk (PRO RG 12/1564); baby in bath, 1884 (PRO COPY 1/370; photograper Henry Johnson, Wood Green); marriage of Alexander McCurry and Charlotte King, 1919 (author's photograph); Sergeant Frederick Marshall of the Queen's Royal (West Surrey) Regiment, c. 1915 (author's photograph); Richard Hodgson, 1907 (PRO COPY 1/515; photographers William Cheetham and James Whittaker, Blackburn); the Countess of Dudley, 1891 (PRO COPY 1/406; photographer Hayman Seleg Mendelson, Bayswater). While every effort has been made to trace the copyright holders, this has not always proved possible because of the antiquity of the images.

Printed in the United Kingdom by Cromwell Press, Trowbridge, Wiltshire

To the memory of
Douglas Godfrey Christian
1923–1974

See the web site for this book at

<www.spub.co.uk/protgi/>

The site includes links to all resources mentioned in the text.

Contents

Preface

One difficulty with any book on the internet and genealogy is deciding what knowledge to presuppose in the reader. I have assumed a reader who is already connected to the internet and is familiar with e-mail and a web browser, but I have not assumed any further internet expertise. For that reason there is detailed discussion of search engines, mailing lists and newsgroups in the later chapters, material which will be familiar to seasoned internet users but which, experience suggests, the relative beginner does not often make the most of. I have not assumed expert knowledge of genealogy, but a thorough genealogy tutorial is beyond the scope of this book. Internet resources for the novice genealogist are mentioned in Chapter 2 but if you are completely, or fairly, new to family history you'll need a good book on off-line genealogy (see p. 9 for recommendations).

It would be impossible here to thank all those who over the years have drawn my attention to particular resources mentioned in the text, or discussed the virtues or otherwise of particular uses of the internet for genealogy. But among those who have frequently alerted me to new web sites are the contributors to *Computers in Genealogy*, particularly David Squire in his regular 'Web Watch' column, and my fellow Genuki maintainers. Eric Probert's 'Computer Intelligence' in *Family Tree Magazine* and Dick Eastman's on-line newsletter have also been invaluable over the years.

I would like to thank David Hawgood and Roland Clare for helpful comments on the draft text.

Particular thanks are due to the Genuki volunteers and Cyndi Howells for creating and maintaining sites which not only saved me a lot of work, but which I have been able to direct readers to again and again for further resources.

Internet addresses

In this book URLs (Uniform Resource Locators) for internet resources have been placed between angled brackets. According to strict citation standards, every resource should begin with a specification of its type: the Public Record Office's home page on the World Wide Web should be cited as **<http://www.pro.gov.uk/>** rather than simply as **<www.pro.gov.uk>**

and all e-mail addresses should begin **<mailto:…>**. However, since browsers manage perfectly well without the '**http//:**', and the @ sign readily identifies e-mail addresses as such, I have allowed myself to omit these. Newsgroup names are discussed in Chapter 10: although they look similar to web page addresses, either the context or the word newsgroup in the text will identify them correctly.

Any hyphen within a URL is part of the reference, not a typographical nicety. There are *never* spaces or line breaks in internet addresses.

Addresses for web pages are *partially* case sensitive. Anything up to the first / is not case sensitive; anything after it must be in the correct case. Usually URLs are all lower case, but note that Genuki in particular uses upper case for county abbreviations (e.g. LAN in all the Lancashire pages) and often has the first letter after a / in upper case.

In general, titles of web sites have been indicated solely by initial capitals, while individual pages are between inverted commas. However, the distinction between a site and page is not always easy to make, and it is difficult to be thoroughly consistent in this respect.

Caveat

Internet resources are in a constant state of flux: official and commercial sites are regularly being redesigned or even reorganized; personal sites are liable to move without warning or even disappear entirely. While print is unable to cope with this, and it is something all internet books have to live with, links to all the resources mentioned in the text are on the web site for this book at **<www.spub.co.uk/protgi/>**, and the aim to is to keep those links up to date.

Since the first printing of this book, a number of sites and pages have disappeared entirely:

- Excite UK (pp. 25ff.) has closed, and the US equivalent at **<www.excite.com>** is of little use to British genealogists. The nearest equivalent is the Open Directory's UK genealogy page at **<dmoz.org/Regional/Europe/United_Kingdom/Society_and_Culture/Genealogy/>**.
- The FRC home page hosted by the PRO (p. 58) no longer exists. However, all the relevant information can be found via the links from **<www.familyrecords.gov.uk/frc.htm>**.
- The History of the British Armed Forces site (p. 88) has closed down.
- The Canadian Forces College's page for military museums (p. 89) has been removed.
- Sheila Webber's collection of links to search engine reviews (p. 154) has been removed.

A few large sites – the British Library, the BBC, and Channel 4 – have undergone significant reorganization, with many pages being moved. Unfortunately these particular sites do not redirect you automatically to the new location of the pages, so go to **<www.spub.co.uk/protgi/>** for up-to-date links rather than typing those given in the text.

At the beginning of March 2002, AltaVista changed its default search option from OR to AND, which means that the figures on p. 147 are no longer accurate for AltaVista's default search, though they are still representative of a typical OR search.

In some cases, a URL has been so long that I have given instructions on how to get to the page rather than give the full URL – on the web site for this book the direct link is usually available, except where this would bypass a page the site-owner needs you to see first.

1 Introduction

The steady growth in the number of people interested in family history may have its roots in greater leisure time, may be a reaction to social and geographical mobility, may even be a response to recent television programmes, but above all it is closely related to the growth of the internet and widening access to it. While the internet has not changed the fundamental principles of genealogical research, it has changed the way in which some of that research is done and what it is possible for the individual genealogist to do with ease.

Transcriptions of primary records, or at least indexes to them, are increasingly available on the internet, and even where records themselves are not on-line the ability to check the holdings of record offices and libraries off-line means that a visit can be better prepared and more productive. Those who have previously made little progress with their family tree because they have lacked the time or mobility to visit archives can pursue their researches much more conveniently, with access to at least some records from their desktop. Likewise, those who live on the other side of the world from the repositories where records of their ancestors' lives are stored can make progress without having to employ a researcher. On-line data is a boon, too, for those who have difficulty reading from microfilm or original records.

Archives have realized that the internet is also a remedy for some of their pressing problems: lack of space on their premises, how to make their collections accessible while preserving them from damage, and the increasing pressure from government to provide wider access to services. In addition, there is the obvious commercial potential: on-line record transcriptions can attract distant and, particularly, overseas users in large numbers, while even those living less far away will use a charged service which saves them time and travel costs.

Genealogists also benefit from the ease with which messages and electronic documents can be exchanged around the world at effectively no cost. It is easier than ever to contact people with similar research interests, and even distant cousins. It is easier than ever, away from a good genealogy library or bookshop, to find expertise or help with some genealogical problem. And if you need to buy a book, there are genealogy bookshops with on-line catalogues and secure ordering.

The fact that any information stored digitally, whether text or image, can be published on the Web easily and more or less free of cost to both publisher and user, has revolutionized the publishing of pedigrees and other family history information. It has allowed individuals to publish small transcriptions from individual records, material which it would otherwise be difficult to make widely available. Individual family historians can publicize their interests and publish the fruits of their researches to millions of others.

The internet has enhanced cooperation by making it possible for widely separated people to communicate easily as a group. While collaborative projects did not start with the internet, the internet makes the coordination of vast numbers of geographically distributed volunteers, such as the 1,500 or so involved in FreeBMD (see p. 32), much easier.

Inevitably, however, the explosion of the internet and what it has made possible for family historians has given rise to unrealistic expectations in some quarters. Stories of messages posted to mailing lists or newsgroups asking, 'Where will I find my family tree on-line?' are not apocryphal.

The fact is that if you are only beginning your family tree, you will have plenty to do off-line before you can take full advantage of what is on-line. For a start, because of privacy concerns, you won't find much information about any ancestors born in the 20th century available on-line, except for addresses, phone numbers and perhaps web sites of living people. Specifically, the birth and marriage records for the last 100 years, without which you will probably not be able to get further back, are not available on-line and are not likely to be, even when there is nothing else left to digitize. And you shouldn't expect to be able to interview your granny by webcam.

Even if you are not going to find all the original records you need on-line, you can still expect to make contact with other genealogists who share your interests. But to make the most of this you will need to have done your own off-line research into recent generations. The reason is that if you're going to discover others on the internet who have done research into your ancestors, they are not likely to be close relations (if they were you'd surely know about them already through your family). Relatives discovered via the internet will be at best third cousins, i.e. descendants of your great-great-grandparents who were born perhaps 100 or so years before you. Unless you know the names of your great-great-grandparents and where they came from, you will not be in a position to establish that you are in fact related to someone who has posted their pedigree on-line.

Of course, if your surname is unusual, and particularly if you know that earlier generations of your family lived in a particular place, you may be able to make contact with someone researching your surname and be reasonably certain that you are related. Or you may be lucky enough to find that someone is doing a one-name study of your surname. In this case, they may already have extracted some or all of the relevant entries in the civil registration records, and indeed may have already been able to link up many of the individuals recorded.

But, in general, you will need to do work off-line before you can expect to find primary source material on-line and before you have enough information to start establishing contact with distant relatives.

However, one thing that is useful to every on-line genealogist is the wealth of general genealogical information and the huge range of expertise embodied in the on-line community. For the beginner, the internet is useful not because there is lots of material on-line, but because there are many places to turn to for help and advice. And this is particularly important for those who live a long way away from their ancestral homes.

All the same, it is important to remember that, whatever and whoever you discover on-line, there are many other sources for family history, both in print and in manuscript, which aren't on-line. If you restrict yourself to on-line sources you may be able to construct a basic pedigree, but you will be seeing only the outline of your family's history. On the other hand, if you are one of those who refuses on principle to use the internet (and who is presumably reading this by accident), you are just making your research into your family history much harder than it need be.

History

With the rapid rate at which new developments are taking place, and the relative novelty of the World Wide Web (which has only been widely used beyond a circle of computer buffs for perhaps four or five years), on-line genealogy might seem to be a new development, but in fact it has quite a history and a number of distinct historical sources.

On the internet itself, on-line genealogy started in the early 1980s with the newsgroup net.roots (which became soc.roots and eventually spawned all the genealogy newsgroups discussed in Chapter 10), and with the ROOTS-L mailing list (which gave rise to RootsWeb **<www.rootsweb. com>**, the oldest on-line genealogy co-operative).[1] But in that period internet access was largely confined to academics and the computer industry, so for many people on-line genealogy meant bulletin boards run by volunteers from their home computers and accessible via a modem and phone line. A system called FidoNet allowed messages and files to be transferred around the world, albeit slowly as each bulletin board called up its neighbour to pass messages on. The only commercial forums were the growing on-line services which originally targeted computer professionals and those in business, but which gradually attracted a more

---

[1] For a history of the newsgroups, see Margaret J. Olson, 'Historical Reflections of the Genealogy Newsgroups' at **<homepages.rootsweb.com/~socgen/Newshist. htm>**. For the history of ROOTS-L and RootsWeb, see **<www.rootsweb.com/ roots-l/>**.

disparate membership. Of these, CompuServe, with its Roots forum, was the most important. One significant feature of these commercial services was the ability to access them from all over the world, in many cases with only a local call, which we now take for granted.

These systems had the basis of what genealogists now use the internet for: conversing with other genealogists and accessing centrally stored files. But the amount of data available was very small and discussion was the main motivation. Part of this was down to technical limitations: with modem speeds a 50th of what we now take for granted, transferring large amounts of data was unrealistic except for the few with deep pockets or an internet connection at work. No government agencies or family history societies had even contemplated an on-line presence, though computer groups were starting to spring up by the end of the 1980s.

What changed this was the World Wide Web, created in 1991 (though it was 1995 before it started to dominate the internet), and the growth of commercial internet services. The innovation of the Web made it possible for a large collection of material to remain navigable, even for the technologically illiterate, while the explosion in public use of the internet drove the requirement for it to be more user friendly.

While the overall picture is therefore very positive, this is not to say that there are no outstanding issues and problems in using the internet, as it is now, for genealogy. Some of these are discussed in the final chapter.

Nevertheless, the result of the developments described above is that, just as computers had done in the 1980s and microfilms before that, the internet is now driving developments in access to genealogical information, which in turn is drawing more people to start researching their family tree.

2 First Steps

What your first steps in on-line genealogy are depends on how much research you have already done on your family tree, and what your aim is.

If you are just beginning your family history, it is best to regard the internet initially as a source of help and contacts rather than as a source of genealogical information about your most recent forebears. The box below gives a simplified outline of the process of constructing a family tree, which is the foundation on which your family history will be built.

1. Interview your elderly relatives and collect as much first- or second-hand information as you can. (Continue doing so, as you find out more in subsequent steps.)
2. Get marriage and birth certificates for your most recently deceased ancestors.
3. From these, work back to the marriages, and then births of the parents of those ancestors.
4. Keep repeating this process until you get back to the beginning of general registration.
5. Once you have names and either places or actual addresses for a date in the 19th century, refer to the census to see:
   (a) whole family groups
   (b) birthplaces and approximate birth years.
6. Once you have found in the census an adult ancestor who seems to have been born before general registration, use the birthplace and date information in the census to locate his or her baptism in a parish register.
7. From this, work back to the marriages, and then baptisms, of the parents of that ancestor in parish registers.
8. Repeat these steps for all your lines of ancestry until you hit a brick wall.

The first three steps can't be done on-line, and it's only once you get back 100 years that you will start to find significant amounts of source material on the internet. Having done your first century the 'hard' way, you will also have a much better understanding of what's involved in constructing a family tree. The material in the 'Tutorials' and 'Getting help' sections below should help you get going.

If you are not new to family history, but have just started to use the internet, your needs will be rather different. Since you will already be familiar with civil registration and census records and know what is involved in researching your family tree, your basic questions will be: What's on-line and where do I find it? Who else is working on my family?

Chapter 3 looks at sites that provide collections of links to genealogy resources, while the two subsequent chapters look at on-line records and the web sites of archives, etc. Chapters 7, 8 and 9 look at internet resources relating to particular aspects of genealogy, while Chapter 11 covers general techniques for finding web sites that have specific information. For making contact with others, look at Chapters 6 and 10.

Whatever stage you are at, it will be worth looking at the discussion groups in Chapter 10, and the information on records and repositories in Chapters 4 and 5.

Tutorials

While the internet cannot match the wealth of introductory books for family historians that will be found in print, there is quite a range of material covering the basics of genealogical research in the British Isles.

The main source for such materials is Genuki which has a page devoted to 'Getting Started in Genealogy and Family History' at **<www.genuki.org. uk/gs/>**. There are individual pages on major topics, such as that for 'Civil Registration in England and Wales' at **<www.genuki.org.uk/big/eng/ civreg/>**.

Genuki is host to three guides for beginners:

- Roy Stockdill's 'Newbies' Guide to Genealogy and Family History' at **<www.genuki.org.uk/gs/Newbie.html>**
- Jeanne Bunting's 'What is Genealogy' at **<www.genuki.org.uk/gs/ Bunting.html>**
- Dr Ashton Emery's 'A-Z Of British Genealogical Research' at **<www. genuki.org.uk/big/EmeryPaper.html>**, presented as a dictionary rather than a connected account.

Genuki also has links to other introductory materials.

The Public Record Office (PRO) has extensive introductory material on its web site. The 'Education' area of the site at **<www.pro.gov.uk/ education/>** links to 'The Learning Curve', which has material for use within the National Curriculum, while 'Pathways to the Past' includes material for grown-ups on local and family history. The family history section has pages devoted to the following topics:

Naming Names and Tracing Places
- Civil Registration
- Stand Up and Be Counted
- What About Births, Marriages and Deaths Before 1837?
- Dissenting Voices
- Britons Born, Married or Dying on Board Ship
- Wills and Death Duty Registers
- Finding Taxpayers
- Ancestors as Investors
- Oath Rolls
- Timeline

People at Work
- Apprentices
- Police
- Customs and Excise
- Coastguards
- Lawyers in the Family
- Other Records about People at Work

The Army and Navy
- Soldiers' Papers
- Tracing Army Officers
- Regimental Diaries
- War Medals
- The British Army Before the First World War
- The Royal Navy: Officers
- Tracing Ratings
- Merchant Seamen
- Crew Lists
- Log Books
- Timeline
- Migrant Ancestors

Migrant Ancestors
- Migrant Ancestors
- Movements of the Poor
- Britons Abroad
- Children on the Move
- Wartime Evacuees
- Immigrants to Britain
- Refugees
- Ships' Passenger Lists

Ancestors and the Law
- Name Changes

- Bankrupts
- Criminal Courts
- Prisoners and Transportation
- Licences and Pardons
- Cases in Chancery
- The Court of Requests

The Society of Genealogists (SoG) has a number of leaflets on-line at <www.sog.org.uk/leaflets/>. Though they are not designed as a coherent introduction to family history, they include 'Starting genealogy' and 'Note taking and keeping for genealogists'. The Federation of Family History Societies (FFHS) has a number of on-line leaflets at <www.ffhs.org.uk/General/Help/>, including 'First Steps in Family History'.

Both the BBC and Channel 4 have introductory material relating to recent television series on family history:

- For the BBC's *Blood Ties* series: 'How to Get Started in Genealogy' at <www.bbc.co.uk/history/programmes/blood/family_1.shtml>
- For Channel 4's *Extraordinary Ancestors* series: <www.channel4.com/nextstep/geno/>.

The Church of Jesus Christ of Latter-day Saints (LDS) has extensive introductory material on its FamilySearch web site at <www.familysearch.org/Eng/Search/RG/frameset_rg.asp> (or go to the home page at <www.familysearch.org> and select Search, then Research Guidance). There are separate 'Search Strategy' pages for England, Wales, Scotland and Ireland. Each of these has links to material on looking for birth, marriages and deaths in the three main periods for genealogical research: general registration, parish registers, and before parish registers (see Figure 2.1). Clicking on the 'For Beginners' tab will take you to general material on:

- Organizing your paper files
- How to find the name of the place where your ancestor lived
- How to find information about the place where your ancestor lived
- How to find maps
- How to find compiled sources

The *Irish Times'* Irish Ancestors site has an excellent range of introductory material relating to Ireland at <scripts.ireland.com/ancestor/browse/index.htm>, including information on the counties and emigration (see Chapter 7) and good pages on the various Irish genealogical records.

Cyndi's List has a 'Beginners' page at <www.CyndisList.com/beginner.htm>, and a collection of links on 'Researching: Localities & Ethnic Groups' which will be useful if you need to start looking for ancestors outside the UK and Ireland. Cyndi's 'How to: tutorials and guides' page at <**www.CyndisList.com/howtotut.htm**> provides an outline of all the introductory materials on six major genealogy sites. All these sites are US-based, so much of the material on specific records will not be of use unless you are tracing American ancestors. However, this page should help you find some of the more general information buried in these sites.

About.com has much tutorial material at <**genealogy.about.com/ hobbies/genealogy**>, including 'Top Ten Genealogy Mistakes to Avoid'.

If you are trying to research ancestry in the British Isles from abroad, Genuki's 'Researching From Abroad' page at <**www.genuki.org.uk/ab/**> will be useful. The SoG has a leaflet 'Notes for Americans on tracing their British ancestry' on-line at <**www.sog.org.uk/leaflets/americans.html**>. Mark Howells 'Guide to Researching Ancestors from the United Kingdom using the LDS Family History Center Resources' at <**www.oz.net/ ~markhow/uksearch.htm**> will also be useful. If you are unfamiliar with the administrative subdivision of Britain into counties and parishes, you should consult Jim Fisher's page 'British Counties, Parishes, etc. for Genealogists' at <**homepages.nildram.co.uk/~jimella/counties.htm**> and Genuki's pages on 'Administrative Regions of the British Isles' <**www.genuki.org.uk/ big/Regions/index.html**>.

Figure 2.1 FamilySearch's Research Guidance page on looking for English Deaths in the period 1538–1837 at <www.familysearch.org>

Getting help

Even with these tutorial materials, you may still have a question you can't find an answer to.

One solution is to use a search engine to find pages devoted to a particular topic (see Chapter 11). However, this can be quite time consuming as you may end up following quite a few links that turn out to be useless before you find what you are looking for.

The various discussion forums discussed in Chapter 10 are ideal places for getting help and advice. But before posting a query to one of these, make sure you read the FAQ (Frequently Asked Questions) – see p. 136. There are a number of lists for beginners, notably GEN-NEWBIE-L 'where people who are new to computers and genealogy may interact'. Information on how to join this list will be found at **<www.rootsweb.com/~jfuller/ gen_mail_info.html>**, and past messages are archived at **<archiver.rootsweb. com/th/index/GEN-NEWBIE>**. However, you should be warned that this is a very busy list with an average of over 50 messages a day.

Ask a Librarian' is an 'on-line reference service' run by CoEast, a public library consortium, at **<www.ask-a-librarian.org.uk>**. You can e-mail a question and you will get a reply within two working days. Before asking a family history question, consult the 'tips on asking your question' page, and don't expect them to search original records on your behalf to find your great grandparents' wedding.

However, there is one really important step that will save you a lot of this trouble: get a good book on family history. If you are a relative beginner, you might start with Anthony J. Camp's *First Steps in Family History*, or the Reader's Digest volume *Explore Your Family's Past*; if you have already made some progress, Mark Herber's *Ancestral Trails* should be on your bookshelf. Contrary to the hype, the internet has not made such publications redundant. There is a lot of good reference material on the internet, and an increasing amount of primary data, but tutorial material is still relatively underdeveloped despite all the sites listed in this chapter.

3 On-line Starting Points

Subsequent chapters in this book are devoted to particular types of genealogical resource or internet tools. This one looks at some of the on-line starting points for genealogy on the internet: sites which provide links to other resources. These go under various names: directory, gateway or portal.

- An internet directory is the electronic equivalent of the Yellow Pages, a list of resources categorized under a number of subject headings.
- A gateway is a directory devoted to a single subject, and may also offer knowledgeable annotation of the links provided as well as additional background information. A gateway is not just a directory; it can be more like a handbook.
- A portal is a site which aims to provide a single jumping-off point on the internet for a particular audience, bringing together all the resources they might be interested in. Like a gateway, a portal may provide information as well as links.

In genealogy, since the audience is defined by its interest in a particular subject, it is not always possible to maintain a clear distinction between gateways and portals. 'Portal' tends to be the preferred term in the case of a site which has some official status or which aims to be definitive. Both gateways and portals tend to be selective and only include links to recommended resources, whereas directories tend to be all-encompassing. (The term 'gateway' is also used in a quite different sense, see p. 133.)

Directories, gateways and portals are not the only way to find information on the internet: general-purpose search engines such as Google **<www.google.com>** and AltaVista **<www.altavista.com>**, discussed in Chapter 11, can also be used to find genealogical material on-line. The differences between directories, gateways and portals on the one hand and search engines on the other are discussed in detail on p. 143. The most important is that directories etc. provide lists of web *sites* while search engines locate individual web *pages*, so the former are better for locating significant resources on a particular topic rather than mere mentions of a subject. This makes them preferable for initial exploration. The fact that the entries are selected, and perhaps helpfully annotated makes

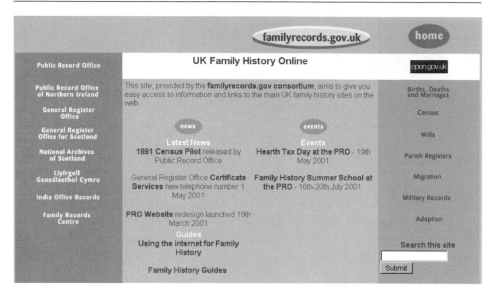

Figure 3.1 The FamilyRecords portal <www.familyrecords.gov.uk>

them even more useful. However, there are certain things they are poor for, notably information published on the personal web sites of individual family historians.

The British Isles

There are two on-line starting points which are essential for British genealogy: the FamilyRecords portal, which is the government's gateway to official web sites of use to family historians; and Genuki, which aims to be comprehensive in its coverage of sites relating to genealogy in the British Isles. In addition, there are a number of other official and unofficial sites which provide starting points for exploring specifically British and Irish internet resources. Sites linking to more general resources are discussed later in this chapter (p. 25).

FamilyRecords

The FamilyRecords portal at <**www.familyrecords.gov.uk**> (Figure 3.1) is run by a consortium made up of the Public Record Office, Public Record Office of Northern Ireland, National Archives of Scotland, the National Library of Wales, the General Register Office, the General Register Office for Scotland and the British Library India Office, and aims to provide links to the web sites of these bodies and to official information. FamilyRecords provides basic information about the major national repositories, including contact details and links to their web sites. There are also brief descriptions of the main types of public record, with links to the bodies that hold them. Although deliberately limited in scope, it provides a good way of locating specific material on the official web sites. The web sites of the individual bodies linked to the FamilyRecords portal are discussed under 'Civil registration' in Chapter 4 (p. 30 ff.) and under 'National archives' in Chapter 5 (p. 58 ff.).

UKonline
While the FamilyRecords portal is restricted to genealogical coverage, there is also a general-purpose official gateway called UKonline at <www.ukonline.gov.uk>.[2] This replaced the government's original gateway at <www.open.gov.uk> in summer 2001. UKonline provides access to all government information on-line, with links to all branches of local and national government. It therefore covers local authorities, county record offices and the like, which are not linked from FamilyRecords. There is a search facility as well as alphabetical indexes of national and local government services.

There is an unofficial directory of government sites at Tagish <www.tagish. co.uk/links/>, which is in some ways easier to use than UKonline.

Ireland
Obviously there is no link from FamilyRecords to official bodies in the Republic of Ireland. However, Genuki, described in the next section, has a comprehensive collection of links to Irish material on-line at <www. genuki.org.uk/big/irl/> and the Irish Ancestors site has links to the major Irish bodies with genealogical material at <scripts.ireland.com/ancestor/ browse/links/libraries.htm>. Irish libraries and archives are covered in Chapter 5, while Irish civil registration is covered in Chapter 4.

Genuki
The most comprehensive collection of on-line information about family history for the British Isles, with an unrivalled collection of links, is Genuki, the 'UK & Ireland Genealogical Service'. Genuki describes itself as 'a virtual reference library of genealogical information that is of particular relevance to the UK & Ireland.' As a reference source, the material it contains 'relates to primary historical material, rather than material resulting from genealogists' ongoing research.' This means it is really a handbook of British and Irish genealogy on-line. But Genuki also functions as a gateway, simply because it has links to an enormous number of on-line resources for the UK and Ireland, including every genealogical organization with a web site.

Genuki has its origins in the efforts of a group of volunteers, centred on Brian Randell at the University of Newcastle and Phil Stringer at the University of Manchester, to set up a web site for genealogical information

---

[2] The 'UKonline' (one word) web site is not to be confused with the Internet Service Provider UK Online (two words).

in 1994 when the World Wide Web was still very young. Genuki has always been an entirely non-commercial and volunteer-run organization; all the pages are maintained by a group of about 50 volunteers on many different web sites, mostly at UK universities or on the personal sites of the volunteers. Many other individuals have provided information and transcripts of primary data. Genuki started as an entirely informal group, but is now a charitable trust.

There are two distinct parts to Genuki.

First, there are a number of pages devoted to general information about family history in the British Isles:

- Frequently Asked Questions (FAQs) – typical queries asked by Genuki users.
- Getting started in genealogy – a range of beginners' guides (or links to them). See 'Tutorials' on p. 6.
- Pages devoted to individual general topics, such as 'Military Records' or 'Immigration and Emigration', all linked from **<www.genuki.org. uk/big/>** (many of these are mentioned in this book).
- Researching from abroad – useful links for those who dwell outside the UK, especially in North America.
- World genealogy – a small collection of links for those researching non-British ancestry.
- Genealogical events relating to UK and Ireland Ancestry (see p. 182).
- Information on Genuki itself – how it is run, the principles on which it is structured.

🖳 United Kingdom
and Ireland

Contents
& Search 📰

**UK & Ireland
Genealogy**

| Guidance for
First-Time Users
of These Pages | | Guidance for
Potential Contributors
to These Pages |

| **Enter this large collection of genealogical information pages for
England, Ireland, Scotland, Wales, the Channel Islands, and the Isle of Man.**		
Getting started in genealogy	Frequently Asked Questions
(FAQs)	Researching UK and Irish genealogy from
abroad
World genealogy, newsgroups and bulletin
boards, etc.	Recent changes to these pages	Upcoming UK & Ireland Genealogical events
(GENEVA)

To report errors found in these pages, please use this list of GENUKI maintainers in order to find the appropriate email
address.

Note: The information provided by GENUKI must not be used for commercial purposes, and all specific
restrictions concerning usage, copyright notices, etc., that are to be found on individual information pages
within GENUKI must be strictly adhered to. Violation of these rules could gravely harm the cooperation that
GENUKI is obtaining from many information providers, and hence threaten its whole future.

Figure 3.2 The Genuki home page <www.genuki.org.uk>

Second, it provides material and links to on-line resources for all the constituent parts of the British Isles, with pages for:

- England, Wales, Scotland, Ireland, the Isle of Man and the Channel Islands
- Every individual county in these areas
- Many individual towns and parishes

The county pages provide links to the web sites of:

- County record offices and other repositories of interest to family historians (see Chapter 5)
- Local family history societies (see Chapter 13)
- County mailing lists (see Chapter 10)
- County surname lists (see Chapter 6), and
- Other on-line resources relating to genealogy in the county

There are also central listings of:

- National genealogical organizations and local family history societies at **<www.genuki.org.uk/Societies/>**
- All mailing lists relevant to British genealogy at **<www.genuki.org.uk/ indexes/MailingLists.html>**
- All county and other surname lists at **<www.genuki.org.uk/indexes/ SurnamesLists.html>**

Most material on Genuki will be found on these geographical pages, which are organized hierarchically. Figure 3.3 shows a diagram of the hierarchy.

Because of the enormous amount of material on Genuki, it is well worth taking the time to look at the 'Guidance for First-Time Users of These Pages' **<www.genuki.org.uk/org/>**, which gives an outline of what Genuki is. There is a more detailed on-line user guide 'How the information on this server is presented to the user' at **<www.genuki.org.uk/org/user.html>**.

A particular virtue of Genuki is that it uses well-defined subject categories, which are based on those used in the LDS Church's library catalogue and have therefore been designed by genealogically aware librarians. Its coherent coverage of every county, with a long-term aim of covering every parish, is the other feature which makes it useful. The list of categories used on Genuki is shown in Table 3.1.

Some of these categories (for example handwriting, politics and government) will be relevant only at the top levels, but topics such as church records, local records and maps should be represented on every county page. Since the list pre-dates the internet, there are no specific categories for internet-related subjects such as surname lists and mailing lists, so Genuki places these under the Genealogy heading.

The Structure of GENUKI.

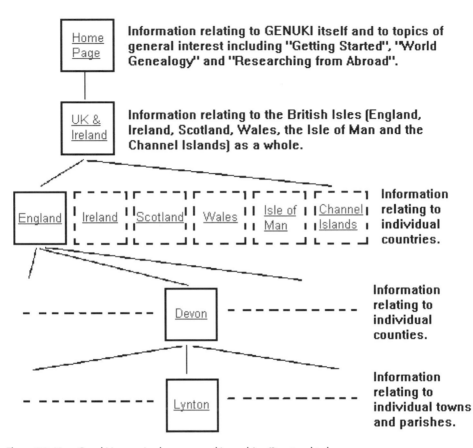

Figure 3.3 How Genuki is organized <www.genuki.org.uk/org/Structure.html>

Once you are familiar with how Genuki is organized, there are other quick ways to get where you want to go. The 'List of Genuki Contents Pages' at **<www.genuki.org.uk/mindex.html>** has links to outline pages for the contents of each county page. These pages lack any description of the material they link to, so they are not intended for beginners or those new to Genuki, but they can provide a quick way of getting to specific material that you know is there.

For a detailed guide to Genuki there is a book, simply called *Genuki*, by David Hawgood, one the Genuki trustees, published by the FFHS. The complete text is available on-line at **<www.hawgood.co.uk/genuki/>**.

Genuki also has a search facility at **<www.genuki.org.uk/search.html>**, discussed on p. 158.

Because Genuki is very comprehensive, it can be easy to overlook the fact that there are some things it does not do. First, it has some deliberate

Table 3.1 Genuki subject headings

Almanacs	Merchant Marine
Archives and Libraries	Migration, Internal
Bibliography	Military History
Biography	Military Records
Business and Commerce Records	Minorities
Cemeteries	(*Monumental Inscriptions – see*
Census	*Cemeteries*)
Chronology	Names, Geographical
Church Directories	Names, Personal
Church History	Naturalization and Citizenship
Church Records	Newspapers
Civil Registration	Nobility
Colonization	Obituaries
Correctional Institutions	Occupations
Court Records	Officials and Employees
Description and Travel	Orphans and Orphanages
Directories	(*Parish Registers – see Church*
Dwellings	*Records*)
Emigration and Immigration	Pensions
Encyclopaedias and Dictionaries	Periodicals
Ethnology	Politics and Government
Folklore	Poorhouses, Poor Law, etc.
Gazetteers	Population
Genealogy	Postal and Shipping Guides
Guardianship	Probate Records
Handwriting	Public Records
Heraldry	Religion and Religious Life
Historical Geography	Schools
History	Social Life and Customs
Inventories, Registers, Catalogues	Societies
Jewish History	Statistics
Jewish Records	Taxation
Land and Property	Town Records
Language and Languages	Visitations, Heraldic
Law and Legislation	(*Vital Records – see Civil*
Manors	*Registration*)
Maps	Voting Registers
Medical Records	Yearbooks

limitations in its linking policy. It does not link to sites which provide information only on an individual family, pedigree or surname. It does not link to commercial sites, unless they also offer useful information free of charge. And finally, if obviously, its links are strictly confined to sites which are relevant to UK and Ireland genealogy. However, as long as what you are looking for is available on-line and falls within Genuki's scope you should expect to find it listed.

Another service Genuki does not provide is answering genealogical queries from individuals. There is a Genuki e-mail address, but this is intended only for reporting errors on the site or drawing attention to new resources not listed on Genuki. See 'Getting help' on p. 10 and Chapter 10 for places to post genealogical queries.

UK Genealogy gateway

The UK Genealogy gateway at **<www.ukgenealogy.co.uk>** is organized in a similar way to Genuki, though it has a more limited amount of material. There are pages for England, Wales, Scotland and Ireland, and a page for each county, giving details of:

- Archives and libraries
- Registration offices
- Local societies
- Mailing lists
- Surname lists
- Lookup exchanges
- Professional researchers
- Useful links

'Essential Web Sites'

The SoG has a small but useful page of 'Essential Web Sites' at **<www.sog.org.uk/links.html>**. While it only has about three dozen links, these cover the core web sites in the following categories:

- General genealogical sites
- Governmental repositories
- Libraries and other national repositories
- Other organizations
- Major on-line data collections

General genealogy gateways

If you have ancestors who lived outside the British Isles you will need to look at some of the general genealogy directories and gateways. And even if all your ancestors were British or Irish, there are good reasons to use other gateways and directories. Since FamilyRecords and Genuki take a strictly geographical approach, you need to look elsewhere for genealogical resources, such as computer software, which are not tied to a particular country or region.

Cyndi's List

The most comprehensive genealogy gateway is Cyndi's List at <www.cyndislist.com>, maintained by Cyndi Howells. You can get an idea of the scope of the list, which has over 100,000 links as of summer 2001, from the 140 or so main categories in Table 3.2.

Unlike Genuki (p. 13) or Yahoo (p. 25), Cyndi's List has a fairly flat structure: most of these headings lead to a single page, while a few act as indexes to a whole group of pages on their subject (these have the word 'index' in their title). So, for example, the main UK page at <www.CyndisList. com/uksites.htm> acts simply as an index to the sub-pages devoted to the various parts of the British Isles, to general UK sites and to British military sites. The advantage of this flat structure is that you don't have go deep into a hierarchy to find what you're looking for; the disadvantage is that the individual pages tend to be quite large and can take a while to download.

However, alongside the main home page, Cyndi provides other, quicker ways to get to where you want once you are familiar with the site. There are four other 'home pages':

- The 'No Frills' index at <www.CyndisList.com/nofrills.htm> is essentially the home page, but with just the headings – no descriptions or update information, and no cross references.
- The 'Alphabetical Category' index at <www.CyndisList.com/alpha.htm> is a complete list of all pages and sub-pages in alphabetical order, with cross references.
- The 'Topical Category' index at <www.CyndisList.com/topical.htm> lists all categories under 11 main headings (Localities, Ethnic Groups and People, Religions, Records, Research Tools and Reference Materials, Help from Others, Marketplace, History, Military, Internet Tools for Genealogy, Miscellaneous).
- The 'Text Only Category' index at <www.CyndisList.com/textonly.htm>.

Once you are familiar with the List, it is much quicker to use these alternative entry points – the main home page is over 120k, while these are under 40k. The smallest is the text-only page at about 30k.

Another way to speed up access to Cyndi's List is to save a copy of the home page to your own hard disk. You will find that clicking on the links from this copy (assuming you are on-line!) will take you to the sub-page without having to wait while the main page loads over the Web. Obviously, you will need to check periodically that no new categories have been added to this top-level page, but the list is fairly well established and stable. It is also worth bookmarking any part of the site that you regularly refer to.

Table 3.2 Categories on Cyndi's List <www.cyndislist.com>

Acadian, Cajun and Creole
Adoption
African-American
America Online – AOL
Asia and the Pacific
Australia and New Zealand
Austria
The Baltic States – Estonia, Latvia
   and Lithuania
Baptist
Beginners
Belgium
Biographies
Births and Baptisms
Books
Calendars and Dates
Canada Index
Canals, Rivers and Waterways
Catholic
Cemeteries and Funeral Homes
Census-related Sites Worldwide
Chat and IRC
Citing Sources
City Directories
Clothing and Costumes
Correspondence
Cousins and Kinship
The Czech Republic and Slovakia
Databases, Search Sites, Surname
   Lists
Denmark
Diaries and Letters
Dictionaries and Glossaries
Eastern Europe
Education
England
Events and Activities
Family Bibles
Famous People
Female Ancestors
Finding People
Finland
France

Genealogy in the Media
Genealogy Standards and
   Guidelines
Germans from Russia
Germany/Deutschland
Greece
Handwriting and Script
Handy On-line Starting Points
Heraldry
Hispanic, Central and South
   America, and the West Indies
Historical Events and People
   Worldwide
Hit a Brick Wall?
House and Building Histories
How To
How To – Tutorials and Guides
Huguenot
Humour and Prose
Iceland
Immigration and Naturalization
Ireland and Northern Ireland
Italy/Italia
Jewish
Kids and Teens
Land Records, Deeds, Homesteads,
   etc.
Languages and Translations
LDS and Family History Centres
Libraries, Archives and Museums
Lookups and Free Searches by
   Volunteers
Lost and Found
Loyalists
Lutheran
Magazines, Journals, Columns and
   Newsletters
Mailing Lists
Maps, Gazetteers and
   Geographical Information
Marriages
Medical, Medicine, Genetics
Medieval

Table 3.2 cont.

Mennonite
Methodist
Microfilm and Microfiche
The Middle East
Military Resources Worldwide
Money
Myths, Hoaxes and Scams
Names
Native American
Netherlands/Nederland
Newsgroups
Newspapers
Norway
Novelties
Obituaries
Occupations
Odds and Ends
Oral History and Interviews
Organizing Your Research
Personal Home Pages
Photographs and Memories
Poland
Poorhouses and Poverty
Presbyterian
Primary Sources
Prisons, Prisoners and Outlaws
Professional Researchers,
    Volunteers and Other Research
    Services
Quaker
Queries and Message Boards
Railroads
Recipes, Cookbooks and Family
    Traditions

Religion and Churches
Reunions
ROOTS-L and RootsWeb
Royalty and Nobility
Scandinavia and the Nordic
    Countries
Schools
Scotland
Search Engines
Ships and Passenger Lists
Societies and Groups
Software and Computers
South Africa
Spain, Portugal and the Basque
    Country
Supplies, Charts, Forms, etc.
Surnames, Family Associations and
    Family Newsletters
Sweden
Switzerland
Taxes
Timelines
Travel and Research
Unique Peoples and Cultures
United Kingdom and Ireland Index
United States Index
Volunteer Online Regional Projects
Wales
Web Rings for Genealogy
Weights and Measures
Western Europe
Wills and Probate
Writing Your Family's History

Even if your genealogical interests are confined to the British Isles, a number of categories and topics on Cyndi's List are worth noting. The pages devoted to individual religious groups will be useful if you have Catholic, Nonconformist or Jewish ancestors (covered in Chapter 7). The 'Software & Computers' page **<www.CyndisList.com/software.htm>** has a very useful collection of links for genealogy software. The Personal Home Pages section **<www.CyndisList.com/personal.htm>** lists almost 4,000 web sites of individuals, while the Surnames page **<www.CyndisList.**

com/surnames.htm> has over 5,000 sites for individual surnames.

Incidentally, Cyndi's List is also available as a book, *Cyndi's List*, from the Genealogical Publishing Company. It was first published in 1999, and includes about 40,000 of the approximately 70,000 URLs provided by the web site, the exclusion being all the personal web sites. A second edition, in two volumes, was published in 2001.

GenWeb

For ancestors from outside the British Isles, you will find a wide coverage of countries and regions on Cyndi's List. But there is also a purely geographical gateway with worldwide coverage in the GenWeb projects. Apart from USGenWeb at **<www.usgenweb.org>** and CanadaGenWeb at **<www.rootsweb.com/~canwgw/>**, which are independent, the remainder are coordinated under the WorldGenWeb project at **<worldgenweb.org>**. In GenWeb, the world is split into a number of regional GenWeb projects, each of which has its own page and coordinates the projects for the individual countries in the region.

In all, there are just under 100 countries, islands or island groups for which there are actively maintained web sites, grouped as listed opposite:

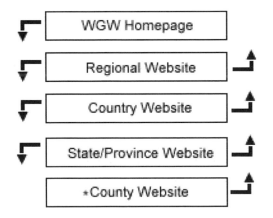

* Not all countries have counties.
The term county is used here in the general sense and refers to the most common political or administrative district in a country. Other names include shires, parish, townlands, states, prefects, rajones, etc.

Figure 3.4 How WorldGenWeb is organized <worldgenweb.org/policy.html>

- Africa (4 countries active)
- Asia (12 countries active)
- British Isles (including the Falkland Islands, Gibraltar, St Helena)
- Canada
- Central Europe (14 countries active – actually northern Europe)
- Caribbean (15 islands active)
- Eastern Europe (11 countries active)
- Mediterranean (9 countries active – actually more like southern Europe, since it excludes African and Middle Eastern states, though it includes Turkey)
- Middle East (5 countries active)
- North America (7 countries active – actually mainly Central America, since it excludes Canada and the USA)
- Pacific (4 'areas' active – Australia and 3 groups of islands – though not every individual island has an active page)
- South America (5 countries active)
- United States

Most of the links to UK and Irish material at <**www.britishislesgenweb.org**> will in fact be found on Genuki, whose county pages are generally more comprehensive. So the real strength of the GenWeb sites, from the point of view of British and Irish family historians, lies in the material relating to former British colonies and those countries from which immigrants came to the UK (see Chapter 7). There is huge variation in the amount of material available: for some countries there is a single page, while for others there are individual pages for administrative subdivisions, for example French *départements*. In general, the level of detail does not go down to the equivalent of individual parishes, though for each US state there are pages for the individual counties. While most of the pages are in English, quite a few are maintained by natives of the countries concerned and are in the local language. Some, notably the Caribbean and South American pages, are available in more than one language.

On the WorldGenWeb projects, the topics on each page are sorted under the following headings:

- History
- Resource Addresses (libraries, archives)
- Society Addresses
- Maps
- Geography
- Culture and Religious History
- Query Board
- Mail List
- Reference Materials (census, deeds, biographies)

Beyond this, the pages do not necessarily have the same layout or look. A useful feature to note is that every GenWeb page has a Query Board where readers can post queries. Such a board is often available for countries which have no maintained web page.

Genealogy Resources on the Internet

One of the longest established genealogy directories on the internet is Chris Gaunt and John Fuller's Genealogy Resources on the Internet site at <www.rootsweb.com/~jfuller/internet.html>. This differs from Genuki, GenWeb and Cyndi's List in that its main division of material is not by subject or by area but by type of access – web, e-mail, etc. This is really a hangover from its origins at a time before web browsers had provided a way of integrating all types of internet resources into a single interface, and when different software was required for each type of resource. This may be the only place where you'll still see references to Gopher and Telnet sites. One of the great virtues of this site is that the pages are designed for very fast downloading, with very simple layouts and few graphics.

The sections devoted to newsgroups and the Web provide excellent starting points and, in particular, the pages on mailing lists (main page at <www.rootsweb.com/~jfuller/gen_mail.html>) are one of the essential genealogy resources on the Web, and one which is repeatedly referred to in this book. Mailing lists are discussed further in Chapter 10.

Another interesting collection of resources listed here are those accessible by e-mail rather than the Web, at <www.rootsweb.com/~jfuller/gen_email.html>. Although many of these started off as services for people with e-mail but without web access (which is nowadays almost no one), there are still some interesting things on this page.

Other genealogy gateways

While Cyndi's List may be the most widely used general genealogy directory, and Genuki is certainly the pre-eminent gateway for UK material, there are many others. Each has its own particular strengths, though many are US-based and are therefore naturally stronger in US resources. There is not enough space here to list them all, let alone describe them in detail. The following represent a small selection:

- About.com's 'Family Tree and Genealogy Research guide' site at <genealogy.about.com/hobbies/genealogy>
- The Genealogy Gateway at <www.gengateway.com>
- Genealogy Links at <www.genealogylinks.net/index.html>
- The Genealogy Pages at <www.genealogypages.com>
- The Genealogy Portal at <www.genealogyportal.com>
- The Genealogy Site Finder at <www.genealogy.com/genealogy/links/>
- I Found It! at <www.gensource.com/ifoundit/>

Specialist gateways

There are also a number of gateways that are not specifically devoted to genealogy but which have links to sites of interest to genealogists. The National Maritime Museum's Port site at **<www.port.nmm.ac.uk>**, for example, has links to naval sites, which may be of interest to those with maritime ancestors. The same is true for several of the military sites mentioned in Chapter 7 – even those with no genealogical information may provide links to other military genealogy sites. The Church Net UK site at **<www.churchnet.org.uk/ukchurches/>** is a gateway to the web sites of present-day churches in the UK.

General directories

In addition to the specifically genealogical gateways discussed so far, the general web directories also provide genealogical links. On the whole, anyone who is sufficiently interested in genealogy to be reading this book will probably find them less useful than the dedicated sites already mentioned, not least since they are not edited and maintained by people with expertise in the subject. However, they can still be of use.

Yahoo
The best known and most widely used directory is Yahoo **<www.yahoo.com>**, which also has a UK version at **<www.yahoo.co.uk>**. This organizes subjects in a hierarchical structure, and the main Genealogy area comes under History, itself a subsection of Humanities. However, companies that sell genealogy products will be found under the Business heading, and genealogy resources for individual countries will be found under the relevant country heading. The main page for genealogy is **<www.yahoo.co.uk/Arts/Humanities/History/ Genealogy>**, but you can get a complete list of relevant Yahoo subject pages by doing a search on *genealogy*. There are, of course, many other areas of Yahoo which will have material of interest to a family historian. The list of genealogy categories on Yahoo is shown in Table 3.3.

Although Yahoo, like other directories and gateways, is selective, its basis of selection is not entirely satisfactory since it depends in part on submissions from web sites that want to be listed. This means the selection does not conform to a coherent policy, so, for example, the Northern Ireland Public Record Office (PRONI) is listed on Yahoo's Genealogy Organisations page, but equivalent bodies in other parts of the UK or the Republic of Ireland, including the PRO, are not listed. Some family history societies are there, but only a small number.

Excite
The UK version of the Excite directory **<www.excite.co.uk>** has genealogy in a similar hierarchy: Library/Arts & Humanities/History/Genealogy &

Table 3.3 Genealogy categories on Yahoo UK <uk.dir.yahoo.com/arts/humanities/history/genealogy>

Beginners' Guides
Chats and Forums
   Chats
   Mailing Lists
   Usenet
GEDCOM
Heraldry
Lineages and Surnames
   Family Reunions
   Irish Clans
   Publications for Sale
   Scottish Clans
   Web Directories
Magazines
Organisations
   PAF Users Groups
   Regional and Ethnic
      Australia
      British Isles
      Canada
      Germany
      Judaism
      Scandinavia
      United States
PAF
   User groups
Reference
   Cemeteries
   Census Records
   LDS Family History Centres
   US Civil War Muster Rolls
Regional and Ethnic Resources
   Acadian
   Armenia
   Australia
   Belgium

Canada
Caribbean
Cuba
Czech Republic
France
Germany
Hispanic and Latino
India
Ireland
Italy
Mexico
Native American
Netherlands
New Zealand
Poland
Religious
Russia
Scandinavia
Scotland
Sweden
Switzerland
Ukraine
United Kingdom
United States
Royal Genealogies
   European Royalty
Shopping and Services
   Commercial Website Directories
   Databases
   Family History Publishers
   Heraldry and Name Histories
   Publications
   Research
   Software
Web Directories

Heraldry. Although it has many fewer sites listed than Yahoo, it actually has a more coherent offering. Specifically, all the sites listed are relevant to the UK, and listings of organizations are much more comprehensive. The other advantage of the Excite directory is that the descriptions of the individual entries tend to be fuller. The categories are shown in Table 3.4.

Table 3.4 Genealogy subject headings on Excite UK

Archives and Records
   English Regional
   National
   Records and Guides
   Scottish Regional
   Welsh Regional
Guides and Directories

Heraldry
Prof. Services
Publications
Societies
   England
   Scotland
Surnames A–Z

4 Sources On-line

The aim of this chapter is to look at what the internet holds in the way of primary source material relevant to all family history research, while Chapter 7 will look at topics (for example, military, emigration) of relevance to particular ancestors, and Chapters 8 and 9 at non-genealogical material of interest to the family historian.

The core of any family history research in the British Isles is the information drawn from the 19th century registrations of births, marriages and deaths, and from the records of christenings, marriages and burials in parish registers starting in the 16th century. Linking these two sources are the census records, which enable an address from the period of civil registration to lead to a place and approximate year of birth in the time before registration. In addition, wills and memorial inscriptions, quite apart from providing additional information, can substitute for missing or untraceable death and burial records.

While the internet is the ideal way of making all this material widely available, particularly to those who are distant from the relevant repositories and major genealogical libraries, the fact is that a huge amount of work is involved in publishing such material on the Web. For example, there may be as many as 100 million births, marriages and deaths registered between 1837 and 1900, and each census includes a record for every member of the population. Nonetheless, at the time of writing there are some substantial data collections on-line, notably the Scottish material on the Scots Origins site <www.origins.net/GRO/>, the LDS Church's FamilySearch site at <www.familysearch.org> and the SoG's datasets at the English Origins site <www.englishorigins.com>. Both the PRO and General Register Office of Scotland (GROS) are engaged in major on-line projects; and in addition to transcriptions by individual genealogists on the Web, there are several large-scale volunteer-run projects to put primary genealogical data on-line.

While the amount of material that is available at present may be quite limited, within a few years we may well see a significant amount of civil registration and census data on-line (even if only in index form), and an increasing amount of material from other genealogical sources.

The funding of such projects is going to be an issue. Volunteer-run projects provide free access to data, but those run by organizations will generally involve commercial partnerships, even where the organizations themselves are volunteer-based, as is the case with family history societies.

While no one expects family history societies to give away their crown jewels, there has been some debate about whether it is appropriate for government agencies already funded by the tax-payer to seek income from charging for access to public records, particularly if some material, such as the 1901 census, will have limited off-line availability. Leaving aside the matter of principle, the fact is that progress on digitizing the nation's historical records will be very much slower if it has to be done from existing funds; and, for most people, the costs of using an on-line service will be less than the costs in time and travel of visiting a repository. There is also an issue about the connected being favoured over the non-connected which, though important, is probably not of immediate relevance to readers of this book. On the other hand, the traditional modes of access to records favour the mobile over those who are less so, and those who happen to live close to repositories. These issues are likely to remain contentious.

Images, transcripts and indexes

There are three main ways in which any textual source can be represented digitally:

- As an image – the original document is scanned.
- In a transcription – the full text of a document is held in a file.
- As an index – a list of names, with or without other details, directs you to the relevant place in a transcription or to the relevant scanned image, or provides you with the full reference to an original document.

Ideally, an on-line index would lead to a full transcription of the relevant document, which could be compared to an image of the original. But for material of any size this represents a very substantial investment in time and resources, and to date very little of the primary genealogical data is so well served. In particular, because images take up much more disk space than text does, images of original documents are not yet very common on-line. Since a transcription takes so much more time to prepare than an index, and still requires an index to be of any use, indexes are by far the most common option on the internet.

This has important implications for how you use the internet for your research: you simply cannot do it all on-line. Except where you have access to scans of the original documents, all information derived from indexes or transcriptions will have to be checked against the original source.

The perfect index would be made by trained palaeographers, familiar with the names and places referred to and thoroughly at home with the handwriting of the period, working with original documents. Their work would be independently checked against the original, and where there was uncertainty as to the correct reading this would be clearly indicated. However, very little of the genealogical material on the Web has been created in this way. The material on-line has been created either in large-scale projects or by individual genealogists, and often working from microfilms not original records. On large-scale projects the data are input by knowledgeable amateurs such as family history society members or by clerical workers, usually without specialist palaeographical skills.

The only case where one can expect a lower error rate is in the transcription of printed sources, such as trade directories, where problems of identifying names or individual letters are less great.

On a more positive note, it is worth remembering that although all indexes are subject to error, the great virtue of on-line indexes is that mistakes can be corrected. In printed or CD-ROM publications this can only be done if and when a subsequent edition is produced.

The upshot of this is that the internet must be treated mainly as a finding aid, just like aids in a genealogical library, not as a substitute for a record office.

However, in the many cases where original records are not indexed on-line, the web sites of the various repositories which hold them will still be worth a visit. Apart from utilitarian information like contact details, opening times, closure dates, etc., essential for any one visiting the repositories, most provide background information about the records and are increasingly making their catalogues available on-line. These sources are discussed in Chapter 5.

Civil registration

England and Wales

Civil registration of births, marriages and deaths started in England and Wales on 1 July 1837, and the original certificates are held in duplicate by the original local register office and by the General Register Office (GRO). The original certificates cannot be seen (for reasons which have been questioned, though not yet legally challenged), but copies can be ordered from the Family Records Centre (FRC). Indexes to the certificates can be consulted at the FRC and on microfiche in county record offices and other genealogical libraries.

Basic information on the FRC is available on the FamilyRecords portal at <www.familyrecords.gov.uk/frc.htm>, which also has information about births, deaths and marriages at <www.familyrecords.gov.uk/BMDmain. htm>. More detailed information is available on the FRC's own pages at <www.statistics.gov.uk/nsbase/registration/family_records.asp> (see Figure 4.1). The most useful pages are probably those relating to 'Contacting the FRC', 'Getting to the FRC', 'Opening Hours & Closure Dates at the FRC'. There is also detailed information about the records the FRC holds.

The FRC's records are not on-line, so the web site does not provide

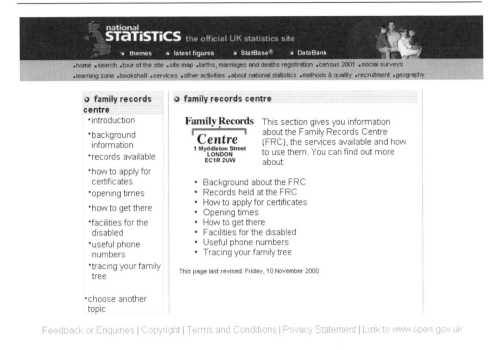

Figure 4.1 Family Records Centre home page at <www.statistics.gov.uk/nsbase/registration/family_records.asp>

access to birth, death and marriage indexes or certificates. Genuki also has information on civil registration, which will be found at **<www.genuki. org.uk/big/civreg/>**, with individual guides to England, Wales and Scotland.

Register offices and registration districts
Even though you may not find any useful data from civil registration on-line, there are some useful on-line resources relating to registration districts which may help in searching the off-line indexes.

For historical information about registration districts, Genuki has a set of pages prepared by Brett Langston at **<www.fhsc.org.uk/genuki/reg/>** which provide details of every registration district in each English or Welsh county, giving:

- Name of the district.
- Date of creation.
- Date of abolition (if before 1930).
- Names of the sub-districts.
- The GRO volume number used for the district in the national indexes of births, marriages and deaths.
- An alphabetical listing of the parishes, townships and hamlets included within its boundaries. If a district covered parts of two or more counties, the areas in each county are listed separately.

- The name(s) of the district(s) which currently hold the records. If two or more offices are listed, the one which holds most records is named first, and the one with least is given last.

There is an alphabetical list of districts at <**www.fhsc.org.uk/genuki/ reg/district.htm**>, and if you are not sure what registration district a particular place is in, consult <**www.genuki.org.uk/big/eng/civreg/places/ index.htm**>. FreeBMD (see the next section) has a list of registration district numbers at <**freebmd.rootsweb.org/districts.html**>.

The names and current contact details of individual register offices will also be found on Genuki, at <**www.genuki.org.uk/big/eng/RegOffice/**>, though this list does not link to the web sites of register offices which have an on-line presence. However, although the site of the Office for National Statistics (ONS) does not have a complete list of register offices on-line it does provide links to those that are, at <**www.statistics.gov.uk/nsbase/ registration/LocalServices.asp**>. The ONS site has detailed information about registering present-day births, marriages and deaths at <**www. statistics.gov.uk/nsbase/registration/default.asp**>. Application forms for copies of certificates can be downloaded from this site in Adobe Acrobat format from <**www.statistics.gov.uk/nsbase/registration/certificates.asp**>.

FreeBMD

In the absence of any official programme to digitize either the original certificates or the GRO indexes, the ONS has given a volunteer project called FreeBMD permission to digitize the indexes for free on-line access. Started in 1999, this project has a large group of volunteers, currently around 1,500, who either transcribe the indexes from microfiche in planned extractions or simply submit entries from their own extractions along with the surrounding entries. Although the project is accepting entries from all years, under the terms of the agreement with ONS only those over 100 years old can be put on-line. By September 2001, the project's database had reached 18 million entries, estimated to be about 18 per cent of the total entries for the period 1837–1900. The pattern of extractions has concentrated on marriages, with relatively few births and fewer deaths; for some years there are few records, while others are nearing completion. Up-to-date information on coverage will be found at <freebmd.rootsweb.org/progress.shtml>.

The material so far collected can be searched on-line. A comprehensive search page (Figure 4.2) allows you to search for a specific person in a chosen place and date range, or to extract all the entries for a particular surname. Figure 4.2 shows a search for all events for the surname Marshall in the Brighton registration district between 1837 and 1850. Figure 4.3 shows the results of this search. Clicking on the links in the district column will take you to information on the registration district, while clicking on the link in the page column brings up a list of all the events on that page in

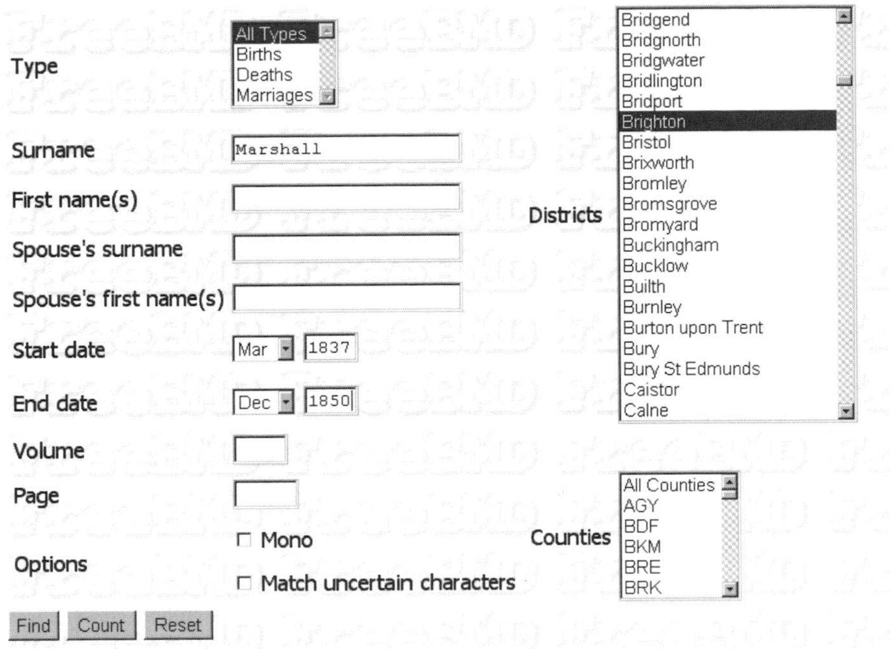

Figure 4.2 The FreeBMD search page at <freebmd.rootsweb.org/cgi/search.pl>. The screenshot shows a search for all Marshall events for Brighton, 1837–50

the original register (*not* the index). Note that the contributor's contact details are provided only for error reporting, and you cannot expect to contact the contributor for full details of the event, since he or she has only looked at the index, not the original certificates. You will need to order any certificate yourself.

FreeBMD is always looking for new volunteers, and details of what is involved can be found on the web site. You can keep up to date with the progress of the project by joining the FreeBMD-News-L mailing list – send a message containing simply the text `subscribe` to **<FreeBMD-News-L @rootsweb.org>**.

Smaller projects

A similar project is CheshireBMD at **<CheshireBMD.org.uk>**, a collaborative venture between Cheshire County Council, Wirral Metropolitan Borough, the Family History Society of Cheshire and South Cheshire Family History Society. This aims to make the indexes to civil registration records for the county freely accessible on-line. At the start of September 2001 index information on 626,985 births, 221,222 marriages and 104,826 deaths was on-line. A useful feature is that clicking on a search result creates a completed application form for submission to the local registration office.

New Query	Revise Query

Surname	First name(s)	Age	District	Vol	Page	Contrib(s)

Deaths Sep 1837

| Marshall | Eliza | | Brighton | 7 | 170 | bdbarnes |
| Marshall | John | | Brighton | 7 | 172 | bdbarnes |

Marriages Dec 1846

| Marshall | Sarah | | Brighton | 7 | 479 | ChrisLloyd |

Figure 4.3 Results of the search in FreeBMD shown in Figure 4.2

On a smaller scale, Mike Foster has created a range of index transcriptions which are available on Genuki:

- Selective transcriptions for South-East England (Suffolk, Essex, East London)
- A complete transcription for the March quarter of 1849
- Transcription for the year 1856 (ongoing)
- Entries missing from the published indexes: 1856, 1858 and 1861

Information about this material and links to it will be found on Genuki at <www.cs.ncl.ac.uk/genuki/StCathsTranscriptions/>.

Finally, on a much smaller scale, the UK BDM Exchange at <www. ukbdm.org.uk> is the only one of the projects that offers access to the information on certificates without the need to order them. The exchange is simply a forum for people who have certificates to post the basic details so that others can contact them for more information. Each entry gives surname, forename, town and county, along with the e-mail address of the submitter who must be contacted for details of the information on the certificate. It also indicates any certificates unwanted by their owners and therefore available for purchase. The site includes some material for baptisms, marriages and burials from parish registers. In September 2001, there were details of almost 30,000 events on the site. Incidentally, HMSO forbids the publication of scanned copies of certificates on the Web.[3]

---

[3] 'Guidance on the Copying of Birth, Death and Marriage Certificates', HMSO Guidance Note No. 7, on-line at <www.hmso.gov.uk/g-note7.htm>.

Scotland

In Scotland, general registration dates from 1 January 1855. The web site of the General Register Office for Scotland (GROS) at **<www.gro-scotland.gov.uk>** is the official on-line source of information about these records.

The situation with the Scottish general registration records is much better than that for England and Wales. Currently, indexes to births, marriages and deaths up to 1900 are available on-line and can be searched for a fee on the Scots Origins site at **<www.origins.net>**, described in more detail in the following section.

There is a project under way to make digital images of all original certificates available on-line, linked to the indexes on the Scots Origins site, by the end of 2003. Details of this programme, which goes by the name of DIGROS (Digital Imaging the Genealogical Records of Scotland's People), can be found at **<www.gro-scotland.gov.uk/grosweb/grosweb. nsf/pages/prdigros>**.

Page last updated: March 200

General Register Office *for* SCOTLAND

The General Register Office for Scotland is the department of the devolved Scottish Administration responsible for the registration of births, marriages, deaths, divorces and adoptions in Scotland, and for carrying out periodic censuses of Scotland's population.

Scots Origins

Search

www.open.gov.uk

Contact Us

What's New ?

Registration

Registering a Birth or Death
Getting Married in Scotland
Adoption
The Scottish Registration Service

Family Records

Searching Historical Records
(including 19th century censuses)

Census - Learning Zone

Scottish Schools Census Project

Jobs during 2001 Census
Frequently Asked Questions

2001 Census

2001 Census Home Page

Medical Research

NHS Central Register
History of NHS Central Register
Vital Events

Demographic Statistics

On-Line Data Library

Figure 4.4 General Register Office for Scotland at <www.gro-scotland.gov.uk>

Scots Origins

The Scots Origins site at <www.origins.net/GRO/> was the first attempt by a government agency in the UK to make a large amount of genealogical material available on-line on a pay-per-view basis. The original material offered was a database of civil registration entries from 1855 (the start of registration in Scotland) to 1900 for births and marriages (giving a 100-year cut-off period), and to 1924 for deaths. Each year will see the extension of these cut-offs by one year. The database also includes entries from the Old Parish Registers (see p. 42). The site is due to be expanded to include all census material over 100 years old (see p. 38).

The project was carried out by a commercial company Origins.net, who converted the data to digital form. They now run the on-line service on behalf of the GROS, while the GROS issues the certificates requested. Interestingly, quite apart from the revenue generated by the on-line service, the GROS reports that income from issuing certificates has increased substantially, and this has undoubtedly been an important factor in the plan to proceed with census material.

Ireland

In Ireland, registration of Protestant marriages dates from 1 April 1845, while full registration began on 1 January 1864. The records for the whole of Ireland up to 31 December 1921 are held by the Registrar General in Dublin, who also holds those for the Republic of Ireland from that date. The equivalent records for Northern Ireland are held by the General Register Office (Northern Ireland). The relevant web sites are at <www.groireland.ie> and <www.groni.gov.uk/index.htm> respectively. The National Archives of Ireland have information on 'Records of births, marriages and deaths' at <www.nationalarchives.ie/birthsmarrdeaths. html>.

None of these records, or indexes to them, are on-line but there is a project in the Republic to digitize the registration service. No plans to place records or indexes on-line has been announced by the Northern Ireland GRO, though certificates can be ordered on-line.

Offshore

The Isle of Man, Jersey, Guernsey, Alderney and Sark have their own civil registration from various dates. At present, only the first two have web sites for the relevant authorities: for the Isle of Man, the Civil Registry at <www.gov.im/deptindex/reginfo.asp>; for Jersey, the Judicial Greffe at <www.judicialgreffe.gov.je>.

The Genuki pages for the Isle of Man <www.genuki.org.uk/big/iom/> and the Channel Islands <user.itl.net/~glen/genukici.html> provide some further information, but I am not aware of any registration data on-line for these islands.

Census records

A census has been taken every 10 years since 1801, except for 1941, and names of individuals are recorded from the 1841 census onwards. The significance of these records for genealogists is that they provide snapshots of family groups on a 10-year basis, and, more importantly, for individuals born before the start of general registration, from 1851 they give a place of birth which makes it possible to trace the line back to the parish registers (an approximate date of birth can be calculated from the person's age).

The starting point for official information relating to the census is the PRO's Census web site at **<www.census.pro.gov.uk>**.

Official census material on-line

The PRO has announced the availability of the 1901 census for England and Wales on-line from the start of 2002, on a pay-per-view basis from the census web site at **<www.census.pro.gov.uk>**. Access to the material is via a free search facility, and there are a number of different things you can search for: a person, an address, a place, a vessel or an institution. The person search is shown in Figure 4.5. Once you have identified the record you want to look at (Figure 4.6), you can pay to see the full census entry for the person found (Figure 4.7). You can then see other people in the same household or view an image of the relevant page in the original enumeration book (Figure 4.8). This latter option allows you to see fuller details than are included on the transcription (some long entries are truncated) and check that the transcription is correct. Payment is by credit card – the charges for individual pages are small, so there is a minimum

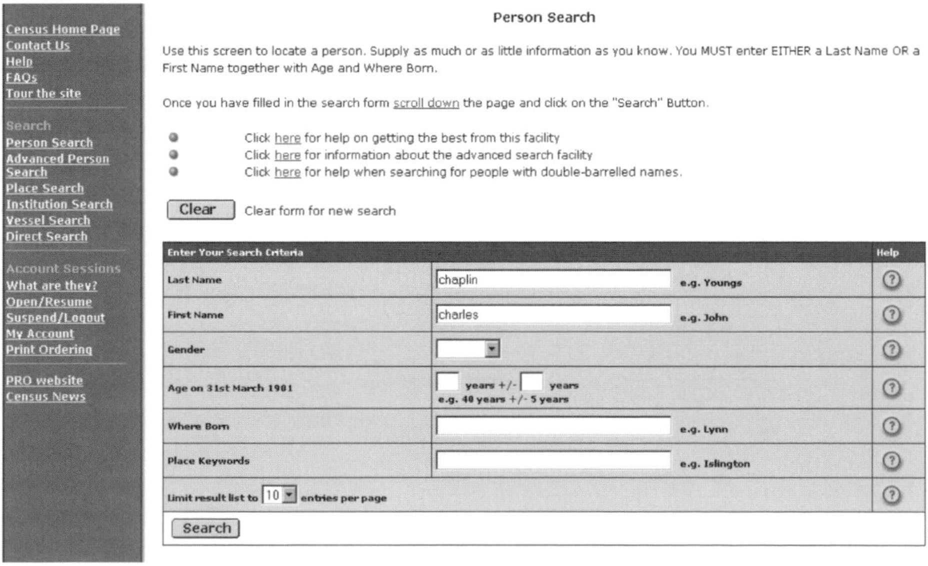

Figure 4.5 1901 census: person search

charge of £5 and you can set a maximum when entering your card details – or via a voucher system, intended for regular users.

The GROS has a similar project under way for the 1901 census as part of DIGROS (see p. 35). In a pilot for this 250,000 pages of the 1891 Scottish

Person Result List

⑦

The query that you entered has returned 100 or more results. To make your search criteria more specific click here.

If you find the text difficult to read because of its size, click here to find out how to enlarge it.

🔲 = View the image of the original document (chargeable).
A Name= View this individual's details (chargeable)
▸ **Results: 31-40 of 151 Matches**

Image	Name	Age	Where Born	Administrative County	Civil Parish	Occupation
🔲	Charles Chaplin	12	Myton Yorkshire	Of York	Haverah Park	
🔲	Charles Chaplin	12	Suffolk Barking	Suffolk	Barking	House Boy
🔲	Charles Chaplin	12	Surrey London	Surrey	Lambeth	Music Hall Artiste
🔲	Charles Chaplin	13	Birmingham	Birmingham	Birmingham	
🔲	Charles Chaplin	13	Woolwich	London	Plumstead	
🔲	Charles Chaplin	14	Essex Little Bromley		Little Bromley	Stockman In Farm
🔲	Charles Chaplin	14	Middlesex Willesden	Middlesex	Willesden	Errand Port
🔲	Charles Chaplin	14	Sussex Brighton	Middlesex	Harrow	
🔲	Charles Chaplin	15	Essex Langford	Essex	Langford	Ordinary Agrl Labourer
🔲	Charles Chaplin	15	Kensington London	London	Kensington	Dressmakers Porter

[<< Prev] [Next >>]

Figure 4.6 1901 census: results of the person search in Figure 4.5

Person Details

Full Transcription Details for **Charles Chaplin**   View Image/Other Household members   [Back to Search Results]

PRO Reference					Schedule Number	
RG Number, Series		Piece	Folio	Page		
RG13		425	97	41	293	

Name			Language
Charles Chaplin			
Relation to Head of Family	Condition as to Marriage	Age Last Birthday	Sex
Servant	S	12	M
Profession or Occupation	Employment Status		Infirmity
Music Hall Artiste	Worker		
Where Born	Address		
Surrey London	94 Ferndale Rd		
Civil Parish	Rural District		
Lambeth			
Town or Village or Hamlet	Parliamentary Borough or Division		
	Brixton		
Ecclesiastical Parish	Administrative County		
St Pauls W Brixton	Surrey		
County Borough, Municipal Borough or Urban District	Ward of Municipal Borough or Urban District		

To find out how much you have spent, click on 'My Account'	Your Session ID is : 567896

What now? you can...

Figure 4.7 1901 census: full census record (transcription) for a person

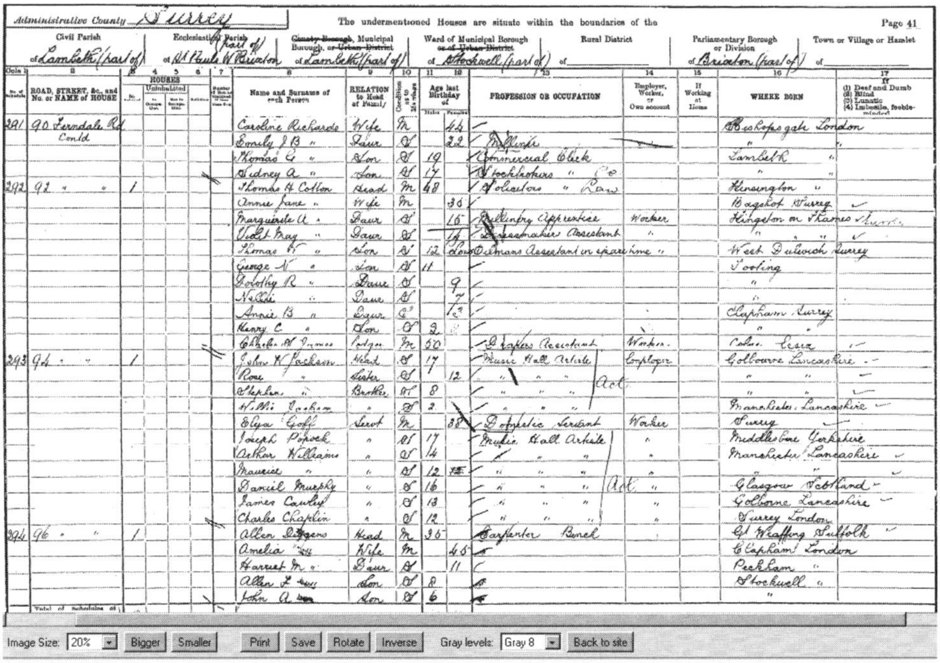
Administrative County of Surrey. The undermentioned Houses are situate within the boundaries of the. Page 41
Civil Parish of Lambeth (part of) — Ecclesiastical Parish of St Paul's W Brixton (part of) — County Borough, Municipal Borough, or Urban District of Lambeth (part of) — Ward of Municipal Borough or of Urban District of Stockwell (part of) — Rural District of — Parliamentary Borough or Division of Brixton (part of) — Town or Village or Hamlet of

No. of Schedule	Road, Street, &c., and No. or Name of House	Name and Surname of each Person	Relation to Head of Family	Condition as to Marriage	Age last Birthday (Males)	Age last Birthday (Females)	Profession or Occupation	Employer, Worker, or Own account	Where Born
291	90 Ferndale Rd Contd	Caroline Richards	Wife	M		44			Bishopsgate London
		Emily J B "	Daur	S		22	Milliner		"
		Thomas G "	Son	S	19		Commercial Clerk		Lambeth "
		Sidney A "	Son	S	17		Stockbrokers "		" "
292	92 " "	Thomas H Cotton	Head	M	48		Solicitors " Law		Kensington "
		Annie Jane "	Wife	M		36			Bagshot Surrey
		Marguerite A "	Daur	S		16	Millinery Apprentice	Worker	Kingston on Thames Surrey
		Violet May "	Daur	S		14	Dressmakers Assistant	"	" "
		Thomas F "	Son	S	12		Dentists Assistant		West Dulwich Surrey
		George N "	Son	S	11				Tooting
		Dorothy R "	Daur	S		9			"
		Nellie "	Daur	S		7			"
		Annie B "	Daur	S		3			Clapham Surrey
		Henry C "	Son	S	2				" "
		Charles W James	Lodger	M	50		Drapers Assistant	Worker	Colne Essex
293	94 " "	John W Jackson	Head	S	17		Music Hall Artiste	Employer	Golborne Lancashire
		Rose "	Sister	S		12	" " "		" "
		Stephen "	Brother	S	8		" " "		" "
		Willie Jackson		S	2		" " "		Manchester Lancashire
		Eliza Goff	Servt	M		38	Domestic Servant	Worker	Surrey
		Joseph Popock	"	S	17		Music Hall Artiste	"	Middlesbro Yorkshire
		Arthur Williams	"	S	14		" " "	"	Manchester Lancashire
		Maurice "	"	S	12		" " "	"	"
		Daniel Murphy	"	S	16		" " "	"	Glasgow Scotland
		James Cawley	"	S	13		" " "	"	Golborne Lancashire
		Charles Chaplin	"	S	12		" " "	"	Surrey London
294	96 " "	Allen Diggens	Head	M	35		Carpenter Bench		Gt Whaddling Suffolk
		Amelia "	Wife	M		45			Clapham London
		Harriet M "	Daur	S		11			Peckham "
		Allen F "	Son	S	8				Stockwell "
		John A "	Son	S	6				"

Image Size: 20% Bigger Smaller Print Save Rotate Inverse Gray levels: Gray 8 Back to site

Figure 4.8 1901 census: image of a page from the original census record

census returns were converted to digital images and linked to four million individual computer index entries, which are already available on the Scots Origins site at **<www.origins.net/GRO/>**.

In the Republic of Ireland some data from the 1901 census is on-line at **<www.leitrim-roscommon.com/1901census/>**. Available data covers all or part of the following six counties: Roscommon, Leitrim, Mayo, Sligo, Westmeath and Galway.

The DIGROS project explicitly aims to convert all earlier Scottish census data for on-line access. The PRO is already intending to make earlier censuses available on-line, and work has already started on the 1881 and 1891 censuses. Up-to-date information about the PRO's plans for digitizing census records will be found at **<www.census.pro.gov.uk>** and in the minutes of the Advisory Panel **<www.census.pro.gov.uk/advisory.htm>**.

FreeCEN

Alongside the official projects there are, as with civil registration, volunteer projects. The most comprehensive of these is FreeCEN, which aims to include all English and Welsh census data from 1841 to 1891. At the time of writing, transcription is well under way, starting with 1891, and the database should be on-line by the time you read this, with the Devon and Cornwall material planned for publication during 2001. The database aims to support the following types of search:

- Search by surname across census years and counties
- Search by place or address
- Display of individual and household details
- 'Neighbourhood scan' – the ability to display adjacent households
- Statistical enquiry – e.g. numbers of carpenters by place name

The project has a home page on RootsWeb at <freecen.rootsweb.org> and a detailed description will be found at <www.john.lerwill.btinternet.co.uk/census/censproc.htm>. There is a status page for each county currently being transcribed. For Devon, which was the pilot county for the project, some of the material has been put on-line (just as text, not in a searchable database) at <www.cs.ncl.ac.uk/genuki/DEV/censusproject.html>.

Other census extracts

There are probably quite a lot of other small collections of census material on the Web, but no major collections. The 2% sample of the 1851 census was available on-line for a while but was removed for copyright reasons. This is, however, available on CD-ROM from S&N Genealogy (see p. 187).

The best way to find any locally based transcriptions is via the relevant Genuki county and parish pages. For example, all the census data for Veryan in Cornwall from 1841 to 1891 is on-line at <freepages.genealogy. rootsweb.com/~dtrounce/veryan.html>. The 1841 and 1871 censuses for Bovingdon in Hertfordshire are on-line at <www.shef.ac.uk/misc/personal/el1scmb/introcen.htm>. Donald MacDonald-Ross has tran-scriptions for a number of small communities in Ross and Cromarty at <freepages.genealogy.rootsweb.com/~coigach/index.htm>. The 1841 census for Corfe, Somerset, is available on Roy Parkhouse's site at <www.parkhouse.org.uk/transcr/Corfe1841.htm>.

Also, you may find that genealogists with web pages devoted to particular surnames include extracts from census records on their sites, though usually only for their own surnames of interest.

Background and finding aids

The PRO has a number of leaflets relating to individual censuses and census records in general, all which are linked from <www.pro.gov.uk/research/leaflets/censusmain.htm>. Genuki has a searchable database of places in the 1891 census at <www.genuki.org.uk/big/census_place.html>, which gives the county, registration district, registration sub-district, PRO piece number and LDS film number (see p. 69) for any place in England, Wales and the Isle of Man.

The Gendocs site shows exactly what information was recorded for each census from 1841 to 1901 at <www.gendocs.demon.co.uk/census.html>, and gives the date on which each census was taken. Genuki has pages on the census for:

- England and Wales: <www.genuki.org.uk/big/eng/CensusR.html>
- Scotland: <www.genuki.org.uk/big/sct/Census.html>
- Ireland: <www.genuki.org.uk/big/irl/#Census>

For Scotland, a useful tool is the on-line index of census microfilms at <www.ktb.net/~dwills/scotref/13311-censusfilms.htm>, which gives the relevant enumeration district(s) and LDS microfilm number for each parish.

Ron Taylor has a substantial collection of census indexes on-line at <rontay.digiweb.com>. They are mainly for 1851 and target those individuals who might be hard to find. The following indexes are provided:

- Strays by County – people found in counties other than their county of birth. This project is in progress but already includes Middlesex, Kent, Essex, Surrey and Lancashire, and counties beginning with A or B; additional counties are being added on a regular basis.
- Strays from Scotland and Ireland – those born in Scotland and Ireland who were not in those countries at the time of the census.
- Strays from France and Germany – those born in France and Germany who were not in those countries at the time of the census. (The majority are British citizens born abroad, but there are also a number of foreign nationals.)
- Visitors – those who were not at their current residence on census night.
- By Occupation – for the more 'mobile' occupations, including policemen, soldiers, fishermen, sailors, doctors, nurses, servants, apprentices.
- Paupers, inmates, convicts, prisoners and prostitutes – most of these people were institutionalized, so were likely to be in unexpected places.

Note that these indexes only indicate the presence of a name, they do not provide further data or references to the original census data – you will need to request a lookup from Ron Taylor, currently charged at $2/£1 per entry.

For Ireland, the National Archives has a brief page of information at <www.nationalarchives.ie/censusrtns.html>, as has the PRONI at <proni.nics.gov.uk/records/census19.htm>. A good guide to the Irish censuses, detailing what is missing and what has survived, is available on the Fianna site at <www.rootsweb.com/~fianna/guide/census.html>.

Because of the amount of Irish census material destroyed, the so-called 'census substitutes' are important. Fianna has a useful guide to these at <www.rootsweb.com/~fianna/guide/cen2.html>, while the National Archives has a briefer description at <www.nationalarchives.ie/titheapplprimvalu.html>. The PRONI has similar information at <proni.nics.gov.uk/records/census18.htm>. It also has a guide to using Griffiths Valuation at <proni.nics.gov.uk/research/family/griffith.htm>.

It is not possible to deal here with census data for countries outside the UK, but Cyndi's List provides links to census sites around the world from <www.cyndislist.com/census2.htm>. Another site that may be useful is Census Links at <www.censuslinks.com>.

Parish registers

The situation with parish register material on-line is generally much less satisfactory than for the civil registration and census records already discussed. The latter are centrally held and recorded on forms which ensure that the structure of the data is consistent and very obvious; they all date at the earliest from the 19th century; and they have generally been kept in fairly good conditions. All this makes digitizing and indexing them a manageable, if mammoth, task. But for parish registers, there is much more variety. First, in England and Wales, at least, they are not held centrally, so no one body can be approached to put them on-line. Second, there is huge variation in their format and preservation, the more so since they cover 300 years up to general registration. And, third, while most genealogists can become accurate readers of 19th-century handwriting, the same cannot be said when it comes to the writing in some of the 18th-century registers, never mind those from the 16th century. Although many parish registers have been transcribed and published in print or typescript, getting the requisite permissions simply to digitize and index these from the hundreds of individuals and groups concerned would be a substantial task, and the right to transcribe and publish parish register material seems to be legally unclear, with some dioceses refusing to allow transcription. All this conspires to make the prospect of a comprehensive collection of on-line parish registers for England and Wales much more distant than it is for civil registration and census records. Nevertheless, some data is available on-line, as well as information that will help you to identify what parish registers remain.

Incidentally, the material in this section refers mainly to the records of the established Church (i.e. of England, Wales, Scotland and Ireland). Other religious denominations are discussed in Chapter 7.

Scottish Old Parochial Registers
Unlike England and Wales, Scotland has collected most of its parish registers in one place, the GROS, and the births/baptisms and banns/marriages dating from 1553 to 1854 (the start of general registration) are all available on-line at the Scots Origins site <www.origins.net/GRO/>.

The GROS web site provides a 'List of the Old Parochial Registers' at <www.gro-scotland.gov.uk/grosweb/grosweb.nsf/pages/opr_cov/>.

A Scottish National Death and Burial Index, aiming to index all recorded pre-1855 deaths and burials in Scotland, is being created by the Scottish Association of Family History Societies in conjunction with its member societies and the GROS. It is not yet clear whether this will be made available on-line.

FamilySearch
The major on-line resource for all parish records is the LDS Church's FamilySearch site at <www.familysearch.org>. The material on this site is

drawn from a number of sources, and it is important to note that not all of it is from transcriptions of parish registers ('controlled extractions', as the LDS calls them). Two of the data collections on the site, Ancestral File and Pedigree Resource File, consist of unverified material submitted by individual genealogists, which is therefore secondary material and of variable reliability – these are discussed in Chapter 6. The collection that contains British parish register extractions is the International Genealogical Index (IGI), originally published on microfiche and then on CD-ROM. A further collection, the Vital Records Index (VRI), has been published on CD-ROM but at the time of writing only the data for Mexico has been put on-line on FamilySearch, though no doubt the British Isles VRI material will join it in due course.

The IGI on FamilySearch is the only substantial collection of parish register records for England and Wales on-line, and as such is one of the essential tools for UK genealogy on the Web. There is also much material for other countries. The majority of the IGI material is for baptisms and marriages, though with some births and a few deaths and burials.

The exact nature of the search options on FamilySearch depends on whether you choose to search in 'All Resources' or in one of the specific data collections. A good reason for choosing the IGI search (see Figure 4.9), apart from the quality of the data, is that it allows you to select not only a country, but also a UK county. You can also choose to look for all events or for just, say, marriages; you can leave the year blank, give a precise year or a range of years. If you are looking for a specific individual, you can also enter the name of the father and/or mother.

Figure 4.9 IGI search page on FamilySearch <www.familysearch.org>

You searched for: Sarah Weymark, Sussex, England, British Isles
Exact Spelling: Off

Results: International Genealogical Index/British Isles (30 matches)

Select records to download - (50 maximum)

☐ **1.** sarah WYMARK - International Genealogical Index
Gender: F Birth: Abt. 1678 <Of Brightling>, Sussex, England

☐ **2.** Sarah WYMARK - International Genealogical Index
Gender: F Birth: Abt. 1700 <Of Brightling>, Sussex, England

☐ **3.** Sarah WYMARK - International Genealogical Index
Gender: F Birth: Abt. 1678 <Of Brightling>, Sussex, England

☑ **4.** Sara WEIMARK - International Genealogical Index
Gender: F Christening: 30 Mar 1739 Pevensey, Sussex, England

☐ **5.** Sarah WYMARK - International Genealogical Index
Gender: F Birth: Abt. 1678 Brightling, Sussex, England

Figure 4.10 Initial search results for the search in Figure 4.9

When the search has been completed, you are presented with a list of search results (see Figure 4.10), with sufficient detail to identify the most plausible matches, and you can then click on the name to get the full details of the record (Figure 4.11).

You can select an individual record or a group of records to download in GEDCOM format (see p. 161), ready to be imported into your genealogy database. Of course, you can also simply save the web page for individual records or the list of search results, though these will have to be saved in text or HTML formats and the data will have to be added to your database manually.

If you are not just looking for a single individual but want to look at a surname in a whole parish, then the information at the bottom of the screen in Figure 4.11 will be useful. This identifies the particular transcription from which this record comes. You can take the batch number, and enter it in the batch number field on the search form (Figure 4.9) to restrict the search to a particular source document – in the example in Figure 4.11 'C042501' indicates the parish registers for Pevensey in Sussex (the link from the 'Source Call No.' takes you to this information). The batch number is also important because it indicates whether a record comes from controlled extractions – in general, numbers that start with a digit are from submissions from Church members, while those starting with a letter are from controlled extractions.

Of course, it would be useful to be able to select the parish straight off without having to run a preliminary search and decode an individual record. You can do this by doing a 'Place Search' in the Family History Library Catalogue, as explained on p. 69. Genuki has detailed instructions

---

Individual Record

FamilySearch™ International Genealogical Index v4.01

British Isles

Select record to download - (50 maximum)

☐ **Sara WEIMARK**
  Sex: F

Event(s):
  Christening: 30 Mar 1739
                 Pevensey, Sussex, England

Parents:
  Father: Edward WEIMARK
  Mother: Jude_

Source Information:

Batch number:	Dates	Source Call No.	Type	Printout Call No.	Type
C042501	1569-1837	0504417	Film	0933425	Film
Sheet:					

Figure 4.11 An individual record in FamilySearch

---

on how to find out batch numbers by this method at <**www.genuki.org. uk/big/FindingBatchNos.html**>. Also, there are a number of sites that list batch numbers for particular counties. The most extensive, at <**freepages.genealogy.rootsweb.com/~tyeroots/index4.html**>, has batch numbers for many counties, and other helpful information about working with batch numbers. Others can be found by looking under the 'Church records' heading on the Genuki county pages. Bear in mind that all these unofficial sites have created their lists by trial and error, and they should be regarded as useful rather than authoritative or comprehensive. Also note that for many parishes there will be more than one batch number.

The facilities on the FamilySearch site can be quite complex to use, but because of the importance of the data it is well worth spending time experimenting and trying out different types of search. You can find more detailed guidance in David Hawgood's *FamilySearch on the Internet* (details at <**www.hawgood.co.uk/fs.htm**>).

FreeReg

FreeReg is another volunteer project, like FreeBMD and FreeCEN, which aims to put UK genealogy data on-line 'to provide free internet searches of baptism, marriage, and burial records, which have been transcribed from parish and non-conformist church registers in the UK.' The project, which can be found at <**freereg.rootsweb.com**>, is still a fairly new one and the number of records it contains compared to the total amount of potential material is still tiny. Even so, the site has some very useful descriptions of the different types of register you are likely to encounter at <**freepages. genealogy.rootsweb.com/~engregisters/home.htm**>.

Other indexes

The National Burial Index for England and Wales was published by the Federation of Family History Societies on CD-ROM in May 2001, but there has been no indication that it will be made available on-line (further information at **<www.ffhs.org.uk/General/Projects/NBI.htm>**).

Many family history societies and individual genealogists have indexes to marriages, burials and, occasionally, christenings. Little of this material has made its way on-line as yet. Most is accessible only for postal searches. However, this situation may change in the next few years as it become easier for societies to charge for on-line access to data. The web sites of family history societies will normally give details of such indexes.

Two important and rare paper collections are to be made available on the SoG's English Origins site (see p. 52):

- Boyd's Marriage Index: 1538–1837 (over 6 million records)
- Boyd's London Burials (50,000 names)

The Marriage Index material for Cambridgeshire, Essex and Suffolk is already on-line, with the remainder to follow in due course.

Wills

Wills are an important source for family historians and there are many printed indexes to them. At the time of writing, the only significant source of on-line will data is the English Origins site at **<www.englishorigins. com>**, which has the following currently available or due for publication in 2001: Bank of England Will Extracts Index, Archdeaconry Court of London Wills Index, Prerogative Court of Canterbury Wills (see pp. 52–53).

The PRO is planning to put records from its class PROB 11, Registered Copies of Wills from 1383 to 1858, on-line in the near future. The wills for 1850 to 1858 are due to go on-line in November 2001 as a pilot, with the remainder of the records to follow in due course.

The Scottish Wills Microsite, **<www.scan.org.uk/aboutus/WillsMicrosite/ willsindex.htm>**, which is part of the Scottish Archive Network, promises 'free access to a comprehensive index of nearly half a million entries to the testaments (wills) of Scots recorded in the Registers of Testaments from the 16th century to 1875', with on-line ordering of will copies. Even without any data, the site is useful as it has good background material on Scottish wills. It also offers historical background material drawn from the wills.

The PRO has three leaflets relating to wills:

- Wills before 1858: where to start **<catalogue.pro.gov.uk/leaflets/ ri2302.htm>**
- Wills and Death Duty Records after 1858 **<catalogue.pro.gov.uk/ leaflets/ri2301.htm>**

- Wills, Probate Records **<catalogue.pro.gov.uk/leaflets/ri2241.htm>**

Probate records since 1858 are under the jurisdiction of the Probate Service whose on-line leaflet at **<www.courtservice.gov.uk/fandl/prob_guidance.htm>** gives details of how to obtain copies.

Memorials

Debt of Honour Register

One of the first important collections of genealogical data for the UK to go on-line was the Debt of Honour Register at **<www.cwgc.org>**. This material, on the web site of the Commonwealth War Graves Commission, is a database of the names of 1.7 million members of the Commonwealth forces who died in the First or Second World Wars. For all those listed there is name, rank, regiment and date of death, with details either of place of burial or, for those with no known grave, of commemoration. The burial information gives not only the name of the cemetery but also the grave reference and instructions on how to get to the cemetery. Some records have additional personal information, usually including the names of parents and the home address. With many cemeteries holding the dead from particular battles and campaigns, there is sometimes historical information which puts the death in its military context. The database also includes information on 60,000 civilian casualties of the Second World War, though without details of burial location.

The initial search page at **<yard.ccta.gov.uk/cwgc/register.nsf>** allows you to specify surname, initials, war or year of death, force (i.e. army, navy, etc.) and nationality. Because there is a maximum of 100 hits it is important, unless you are looking for an unusual name, to give as much

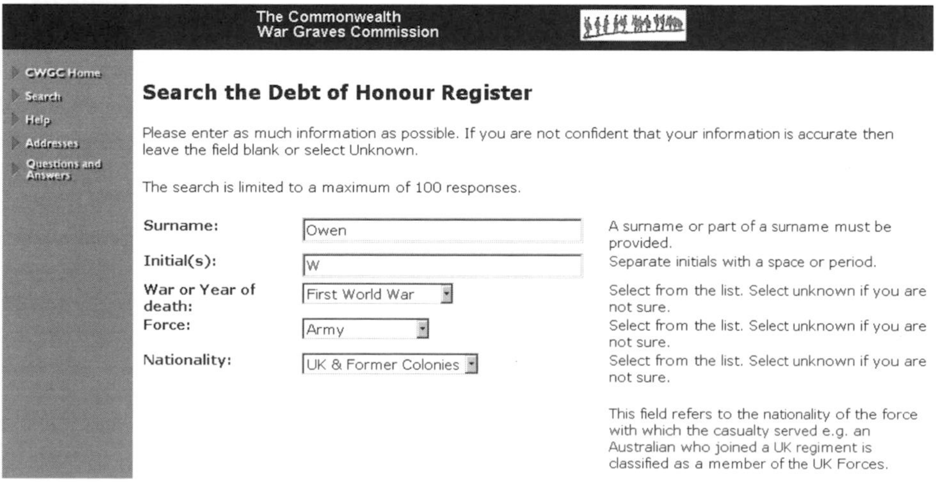

The Commonwealth War Graves Commission

CWGC Home
Search
Help
Addresses
Questions and Answers

Search the Debt of Honour Register

Please enter as much information as possible. If you are not confident that your information is accurate then leave the field blank or select Unknown.

The search is limited to a maximum of 100 responses.

Surname:	Owen	A surname or part of a surname must be provided.
Initial(s):	W	Separate initials with a space or period.
War or Year of death:	First World War	Select from the list. Select unknown if you are not sure.
Force:	Army	Select from the list. Select unknown if you are not sure.
Nationality:	UK & Former Colonies	Select from the list. Select unknown if you are not sure.

This field refers to the nationality of the force with which the casualty served e.g. an Australian who joined a UK regiment is classified as a member of the UK Forces.

Figure 4.12 Search form for the Debt of Honour Register at <yard.ccta.gov.uk/cwgc/register.nsf>

The Commonwealth War Graves Commission			
OWEN, W A	Private	King's Own (Royal Lancaster Regt.)	28th Sep 1918
OWEN, W A E	Private	Royal Warwickshire Regiment	25th Apr 1915
OWEN, W C	Private	Duke of Wellington's (West Riding Regt.)	30th Apr 1918
OWEN, W C	Private	Welsh Regiment	12th May 1917
OWEN, W C	Corporal	Royal Warwickshire Regiment	18th Jul 1918
OWEN, W C	Gunner	Royal Field Artillery	15th Sep 1914
OWEN, W C	Private	London Regiment	2nd Apr 1918
OWEN, W D	Sapper	Royal Engineers	13th Nov 1917
OWEN, W D	Second Lieutenant	Welsh Regiment	11th Oct 1918
OWEN, W E	Private	London Regt (Artists' Rifles)	23rd Mar 1918
OWEN, W E	Private	South Wales Borderers	23rd Jul 1916
OWEN, W E	Private	Lincolnshire Regiment	7th Sep 1917
OWEN, W E	Private	King's Shropshire Light Infantry	21st Sep 1917
OWEN, W E	Lance Corporal	King's Own Yorkshire Light Infantry	2nd Dec 1917
OWEN, W E	Lance Serjeant	Durham Light Infantry	24th Aug 1918
OWEN, W E S	Lieutenant	Manchester Regiment	4th Nov 1918
OWEN, W F	Private	Royal Fusiliers	7th Jun 1917
OWEN, W G	Private	Cheshire Regiment	10th Aug 1915
OWEN, W G	Private	Welsh Regiment	25th Nov 1917
OWEN, W G	Private	Welsh Regiment	18th Jul 1916
OWEN, W G	Private	Northumberland Fusiliers	26th Oct 1917

Figure 4.13 Search results in the Debt of Honour Register

detail as possible. Figure 4.12 shows a search for the record of the war poet Wilfred Owen. From the details given, the database reports there are 148 records, of which only the first 100 are shown (Figure 4.13). If you know the regiment and approximate rank of the person you're looking for, it should not take too long to identify the relevant record. Knowing that Wilfred Owen was an officer, and that he was killed near the end of the war, you can quickly identify him as the lieutenant in the Manchester Regiment who died on 4 November 1918. If he had not been in this initial listing it would have been necessary to rerun the search for individual years of the war. The list of search results links to a page giving the details for each soldier listed. In the case of Wilfred Owen (see Figure 4.14), in addition to the basic details of rank, regiment and date of death, the record shows the names of his parents and their address, along with some further biographical information. The bottom part of the screen gives details of the cemetery and grave, as well as information about the campaigns from which the cemetery holds the dead.

Monumental inscriptions
While monumental inscriptions are not official records, their close connection with the deceased means that they can provide family information not given by a death certificate, and can make up for a missing entry in a burial register.

While quite a few family history societies have projects to transcribe monumental inscriptions, little of this material seems to be available on the Web, and many FHS web sites simply give details of coverage and how to submit requests by post. Where such material is on-line, you should be able to find a link on the relevant Genuki county or parish page.

The Commonwealth War Graves Commission	

In Memory of

WILFRED EDWARD SALTER OWEN MC

Lieutenant
5th Bn., Manchester Regiment
who died on
Monday, 4th November 1918. Age 25.

Additional Information: Son of Mr. and Mrs. Tom Owen, of "Mahim", Monkmoor Rd., Shrewsbury. Native of Oswestry. Enlisted in The Artists' Rifles in October 1915. Commissioned into the Manchester Regiment in June 1916. Was a poet of repute, although during his lifetime, only a few of his poems appeared in print. The 'Atheneum' of December 1919, nominated Owen's work "Strange Meeting" as the finest of the war.

Commemorative Information

Cemetery: ORS COMMUNAL CEMETERY, Nord, France
Grave Reference/   A. 3.
Panel Number:
Location: The village of Ors is between Le Cateau and Landrecies. The Communal Cemetery lies to the north-west of the village. It should not be confused with Ors British Cemetery which is 1 kilometre north-east of the church.

Historical Information: Ors was cleared by the 6th Division on the 1st November, 1918. There are now over 60, 1914-18 war casualties commemorated in this site. Of these, a small number are unidentified. The plot covers an area of 189 square metres.

Display Record of Commemoration

Figure 4.14 Commemoration Record for Wilfred Owen in the Debt of Honour Register

The National Inventory of War Memorials is a joint project of the Imperial War Museum and the Royal Commission on the Historical Monuments of England. The inventory, holding information on Britain's estimated 50,000–60,000 war memorials, is to be published in November 2001. Although the Debt of Honour Register is a more useful source of genealogical information, the NIWM will include information on memorials for earlier conflicts like the Crimean and Boer wars. Initially available only on-site at the Museum, the project is to go on-line when funding permits. Details can be found on the Imperial War Museum web site at <www.iwm.org.uk/collections/niwm/>.

Rod Neep has pages on recording and publishing memorial inscriptions at <www.neep.demon.co.uk/mis/>. The Welsh Family History Archive has a useful page on Welsh Words and Phrases on Gravestones at <home.clara.net/wfha/wales/welsh-phrases.htm>.

Printed sources

Other unofficial sources which can provide information about the lives or deaths of ancestors are printed materials. Of these, newspapers and trade directories are probably the most important general publications, though there are also, of course, directories for a number of professions.

Newspapers

While most historical editions of newspapers must be read in the libraries discussed in Chapter 5, whose catalogues will provide details, there is some material on-line. The Genuki county pages are a good way of finding links to local newspapers on-line, and Cyndi's List has a 'Newspapers' page at <www.CyndisList.com/newspapr.htm>. There are, of course, many sites relating to present-day newspapers including Kidon Media-link, which has links to the web sites of UK newspapers at <www.kidon.com/media-link/unitedkingdom.shtml>, and All the World's Newspapers, which has comprehensive listings for all countries at <www.onlinenewspapers.com>.

The British Library Newspaper Library web site has a lot of information about British newspapers at <www.bl.uk/collections/newspaper/>, and has links for present-day newspapers on-line including: London National Newspapers, Scottish Newspapers, Irish Newspapers, English and Welsh Newspapers, Channel Islands and Isle of Man Newspapers, Newspapers Around the World, and Other Newspaper Libraries and Collections. The BL Newspaper Library Catalogue is on-line at <prodigi.bl.uk/nlcat/>, and the web sites for other major libraries and archives discussed in Chapter 5 will have sections on their newspaper holdings.

Probably the most important on-line historical newspaper material is the 'Internet Library of Early Journals', a joint project by the universities of Birmingham, Leeds, Manchester and Oxford to place on-line digitized copies of 18th- and 19th-century journals, in runs of at least 20 years. The project, at <www.bodley.ox.ac.uk/ilej/>, currently includes:

- *Gentleman's Magazine*
- *The Annual Register*
- *Philosophical Transactions of the Royal Society*
- *Notes and Queries*
- *The Builder*
- *Blackwood's Edinburgh Magazine*

The University of Rochester (New York) has copies of some 17th-century editions of the *London Gazette* on-line at <www.history.rochester.edu/London_Gazette/>.

Alongside digitized newspapers there are some on-line indexes, which are generally the work of individuals and therefore inevitably limited in scope. Examples include the *Belfast Newsletter*, 1737–1800 at <www.ucs.louisiana.edu/bnl/>, the *Surrey Advertiser* for 1864 and 1865 at <newspaperdetectives.co.uk>; and selected years for 12 West Country newspapers at <freespace.virgin.net/paul.mansfield1/paul001.html>.

Trade directories

Alongside newspapers the other major printed source, particularly for ancestors who were in trade, are 19th-century directories. These are increasingly being digitized and published on CD-ROM, but a number are available either complete or in part on the Web.

There are three approaches to putting this material on-line. The simplest is a name index to the printed volume, such as that for Pigot's *Commercial Directory for Surrey* (1839), which is on the Genuki Surrey site at <www.gold.ac.uk/genuki/SRY/>. This simply provides text files with page references for names and places. Rod Neep, who publishes directories on CD-ROM, has name and page indexes for several of his publications at <www.archivecdbooks.com/books/indexes/>. While not a substitute for on-line versions of the directories, these listings at least indicate whether it is worth locating a copy of the directory in question.

Another approach is to place scanned images on the Web, along with a name index, as on Nicholas Adams' site, which provides Pigot's 1830 and 1840 directories for Herefordshire at <freepages.genealogy.rootsweb.com/~nmfa/genealogy.html> (see Figure 4.15).

Finally, some sites offer a full transcription along with a name index, such as Rosemary Lockie's pages devoted to the 1835 Pigot's *Commercial Directory for Derbyshire* at <www.genuki.org.uk/big/eng/DBY/Pigot 1835/about.html>.

There are also some partial transcriptions, usually for individual towns or cities, such as Brian Randell's material for Exeter at <www.cs.ncl.ac.uk/genuki/DEV/Exeter/White1850.html> taken from White's *Devonshire* directory of 1850, or Ann Andrews' extracts for a group of Derbyshire parishes from Kelly's 1891 directory at <ds.dial.pipex.com/town/terrace/pd65/dby/kelly1891_index.htm>. David Foster's Direct Resources site at <www.direct-resources.co.uk> has brief extracts from a large number of directories on-line, with the full transcriptions available on CD-ROM. Familia (p. 66) has details of the trade-directory holdings of public libraries.

A major on-line initiative due for completion in December 2002 is the 'Digitisation of Local Directories' project financed by the New Opportunities Fund and housed at the University of Leicester (see <www.nof-digitise.org>). This aims to put trade directories for counties and towns throughout England and Wales on-line.

Since directories were compiled on a county basis, the easiest way to find them on-line is to look at the relevant county page on Genuki. Alternatively, you could use a search engine to search for, say, [Directory AND Kelly AND Norfolk] or [Directory AND Pigot AND Lancashire] to locate the publications of the two main 19th-century directory publishers. You may also find information about county directories on county record office web sites. (See Chapter 11 for information on search engines and formulating searches.)

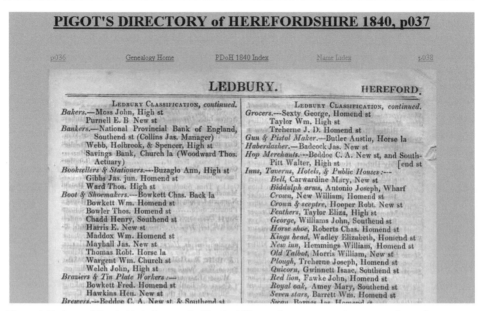

Figure 4.15 Scan of Pigot's 1840 directory for Herefordshire at <freepages.genealogy.rootsweb.com/ ~nmfa/genealogy.html>

Major data collections

Sites devoted to particular collections of data, such as Scots Origins, the 1901 Census, and the Debt of Honour Register have been discussed above. But there are two major sites which have more varied collections of data and do not fall simply into one or other of these categories.

English Origins

The English Origins site at **<www.englishorigins.com>** went live at the end of 2000. It contains data from the collections of the SoG, and the on-line service is run by Origins.net, the company that runs Scots Origins on behalf of the GROS. The complete list of datasets either already available or in preparation is:

- Marriage Licence Allegations Index 1694–1850 (670,000 names)
- Bank of England Will Extracts Index 1717–1845 (61,000 names)
- Archdeaconry Court of London Wills Index 1750–1800 (5,000 names)
- London City Apprenticeship Abstracts 1568–1850 (170,000 names)
- London Consistory Court Depositions Index 1700–1717 (3,200 names)
- Boyd's Marriage Index 1538–1837 (over 6 million records)
- Apprentices of Great Britain: 1710–74 (over 600,000 records)
- Boyd's Inhabitants of London: 14th–19th centuries (60,000 families)
- Boyd's London Burials (50,000 names)

- Prerogative Court of Canterbury Wills 1750–1800 (333,000 records)

The first five are already on-line in their entirety at the time of writing and the others are in preparation. Boyd's Marriage Index, with its six million records, is probably the most significant on-line data collection for England after the 1901 census, and will take some time to complete. Some counties are already available, and others will go on-line as they are ready. The range of London records will make this site invaluable to those with ancestors from the City.

English Origins is a pay-per-view site. Access costs £6 per session, which is a period of 48 consecutive hours during which you can access a maximum of 150 records. Once you have used your allocation you can pay for a new session, but if you do not use your allowance of 150 records in 48 hours, 'unused' records are carried forward for the next time you use the system. Members of the SoG have one free session per quarter.

You can search in individual datasets or across the entire collection. If you do the latter, you will get a screen like that in Figure 4.16 which indicates how many records were found in each dataset. You can then view the results for a single dataset, or refine your search. Figure 4.17 shows the details for the Bank of England Wills. In this case, since a will is a substantial document, you cannot read the will itself on-line but must order a hard copy from the SoG. In other cases, such as the City of London

English Origins Indexes	Records		
Vicar-General Marriage Licence Allegations (1694-1850)	55	View Records	*Detailed Search*
Faculty Office Marriage Licence Allegations (1701-1850)	67	View Records	*Detailed Search*
Bank of England Will Extracts (1717-1845)	10	View Records	*Detailed Search*
Archdeaconry Court of London Wills (1700-1807)	0	No Records	*Detailed Search*
London City Apprenticeship Abstracts (1568-1850)	16	View Records	*Detailed Search*
London Consistory Court Depositions (1700-1713)	0	No Records	*Detailed Search*

Figure 4.16 General search in English Origins at <www.englishorigins.com>

ENGLISH
ORIGINS |
home origins.net info help log out
in association with the Society of Genealogists

Bank of England Will Extracts index: search results

new search?   return to main search page   view images of sample original documents

| Surname **Collyer** |
| Forename |
| Year **1568** to **1850** |

If you are ordering a hard copy of a document, please make a note of the Order Number (on the order button). This number should be quoted in case of any problem.

Description	Book	Date	Reg	Film	Order Extract
COLLYER Andrew. Coach Master of Farnham,Surrey	47 A-I	1836	9934		Order 1006033
COLLYER Ann. Widow of Manchester St,Manchester Sq	37 A-I	1831	7925		Order 1006034
COLLYER Edward. Gent of Church Court,Strand	25 A-I	1826	5518		Order 1006035
COLLYER John Weaver of Covent Garden	5	1760-74	2482	63/2	Order 0005741
COLLYER John. Tailor of Guildford,Surrey	8 A-K	1812	2353		Order 1006036
COLLYER Joseph. Gent of Grays Inn Rd	31 A-I	1828	6606		Order 1006037
COLLYER Margaret Widow of Homerton Hackney	30	1777-81	4442	59/4	Order 0005742
COLLYER Nathaniel. Esq of Park Pl,St James's St	13 A-I	1819	2670		Order 1006038
COLLYER Samuel Carpenter of Crutched	33	1763-1804	390	60/4	Order 0005743

Figure 4.17 The records found in the Bank of England Wills in the search in the previous figure

Description
Christian David, son of David, Spitalfields, Middlesex, turner, to William Cowley, 7 Feb 1722/3, Distillers' Company
Christian James, son of James, Old Street (St Luke), Middlesex, labourer, to James Budgen, 10 Apr 1790 [free], Curriers' Company
Christian John, son of Edward, Christ in Aire, Isle of Man, clothier, to Samuel Gunn, 19 Jul 1693 [19 Feb 1694 discharged] Coachmakers' and Coach Harness Makers' Company
Christian Twigden, son of Hugh, Spratton, Northamptonshire, tailor, to Thomas Kente, 13 Jul 1620, Farriers' Company
Christian William, son of Anthony, St Clement Danes, Middlesex, to Joseph Garth, 18 Jun 1772, Coachmakers' and Coach Harness Makers' Company

Figure 4.18 Records for the surname Christian in the City of London Apprenticeship records on English Origins

Apprentices, most of the genealogically significant information is given in the results (see Figure 4.18).

Ancestry.com

The Ancestry web site **<www.ancestry.com>** is the largest commercial collection of genealogical data. It holds over 2,000 separate datasets, many of them derived from printed materials which may be more or less difficult to find outside a major genealogical library. While the overwhelming majority of these are of interest only to those with US ancestry (the datasets include all the US census data), there are a number which may be useful to UK genealogists, for example:

- Cambridge University Alumni, 1261–1900

- Historic Families of Scotland
- Irish Flax Growers List, 1796

In addition, there are collections of obituaries from recent issues of dozens of UK national and regional newspapers.

Although Ancestry is a commercial service, some of the databases are free of charge and there are regular free offers where a particular database, which is normally only for subscribers, can be accessed free for a limited period (usually a couple of weeks). The front page of Ancestry lists the paid databases currently being offered on this basis.

If a branch of your family emigrated to North America, databases such as the following might be of interest:

- English Origins of American Colonists
- Scots-Irish in Virginia
- New England Founders
- New England Irish Pioneers
- Pennsylvania Irish Quaker Immigrants, 1682–1750

The easiest way to see if Ancestry has anything of interest is simply to search across all databases for a particular name, from the search box on the front page (Figure 4.19). Unfortunately, while Ancestry allows you to search on individual US states, there is only a single option for all non-US datasets. This brings up a page summarizing the various types of database in which the name has been found (Figure 4.20).

You can then inspect more detailed listings. Figure 4.21 shows an expanded listing with details of the individual databases containing the name Robert Blackburn, along with the number of references in each. Those marked 'Free' could be looked at immediately, while you would have to become an Ancestry subscriber for those marked 'Paid'. Note that Ancestry is not a pay-per-view system, and a monthly or quarterly subscription provides access to all paid databases (with the exception of the US census, for which there is a separate subscription).

On the whole, the Ancestry databases are likely to be of most use to those who have US ancestors or who are conducting a one-name study, though as you can see from the example, a single search over a whole range of telephone books could be very useful.

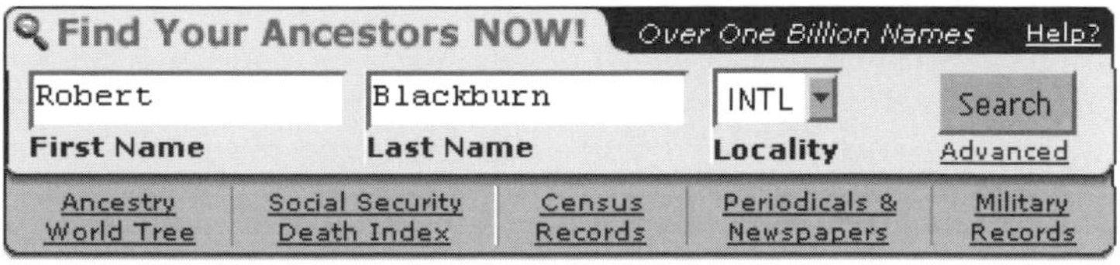

Figure 4.19 Ancestry search form

Search Results for Robert Blackburn in Non-Us

Thinking about subscribing? For as little as $5 per month, gain access to ALL Ancestry databases, 30-Day Money Back Guarantee. Click to subscribe!

❷ **Free** Ancestry World Tree entries for ROBERT BLACKBURN

❷ **Free** View entries in the BLACKBURN Message Boards

❷ **Free** Visit the BLACKBURN Surname Community

❷ **Free** Create a FREE website for the BLACKBURN family!

❷ **New!** Search our Images Online™ Collection for ROBERT BLACKBURN

❷ **New!** Search databases at RootsWeb.com for ROBERT BLACKBURN

Your Search Returned Results in the Following Categories:

📁 Census Records

📁 Immigration & Naturalization Records

📁 Periodicals & Newspapers

📁 Court, Land, & Probate Records

📁 Directories

Figure 4.20 Initial search results on Ancestry

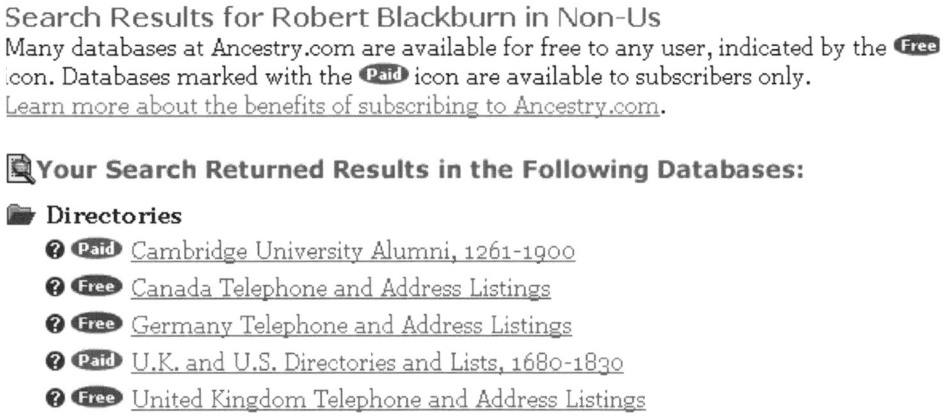

Search Results for Robert Blackburn in Non-Us

Many databases at Ancestry.com are available for free to any user, indicated by the **Free** icon. Databases marked with the **Paid** icon are available to subscribers only. Learn more about the benefits of subscribing to Ancestry.com.

Your Search Returned Results in the Following Databases:

📁 **Directories**

❷ **Paid** Cambridge University Alumni, 1261-1900

❷ **Free** Canada Telephone and Address Listings

❷ **Free** Germany Telephone and Address Listings

❷ **Paid** U.K. and U.S. Directories and Lists, 1680-1830

❷ **Free** United Kingdom Telephone and Address Listings

Figure 4.21 Further details of the search results under Directories

However, one database of very general usefulness, though it does not contain primary genealogical sources, is the Periodical Source Index (PERSI), an index to articles from 5,000 genealogical journals and other publications in the US and abroad, with about 1.48 million entries. PERSI is a paid database and is accessible from **<www.ancestry.com/search/rectype/periodicals/persi/main.htm>**.

A full list of databases available on Ancestry can be found at <www.ancestry.com/search/rectype/alldblist.asp>.

Other records

There are, of course, many other types of record of interest to genealogists, whether they be general records, such as those relating to taxation or property ownership, or records for specific groups of people, such as those relating to service in the armed forces or other occupational records.

Where this material belongs to the nation's official records, the web sites of the national archives will give details of any large-scale plans for digitization (see p. 58 ff.). But even where there are no such plans, many individuals and groups are publishing small collections of data from such records on-line. These tend to be piecemeal digitizations, rather than the publication of complete national datasets, and some are discussed under the relevant topic in Chapter 7 or under 'Local and social history' in Chapter 9.

RootsWeb has a facility for users to upload data into its user-submitted data area. There are about 30 small datasets for the British Isles, details of which are at **<userdb.rootsweb.com/contributors.html>**.

5 Archives and Libraries

Archives and libraries are often seen as the antithesis of the internet, but this is largely illusory, certainly from the genealogical point of view. Only a small number of British genealogical resources are reproduced as images on the Web, and almost all the material currently available is in the form of indexes. This means that you will need to go to the relevant archive or a suitable library to check the information you have derived from on-line sources against original documents (or microfilms of them). It will take years before all the core sources are completely available on-line. Technologically, it is in fact a trivial matter to take records which have already been microfilmed and put images of them on-line. But to be usable such on-line images need to be supported by indexes, if not transcriptions, and the preparation of these requires substantial labour and investment.

If you are going to look at paper records, then catalogues and other finding aids are essential. Traditionally, these have been available only in the reading rooms of record offices themselves, and so you spend a significant part of any visit checking the catalogues and finding aids for whatever you have come in search of. But the Web has allowed repositories to make it much easier to access information about their collections and facilities. At the very least, the web site for a record office will give a current phone number and opening times. Larger sites will provide descriptions of the holdings, often with advice on how to make the most of them. Increasingly, you can expect to find catalogues on-line and, in some cases, even place orders for documents so that they are ready for you when you visit the repository.

All this means you can get more out of a visit to a record office, because you're able to go better prepared. You can spend more time looking at documents and less trying to locate them. And if you can't get to a record office, you will be able to give much more precise information than previously to anyone who is visiting it on your behalf.

This chapter looks at what the major national repositories and the various local bodies provide in the way of on-line information.

National archives

The Family Records Centre
Particularly if you are just starting to research your genealogy, the web site of the Family Records Centre (FRC) at **<www.pro.gov.uk/about/frc/>** will be

worth a visit. Bear in mind that the records held there are not on-line, so the web site does not provide access to birth, death and marriage indexes or certificates. The General Register Office for Scotland is at **<www.gro-scotland.gov.uk>** and the General Register Office (Northern Ireland) at **<www.nics.gov.uk/nisra/gro/>**. These bodies are discussed in more detail under 'Civil registration' in Chapter 4 (p. 30 ff.).

The Public Record Office

The PRO web site at **<www.pro.gov.uk>** has a number of sections relevant to genealogists. There is a main Family History page at **<www.pro.gov.uk/research/familyhistory.htm>**, with an 'Easy Search' facility at **<www.pro.gov.uk/research/easysearch/>** to help you find relevant material.

For detailed information, the PRO's records for individual areas of interest the Research Information Leaflets should be consulted. There are over 300 of these on-line, all linked from an alphabetical index at **<www.pro.gov.uk/leaflets/Riindex.asp>**. For a more informal introduction to family history research at the PRO, see the Family History section of the 'Pathways to the Past' area of the site at **<www.pro.gov.uk/pathways/FamilyHistory>** (from the home page follow the 'Education' link.) A list of the topics in this area is given on pp. 7–8.

The site has links to the FRC and offers an on-line bookshop. In addition, you can expect to find links to any major projects relating to records of genealogical interest (currently, the 1901 census and First World War Soldiers' Documents).

The 'Visiting the PRO' page at **<www.pro.gov.uk/about/visit.htm>** covers all you need to know when visiting the PRO, including details of opening hours and advice on planning your visit.

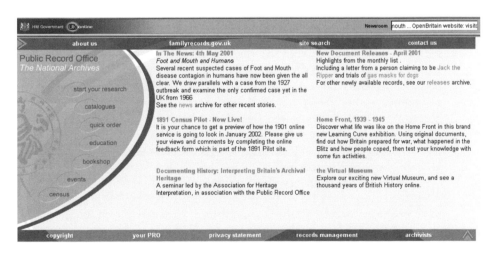

Figure 5.1 Public Record Office home page

Figure 5.2 The Easy Search page on the PRO site at <www.pro.gov.uk/research/easysearch/>

The on-line catalogue

One of the most important facilities on the PRO web site is the on-line catalogue at **<catalogue.pro.gov.uk>**, with well over eight million entries. There are two ways to use the catalogue: you can browse or you can search.

In browsing, you start from the list of all the Lettercodes denoting the various government departments which created the records in question, and you will then get a list of all the individual document classes from that department. Figure 5.3 shows the start of the list of Lettercodes, and Figure 5.4 shows the start of the list of all the document classes for Admiralty Records (Lettercode ADM), which would be of interest if you had an ancestor who served in the Royal Navy. The titles of the classes are sometimes rather terse, but clicking on the classmark will bring up a description of the class in the right-hand frame of the browser window. Clicking on the link from the class title brings up a list of all the individual pieces within that class – Figure 5.5 shows the start of the list for ADM 11, Officers' Service Records.

Of course, this is all very well if you are familiar with the records in question, or are working with a reference book. If not, it is probably easier to enter the catalogue via the Search option. You can search on up to three keywords, and the results will show all the classes whose titles or descriptions contain the relevant words. Each of these entries will link to a detailed list of piece numbers as in Figure 5.5.

Public Record Office Online Catalogue

home | login | browse | hits | help   go to reference [   ] go

help

Catalogue Browser

View departments by :   Reference / Title
Summary screen display :   On / Off
Browse from reference :   [   ] go

1	2	3	4	5	6	7	Title/Scope and content	Covering dates
+	A						Records of the Alienation Office	1571-1858
+	AB						Records of the United Kingdom Atomic Energy Authority and its predecessors	1939-1999
+	ACT						Records of the Government Actuary's Department	1870-1979
+	ADM						Records of the Admiralty, Naval Forces, Royal Marines, Coastguard, and related bodies	1205-1992
+	AE						Records of the Royal Commission on Historical Monuments (England)	1908-1991
+	AF						Records of the Parliamentary Boundary Commissions for England and Wales	1938-1990
+	AH						Records of the Location of Offices Bureau	1963-1979
+	AIR						Records created or inherited by the Air Ministry, the Royal Air Force, and related bodies	1862-1985

Summary of ADM
Records of the Admiralty, Naval Forces, Royal Marines, Coastguard, and related bodies

more

Covering dates
1205-1992
Scope and content
Records of the Admiralty, Naval Forces, Royal Marines, Coastguard, and related bodies concerning all aspects of the organisation and operation of the Royal Navy and associated naval forces.

Figure 5.3 List of PRO Lettercodes

Public Record Office Online Catalogue

home | login | browse | hits | help   go to reference [   ] go

−	ADM			Records of the Admiralty, Naval Forces, Royal Marines, Coastguard, and related bodies	1205-1992	
	+	Division within ADM		Records of the Navy Board and the Board of Admiralty	1563-1985	
		+	ADM 1	Admiralty, and Ministry of Defence, Navy Department: Correspondence and Papers	1660-1976	31024
		+	ADM 2	Admiralty: Out-Letters	1656-1859	1756
		+	ADM 3	Admiralty: Minutes	1657-1881	286
		+	ADM 4	Admiralty: Letters Patent, Lord High Admiral and Lords of Admiralty Appointments	1707-1964	410
		+	ADM 5	Admiralty and predecessors: Letters Patent, Navy Board, Transport Board, Vice-Admiralty and Commissi ...	1746-1890	85
		+	ADM 6	Admiralty: Service Records, Registers, Returns and Certificates	1673-1960	476
		+	ADM 7	Admiralty: Miscellanea	1563-1953	1005
	+	Division within ADM		Records of HM Ships	1669-1971	
		+	ADM 8	Admiralty: List Books	1673-1909	174
	+	Division within ADM		Records of Service	1660-1972	
		+	ADM 9	Admiralty: Survey Returns of Officers' Services	1817-1848	61
		+	ADM 10	Admiralty: Officers' Services, Indexes and Miscellanea	1660-1851	16
		+	ADM 11	Admiralty: Officers' Service Records (Series I)	1741-1897	89
	+	Division within ADM		Records of the Navy Board and the Board of Admiralty	1563-1985	

Summary of ADM 11
Admiralty: Officers' Service Records (Series I)

more

Covering dates
1741-1897
Scope and content
This series includes some original returns of officers' services (including surgeons, chaplains, etc.) in addition to various entry books and compilations of the same and of the appointments of commissioned and warrant officers. It includes also some registers of commissions and warrants entered under the

Figure 5.4 Class list for Admiralty Records

The on-line catalogue is very straightforward to use, but it cannot simplify the organization of records themselves, which have been created independently by individual government departments over 900 or so years. In order to make the most of the catalogue, you will need to be familiar with the way in which the records you are looking for are organized. There are Research Information Leaflets for all the major classes of records of

1	2	3	4	5	6	7	Title/Scope and content	Covering dates	Last Piece Ref.
⊟	ADM						Records of the Admiralty, Naval Forces, Royal Marines, Coastguard, and related bodies	1205-1992	
	⊟	Division within ADM					Records of Service	1660-1972	
		⊟	ADM 11				Admiralty: Officers' Service Records (Series I)	1741-1897	89
			⊞	Subseries within ADM 11			*Pieces without a sub-series parent*		
				⊞	ADM 11/1		Commission Branch precedents and draft statements of services of candidates for promotion.	c.1841-1861	
				⊞	ADM 11/2		Survey of Masters' Services, Nos.3-249.	1833-1835	
				⊞	ADM 11/3		Survey of Masters' Services, Nos.250-492.	1833-1835	
				⊞	ADM 11/4		Analysis of masters' eligibility for half-pay.	c.1831	
				⊞	ADM 11/5		Analysis of masters' half-pay list.	1819	
				⊞	ADM 11/6		Analysis of masters' services, annotated to 1847.	1822	
				⊞	ADM 11/7		Survey of Masters' Services, Nos.4168-4400.	1851	

Figure 5.5 List of piece numbers for the class ADM 11

interest to genealogists, as well as the PRO's *Tracing Your Ancestors in the Public Record Office* and specialist publications on individual classes of record. A useful feature of the on-line catalogue search is that the search results start with a list of relevant PRO leaflets.

National Archives of Scotland

The National Archives of Scotland has a web site at **<www.nas.gov.uk>**, with a Family History section at **<www.nas.gov.uk/family_history.htm>**. At the time of writing there is no on-line catalogue, but one is being developed for mid-2002 as part of the Scottish Archive Network (see p. 72). The site offers a comprehensive collection of leaflets in Adobe Acrobat (PDF) format, covering: adoption, buildings, crafts and trades, crime and criminals, customs and excise, deeds, divorce, education, emigration, estate records, inheriting lands and buildings, lighthouses, military records, the poor, publications, sasines, taxation records, valuation rolls, and wills and testaments. There is also a Family History FAQ ('frequently asked questions') page covering the National Archives' holdings and services relevant to family historians.

The Public Record Office of Northern Ireland

The Public Record Office of Northern Ireland (PRONI) has a web site at **<proni.nics.gov.uk>**. The site offers extensive information for genealogists, including descriptions of the major categories of record and about two dozen leaflets on various aspects of Irish genealogical research. Links to all these aids are provided on the Records Held page at **<proni.nics.gov.uk/**

records/records.htm>. The 'Introductions to the Major Collections' page at <proni.nics.gov.uk/records/listing.htm> links to descriptions of the main collections of private papers held by PRONI. There is also an FAQ at <proni.nics.gov.uk/question/question.htm>.

The site does not offer a full on-line catalogue, but has four on-line indexes of use to genealogists:

- The Geographical Index (for locating any administrative geographical name, with Ordnance Survey Map reference number)
- The Prominent Person Index
- The Presbyterian Church Index
- The Church of Ireland Index

The last two cover only those records which have been microfilmed by PRONI. There are plans to add other church records, school records and pre-1858 wills.

National Archives of Ireland

The National Archives of Ireland web site at <www.nationalarchives.ie> has no on-line catalogue, but there are several on-line databases of interest to genealogists:

- Ordnance Survey Parishes Index
- Ireland-Australia Transportation
- National School Roll Books and Registers

All these can be accessed from <www.nationalarchives.ie/onlinesearch. html>. There is a collection of guides to various aspects of Irish genealogy at <www.nationalarchives.ie/genealogy.html>.

Historical Manuscripts Commission

The web site of the Royal Commission on Historical Manuscripts has two resources of interest to family historians. The National Register of Archives (NRA) has an on-line index at <www.hmc.gov.uk/nra/nra2. htm>. This contains reference details for around 150,000 people, families and corporate bodies relating to British history, with a further 100,000 related records. The materials themselves are held in record offices, university libraries and specialist repositories. The NRA catalogue gives details of location and availability. The search engine allows you to search by:

- Corporate Name – combined search of the Business Index and the Organisations Index
- Personal Name – combined search of the Personal Index and the Diaries and Papers Index

- Family Name
- Place Name – lists businesses, organizations and other corporate bodies by place

Figure 5.6 shows the results of a place name search in the NRA, while Figure 5.7 shows the full details for one of the search results. Note that it not only gives the repository but also the reference number used by the record office in question.

Of more specialist interest is the Manorial Documents Register (MDR) at **<www.hmc.gov.uk/mdr/mdr.htm>**, which provides a record of the whereabouts of manorial documents in England and Wales. Although most of the MDR is not computerized certain sections are available on-line, including Wales and parts of England.

Other archives

The ARCHON (Archives On-line) site at **<www.hmc.gov.uk/archon/ archon.htm>** acts as a gateway for archives. The site is hosted by the Historical Manuscripts Commission (see previous section) and its intention is to provide 'information on all repositories in the United Kingdom and all those repositories throughout the world which have collections of manuscripts which are noted in the indexes to the UK National Register of Archives.' It is particularly useful because it allows

Figure 5.6 Place name search in the National Register of Archives

Historical Manuscripts Commission

UK National Register of Archives

Robert Plumley, coal merchant
Pevensey, Sussex

1844-70 : memorandum book
East Sussex Record Office
Reference : PLU
NRA 6462 Plumley

1 record noted.

Where reference is made to an NRA number, a catalogue is filed in the National Register of Archives and may be consulted in our public search room.

Figure 5.7 Full entry for a record in the NRA

you to search for all archives in a given town or county, and provides links to the web sites of all county record offices.

'Archives in Focus'
'Archives in Focus' on the HMC's web site at **<www.hmc.gov.uk/focus/>** has a different purpose from those mentioned so far, aiming not to provide links to archives or archive material but to explain to the non-specialist what archives are and why they are useful. The 'Your History' section of the site has material relating to the use of archives in family history. The 'Teaching Resources' section offers an annotated list of some of the best digitized material on UK archive web sites by way of example.

The national libraries

The British Library has a number of collections of interest to genealogists. The home page of the BL web site is at **<portico.bl.uk>**, while the library catalogue is at **<blpc.bl.uk>**. The British Library Newspaper Library at Colindale has its own catalogue at **<prodigi.bl.uk/nlcat/>** with over 50,000 newspaper and periodical titles from all over the world, dating from the 17th to the 21st century. Each entry in the web catalogue contains full details of the title (including any title changes), the place of publication (the town or city and the country) and the dates which are held. The Oriental and India Office Collections do not have an on-line catalogue, but a description of holdings will be found at **<www.bl.uk/collections/oriental/>**.

The National Library of Scotland has a web site at **<www.nls.uk>** with a number of on-line catalogues linked from **<www.nls.uk/catalogues/**

online/index.html>, though not all of its material is included in these as yet.

The National Library of Wales web site at **<www.llgc.org.uk>** provides links to a number of on-line catalogues at **<www.llgc.org.uk/cronfa/ index_s.htm>**. The most important of these is the ISYS free text-search system, as it includes an index of applicants for marriage licences from 1616 to 1837. The search page for ISYS is at **<www.llgc.org.uk:81/ isysmenu.htm>**.

The National Library of Ireland has a web site at **<www.nli.ie>**, with a family history section at **<www.nli.ie/fr_servfamily.htm>**. There are several on-line catalogues, searchable separately or combined, all linked from **<www.nli.ie/fr_cata2.htm>**.

County record offices

There are several ways to locate a county record office (CRO) web site. The simplest is to use Genuki: each Genuki county page provides a link to relevant CROs, and may itself give contact details and opening times. The ARCHON site (see p. 64) allows you to locate a record office by county or region. Finally, CROs can be found via the web site of the relevant county council (you may even be able to make a guess at its URL, as it will often be something like **<www.essexcc.gov.uk>**) or via the UK government portal at **<www.ukonline.gov.uk>** (see p. 13), which links to the web sites of all arms of national and local government.

There is a wide variation in what CROs provide on their web sites. At the very least, though, you can expect to find details of location, contacts and opening times, along with some basic help on using their material. However, increasingly they offer background material on the area and specific collections, and even on-line catalogues.

Public libraries

Public libraries, although they cannot vie with county record offices for manuscript material, have considerable holdings in the basic sources for genealogical research.

The UK Public Libraries Page at **<dspace.dial.pipex.com/town/square/ ac940/ukpublib.html>** provides links to the web sites of public libraries, and to their OPACs (On-line Public Access Catalogues) where these are available over the internet.

However, a more useful starting point for genealogists is the Familia web site at **<www.familia.org.uk>**. This site is designed to be a comprehensive guide to genealogical holdings in public libraries, with a page for every local authority in the UK and the Republic of Ireland, listing the principal public libraries within the authority which have family history resources, along with contact details, opening times, etc. It then

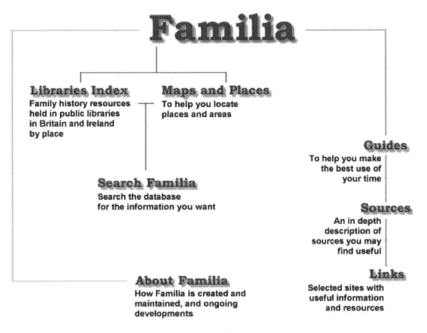

Figure 5.8 Familia home page at <www.familia.org.uk>

outlines the genealogical holdings under the following main headings:

- Births, deaths and marriages
- Census records
- Directories
- Electoral registers
- Poll books
- International Genealogical Index
- Unpublished indexes
- Parish registers
- Periodicals
- Published transcripts
- Other materials

There are also details of any research services offered. While not all local authorities have provided detailed information on their family history material via Familia, over 80 per cent of them have. Figure 5.9 shows part of the entry for the London Borough of Bromley, with details of its directory and electoral register holdings.

6. Directories

6(a) County and Regional Directories

Kent (and some Home Counties) 1840-1938 - incomplete series

6(b) City and Town Directories

Bromley 1866-1962
Beckenham 1897-1939 (some including Anerley and Penge)

6(c) Telephone Directories

Bromley 1952 to date
Orpington 1967-1970. Included in Bromley 1972-

7. Electoral registers and polls books

7(a) Electoral Registers

Beckenham 1925- last non-current year
Bromley 1905-70 (continued as Ravensbourne 1971-)
Chislehurst 1912-
Orpington 1939-
Penge 1899-1947 (continues as part of Beckenham)
N.B. The Reference Library has current registers

Figure 5.9 Part of the Familia page for the London Borough of Bromley

A useful resource for those who have no internet connection of their own is the 'Get Online' listing of public libraries with internet access at <www.peoplesnetwork.gov.uk/netbase/>.

University libraries

While university libraries are not of major importance for genealogical research, all have special collections which may include personal papers; and many have collections of local material which, while unlikely to be of use in constructing a pedigree, may be of interest to the family historian looking for information on an area.

There is no single central index to university library holdings but COPAC is a major consortium of, currently, 23 university libraries, including three of the four copyright libraries (Cambridge University Library, the Bodleian in Oxford, and Trinity College, Dublin). The COPAC web site at <www.copac.ac.uk> provides access to a consolidated catalogue for all member institutions.

However, all university libraries are included on the ARCHON site at <www.hmc.gov.uk/archon/archon.htm>, which provides contact details and has catalogue entries for archival material (i.e. not books or periodicals) relating to individuals, families and organizations. The Archives Hub at <www.archiveshub.ac.uk> is a relatively new site which offers descriptions of archive material in university libraries. Launched in March 2001, it aims to cover 15,000 collections in 30 UK universities.

Bear in mind that university libraries are not open to the general public and that you will normally need to make a written application in advance in order to have access, particularly in the case of manuscript material.

Family History Centres

The LDS Church's Family History Centres (FHCs) are valuable not just because they hold copies of the IGI on CD-ROM, microfiche of the GRO indexes, and other materials, but because any UK genealogical material which has been microfilmed by the Church can be ordered for viewing in an FHC, and this includes many parish registers.

Contact details for FHCs are available at the FamilySearch site at <www.familysearch.org> – clicking on the Library tab (at the top of most main screens) and then selecting Family History Centres will lead to a search page. Genuki provides a quick way to get listings from this search facility: the page at <www.genuki.org.uk/big/LDS/> has links which will search automatically for all FHCs in England, Scotland, Ireland and Wales on the FamilySearch site. There is also an unofficial list, maintained by an individual member of the LDS Church at <www.lds.org.uk/genealogy/fhc/>, which appears to be more up to date. This has a complete listing of towns on the main page, making a search unnecessary.

The key to exploiting this immense wealth of material is the Family History Library (FHL) catalogue, which can be consulted on-line at the FamilySearch site. The search page at <www.familysearch.org/Eng/Library/FHLC/frameset_fhlc.asp> offers searches by place, surname, or, for published works, author. If you search by place, you will get a list of the various types of records available for it. Figure 5.10 shows the initial results of a place search for Lenham in Kent, while Figure 5.11 shows the expanded entry for Church Records, with descriptions of the various items available.

In order to find the microfilm reference for one of the entries, you need to click on it to bring up the 'Title Details' screen (Figure 5.12). This tells you the repository where the material is held (or was at the time of filming), together with the repository's reference for the material. This means you could even use the FHL catalogue as a partial catalogue to county record offices.

Finally, clicking on the 'View Film Notes' button at the top left brings up detailed information on the microfilms relating to this item (Figure

Place Details	FAMILY HISTORY LIBRARY CATALOG	THE CHURCH OF JESUS CHRIST OF LATTER-DAY SAINTS

View Related Places

Place:	England, Kent, Lenham
Topics:	England, Kent, Lenham - Census England, Kent, Lenham - Church records England, Kent, Lenham - Church records - Indexes England, Kent, Lenham - Land and property England, Kent, Lenham - Manors England, Kent, Lenham - Manors - Court records England, Kent, Lenham - Occupations England, Kent, Lenham - Poorhouses, poor law, etc. England, Kent, Lenham - Taxation

Figure 5.10: Search results for Lenham, Kent in the FHL catalogue

Topic Details	FAMILY HISTORY LIBRARY CATALOG	THE CHURCH OF JESUS CHRIST OF LATTER-DAY SAINTS

Topic:	England, Kent, Lenham - Church records
Titles:	Archdeacon's transcripts, 1564-1813; Bishop's transcripts, 1811-1905 Church of England. Parish Church of Lenham (Kent) Births and baptisms, 1779-1837 Independent Church (Lenham) Bishop's transcripts, 1874-1908 Church of England. Chapelry of Charing Heath (Kent) Churchwarden accounts and vestry minutes, 1681-1918 Church of England. Parish Church of Lenham (Kent) Parish register extracts, 1559-1905 Church of England. Parish Church of Lenham (Kent) Record of members, 1849-1860 Church of Jesus Christ of Latter-day Saints. Lenham Hill Branch (Kent) Record of members, ca. 1795-1877 Church of Jesus Christ of Latter-day Saints. Bromley Branch (Kent)

Figure 5.11 Search results for Lenham, Kent in the FHL catalogue – Church records

5.13), with an exact description of what is on each film, together with the film reference which you can now use to order the film at an FHC.

The Society of Genealogists

The Society of Genealogists is home to the premier genealogical library in the country. Its library catalogue has been converted to an OPAC system with the aid of a Heritage Lottery Fund grant. At present, this catalogue is only available in the Society's library, but it is likely to be put on-line at some point in the future, possibly as part of the English Origins site (though access will be free of charge).

However, the Society already has details of one important section of its holdings on-line on its own web site: the list of more than 11,000 parish register copies in its library can be found at **<www.sog.org.uk/prc/>**. There

Title Details	FAMILY HISTORY LIBRARY CATALOG	THE CHURCH OF JESUS CHRIST OF LATTER-DAY SAINTS

View Film Notes

Title:	Archdeacon's transcripts, 1564-1813; Bishop's transcripts, 1611-1905
Authors:	Church of England. Parish Church of Lenham (Kent) (Main Author)

Notes:	Microreproduction of original records housed at the Canterbury Cathedral Archives, Canterbury, Kent.
	Some early pages damaged.
	The church was named for St. Mary.
	Canterbury Cathedral Archives no.: DCa/BT/112; DCb/BT1/141; DCb/BT2/174

Subjects:	England, Kent, Lenham - Church records

Format:	Manuscript (On Film)
Language:	English
Publication:	Salt Lake City : Filmed by the Genealogical Society of Utah, 1991-1992
Physical:	on 4 microfilm reels ; 35 mm.

Figure 5.12 FHL catalogue search – Title Details

Film Notes	FAMILY HISTORY LIBRARY CATALOG	THE CHURCH OF JESUS CHRIST OF LATTER-DAY SAINTS

View Title Details

Title:	Archdeacon's transcripts, 1564-1813; Bishop's transcripts, 1611-1905
Authors:	Church of England. Parish Church of Lenham (Kent) (Main Author)

Note	Location Film
Archdeacon's transcripts: Baptisms, marriages and burials 1564-1813 (missing: 1565/6, 1570/1, 1573/4, 1578/9, 1594/5, 1629/30, 1633/4, 1640/1-1660/1, 1664/5, 1665/6, 1670/1, 1774/5, 1775/6)	FHL BRITISH Film 1751918 Item 3
Bishop's transcripts: Baptisms, marriages and burials 1611-1813 (missing: 1613/4, 1621/2, 1627/8, 1631/2, 1640/1, 1642/3-1662/3, 1716/7, 1795/6)	FHL BRITISH Film 1736839 Item 3
Bishop's transcripts contd.: Baptisms,marriages and burials 1813-1824	FHL BRITISH Film 1786623 Item 6
Bishop's transcripts contd.: Baptisms and burials 1824-1873, 1876-1882, 1897-1898, 1904-1905 Marriages 1824-1837	FHL BRITISH Film 1786624 Item 1

Numbers 1-4 of 4 film notes

Figure 5.13 FHL catalogue – Film Notes

is a page for each county giving for each parish the dates for which there are copies and the shelf mark in the Society's library.

Future developments

The development of electronic sources and finding aids is being taken seriously by all those involved with historic documents. Access to Archives (A2A) is a national project, funded by government and the Heritage Lottery Fund, to 'create a virtual national archives catalogue, bringing together a critical mass of information about the rich national archival heritage and making that information available globally from one source via the World Wide Web.' Information about A2A will be found on the PRO web site at <www.pro.gov.uk/archives/A2A/>.

There is a similar project north of the border: the Scottish Archive Network (SCAN), at <www.scan.org.uk>, is funded by the Heritage Lottery Fund and the Genealogical Society of Utah, and has a three-year project to 'revolutionise access to Scottish Archives, their catalogues and contents.' Among its aims are the linking of archives large and small, public and private, throughout Scotland, and the creation of a unique knowledge base on Scottish history and culture.

While it may be a very long time before all genealogical records are on-line, it looks as if there will be a comprehensive network of catalogues for the repositories that hold them within the fairly near future.

6 Surnames and Pedigrees

The resources discussed in Chapter 4 contain direct transcriptions of, or indexes to, primary genealogical sources. But alongside these are 'compiled' sources, the material put together by individual genealogists. Many people are now putting their pedigrees on-line – Chapter 12 explains how to do this yourself, and Chapter 11 looks at how to locate personal web sites that have genealogical information. But there are a number of major sites to which people can submit details of the surnames they are interested in, or even entire pedigrees without creating their own web site, so that others can contact them. Sites devoted to general information about surnames are discussed in Chapter 9.

Surname interests

One of the best ways to make progress with your family tree is to contact others who are interested in the same surnames. In some cases you will end up encountering cousins who may have considerable material relating to a branch of your family, but at the very least it is useful to find out what resources others have looked at. If you find someone who is doing a one-name study, they may even have extracts from primary sources which they might be prepared to share with you.

Before the advent of the internet, finding such contacts was quite difficult. It involved checking a range of published and unpublished sources, looking through the surname interests in family history magazines and consulting all the volumes of directories such as the annual *Genealogical Research Directory*. You will still need to do all this, of course, not least because many genealogists are not on-line and this is the only way to find out about *their* researches. The SoG's leaflet 'Has it been done before?' at **<www.sog.org.uk/leaflets/done.html>** has a comprehensive overview of the various off-line resources to check.

County surname lists

If you have already made some progress with your family history and have got back far enough to know where your ancestors were living 100 or so years ago, then you should check the relevant county surname list – a directory of genealogical research interests for a particular county. There is a surname list for almost every county in the UK and Ireland, and

Genuki keeps a central list of these at <**www.genuki.org.uk/indexes/ SurnamesLists.html**>.

Surname lists do not provide genealogical information as such: they are just registers of interests, like a printed research directory, and give for each surname the e-mail address of the researcher who submitted it, and usually a date range for the period of interest (see Figure 6.1). Some lists also have links to the web sites of submitters.

For other countries, Cyndi's List has further surname lists at <**www.CyndisList.com/database.htm#Locality**>, but do not expect to find the same level of coverage as there is for the UK.

In addition to the county surname lists, there are a number of surname lists relevant to UK emigration and immigration. These are discussed in Chapter 7 (see p. 91 ff).

You should consider submitting your surname interests to the relevant county lists so that other people can contact you. The exact method of doing this varies from list to list: on some there is a web page with a submission form; on others you will need to e-mail the list-maintainer. Be sure to follow the instructions, as many list maintainers expect you to submit your interests in a particular format (to make processing of submissions easier to automate) and may ignore something sent in the wrong format.

One problem with surname lists is that someone may submit a surname and then forget to change their contact details if they change their

Sussex Surname Interest List

This list is compiled by Chris Broomfield. Submit your Names or Email additions & corrections to me.

New and changed entries this month shown in yellow

Last modified 07 July 2001

H

HAARNACK,Brighton,c1920s	Moira Bonnington
HABGOOD,Ashburnham,1700-1800	Michael Butler
HABGOOD,Ashburnham; all,1700-1800	Katherine Luck
HABGOOD,Hellingly,-1810	Michael Butler
HACK,All,all	Chris Wooderson
HACKETT,Chichester,1800-1900	David Hackett
HACKNEY,Warbleton,c1830	A Hackney
HADLEY,Ticehurst,1770	Karen Langridge
HAFFENDEN,All,1900	Enid Haffenden
HAFFENDEN,Arlington,1863	Karen Langridge

Figure 6.1 Part of the Sussex Surnames List <www.np03.dial.pipex.com/surnames/ssx/ssxname.htm>

e-mail address, so you will occasionally find contact details that are no longer valid. Unfortunately there is nothing you can do about this – it is a fact of life on the internet – and there is no point in asking the surname list manager where a particular submitter can be contacted if their stated e-mail address is no longer valid.

The Guild of One-Name Studies

The Guild of One-Name Studies at **<www.one-name.org>** is an organization for those who are researching all people with a particular surname, rather than just their own personal pedigree. It has a searchable Register of One-Name Studies on-line at **<www.one-name.org/ register.shtml>**, which gives a contact address (not necessarily electronic) for each of the 7,000 or so surnames registered with the Guild.

Unlike the county lists, the surname interests registered with the Guild cover the whole world – this is, in fact, a requirement for membership of the Guild. So, even though the person who has registered a particular one-name interest may not have ancestors in common with you, there is still a good chance that they have collected material of interest relating to your surname. In particular, a Guild member is likely to have a good overview of the variants of their registered surname. This means that the Guild's list of surnames is worth checking even, or especially if, you are only just starting your researches, whereas the county surname lists are probably not very useful until you have got back three or four generations.

RootsWeb

One of the most useful sites for surnames is RootsWeb at **<www.rootsweb.com>** which has a wide range of surname-related resources, all linked from **<resources.rootsweb.com/~clusters/surnames/>**. There is a separate page for each listed surname with:

- Links to personal web sites at RootsWeb which include the name
- Search forms for a number of databases hosted by RootsWeb
- Links to any mailing lists for the surname (see below)

The most general surname resource at RootsWeb is the Roots Surname List (RSL) at **<rsl.rootsweb.com>**. This is a surname list attached to the ROOTS-L mailing list, the oldest genealogy mailing list on the internet, and contains about a million entries submitted by around 200,000 individual genealogists. You can enter a geographical location to narrow your search, using Chapman county codes and/or three-letter country codes (see Figure 6.2 for some examples) – there is a list of standard codes at **<helpdesk.rootsweb.com/help/abbrev2.html>**. However, you may need to do a couple of searches to make sure you find all relevant entries as some people spell out English counties in full or use the two-letter country code UK. If you check the list regularly, a useful feature is that you can

Surname	From	To	Migration	Submitter
Marshall	1000	1889	"SouthBank,ENG>Cleveland,OH"	lindonm
Marshall	1126	1248	WLS>ENG	mcgraw
Marshall	1500	1641	Ilminster,ENG>Exeter,ENG>NewHaven,CT,USA	brucew
Marshall	1500	1600	ENG	seejay
Marshall	1500s	1619	Quarrington,LIN,ENG	edharr
Marshall	1502	1641	ENG	varya
Marshall	1502	1641	"SOM>DEV,ENG>NewHaven,CT"	ktonks
Marshall	1576	1641	ENG>MA,USA	silvie
Marshall	1580	----	LIN,ENG	bchapman
Marshall	1584	now	BKS, ENG	shanan
Marshall	1595	now	LND,ENG>MA,USA>AnnapolisCo,NS,CAN	behall
Marshall	1595	1636	ENG>MA,USA	spencer
Marshall	1596	now	ENG>MA,USA	horvat1
Marshall	1598	1650	ENG>MA	maryl
Marshall	1600	now	LIN,ENG	lkfergus
Marshall	1600	1733	ENG>Westfield,MA,USA	mrstamil
Marshall	1600	now	ENG>VA>JohnsonCo>CarterCo,KY	af15469

Figure 6.2 The results of a search for MARSHALL in ENG in the Roots Surname List

restrict your results to those added or updated recently. As you can see from Figure 6.2, the submitter details are not given on the search results page, but there is a link to them from the user ID given in the 'submitter' column.

Discussion forums

Mailing lists, newsgroups and other types of discussion forum are described in detail in Chapter 10, but it is worth noting here that there are many of these devoted to individual surnames. Even if you do not participate in any of them, it will be well worth your while to look through the archives of past messages to see if anyone else is working on the same family or on the same geographical area.

John Fuller's list of mailing lists has links to surname lists at <www.rootsweb.com/~jfuller/gen_mail.html#surnames>. Many of the surname lists are hosted by RootsWeb and can be found either from the general list of mailing lists at <lists.rootsweb.com> or via the individual surname pages at <resources.rootsweb.com/~clusters/surnames/>. RootsWeb also has message boards for thousands of surnames.

Pedigree databases

The surname-interest resources do not provide genealogical information, they simply offer contact details for other genealogists who may share your interests. But there are several sites which allow genealogists to make their pedigrees available on the Web. You can, of course, do this by creating your own web site, as discussed in Chapter 12, particularly if you want to publish more comprehensive information. But if you just want to make your pedigree available on-line, these sites provide an easy way to do it. (Some of the issues as to whether you should submit your own pedigree to one or more of these sites, and how to do so, are discussed in Chapter 12.) Even if you do not make your own pedigree available, many others have, and it is worth checking these sites for overlap with your own family tree.

There is not space here to give more than a brief account of some of the most important sites, but for a comprehensive list of pedigree databases consult the 'Databases, Search Sites, Surname Lists' page on Cyndi's List at <www.cyndislist.com/database.htm>.

Free databases

FamilySearch at <www.familysearch.org> has been discussed as a source of record transcriptions in Chapter 4 (p. 42), but the site also includes two data collections with user-submitted information. Ancestral File goes back to 1978, starting life as a CD-ROM collection, initially as a way for members of the LDS Church to deposit the fruits of their researches but in fact open to submission from anyone with genealogical information. The Pedigree Resource File is a more recent database compiled from

Figure 6.3 An individual record in Ancestral File

submissions to the FamilySearch web site and also published on CD-ROM.

In Ancestral File a successful search on an individual name brings up an individual record with links, on the left, to a full pedigree, a family group record and submitter details (see Figure 6.3).

In the Pedigree Resource File a search produces a similar individual record with details of the submitter, but no link to a pedigree. A useful feature is that it gives you the submission number – clicking on this will do a search for all individuals in the same submission. Unfortunately, there is only a postal address for submitters in these two FamilySearch databases, no e-mail address.

As discussed in Chapter 4, you can search all four FamilySearch databases at once by selecting All Resources from any of the search pages (see Figure 4.9), and the results are then listed separately for each database.

Ancestry has a pedigree database called Ancestry WorldTree at <www.ancestry.com/search/rectype/usersub/worldtree/main.htm> containing about 80 million names in submitted pedigrees. The WorldTree database is freely accessible and does not require a subscription to Ancestry. Other Ancestry databases are discussed in Chapter 4 (p. 54), and if you do a general name search on Ancestry the results will include any relevant material for WorldTree.

RootsWeb's WorldConnect Project at <worldconnect.genealogy. rootsweb.com> has a searchable database of 25,000 submitted files containing over 60 million names. As with other RootsWeb material, no subscription or payment is required.

A useful tool for searching free databases is Rob Kuijsten's Genealogy Surname Navigator, which has a page for UK records at <www.kuijsten. net/navigator/uk/>. This can be used to submit name searches to a number of different databases all from the same search page. It currently includes:

- Ancestral File
- Ancestry World Tree
- Anglo-Indian family history
- FreeBMD 1837–1899
- GeneaNet
- IGI
- RootsWeb Surname List UK
- United Kingdom And Ireland Records (RootsWeb)

Similar pages are available for other countries via links from this page.

Subscription databases

GenServ, started by Cliff Manis in 1991 (before the invention of the Web) as an e-mail only service, is among the oldest pedigree databases on the internet. It is a subscription system at <www.genserv.com>, with over 20 million individuals in more than 15,000 submitted files. It is a slightly unusual service in that you must submit some of your own material in order to subscribe. Once you have done this you can have a free two-month trial subscription, while a regular subscription is £8 per year, which allows you to do unlimited searches. Details of how to subscribe are given at <www.genserv.com/gs/gsh2sub.htm>. A more limited trial (one surname search for any one e-mail address) is available under the 'Sample Search' option. There is also a demo version on a more limited database 'designed for non-members to sample the full range of searching and reporting capabilities available' at <demo.genserv.com>.

World Family Tree is a subscription database (also available on CD-ROM) at <familytreemaker.genealogy.com/wfttop.html> with about 125 million individuals in around 200,000 pedigrees. There is a free search facility, but you need to subscribe in order to view any matching pedigrees. The site has been criticized for charging for access to freely submitted pedigrees, and the charges ($19.99 per month, $79.99 per year) are quite high if you are only to use the site occasionally. However, you can use the site as an index to the CD-ROMs which means you can buy only those which hold material of interst to you, or look for them in a library.

GENDEX

GENDEX at <www.gendex.com> is rather different from the sites mentioned so far, in that it does not store pedigrees at all, but acts as a central registry for pedigrees on personal web sites. It currently holds details of almost 30 million individuals from around 9,000 web sites. GENDEX was developed by Gene Stark as a feature of his GED2HTML program, one of the most widely used programs for converting a GEDCOM file into an on-line pedigree (see p. 162). But it is also used by many other pieces of software that can create family trees for the Web. Anyone who creates a set of web pages using software with GENDEX facilities can have the individuals on their web site automatically added to the index at GENDEX.

GENDEX can either be used free or you can register for more sophisticated search facilities at a cost of $10 per 1,000 search hits.

Limitations

One point to bear in mind is that the majority of the individuals in these databases were born in the US, so in spite of the amount of material you should not be surprised if you do not find matches for your UK ancestors in them. However, as many American pedigrees have some roots in the British Isles, it is still well worth checking them. Also, as more British genealogists submit their family trees to such sites, they will become more useful for British genealogy.

The material on these sites consists entirely of submissions from individual genealogists. This means that the completeness and accuracy of information is highly variable (though some sites do basic consistency checks on material submitted in order to detect obvious errors, such as a death date earlier than a birth date). Ancestral File, for example, contains a dozen submissions with an incorrect birth date for Isaac Newton, who any reference book will tell you was born on Christmas Day 1642. You should therefore look at these databases as a way of contacting people with similar interests, rather than as direct resources of data. You should never directly incorporate such material into your own genealogy database without thorough checking. In some cases this will be simple – the example in Figure 6.3 gives a christening date and parish, which should be easy to check; in others the information may be of little value – say just a year and a country. Of course, it may be that the person who has submitted the information has a substantial collection of supporting material, particularly as some genealogists are wary of putting *all* their information on-line. And the advantage of these databases over the surname resources discussed earlier in this chapter is that they provide information about individuals and families, not just about surnames. This should make it fairly easy to establish whether the submitter is interested in the same family as you, something that may be particularly important for a common surname.

Locating people

The surname lists and databases already discussed will put you in touch with other genealogists who have made their researches – or at least their research interests – public, but you can also use the internet to locate long-lost relatives or their descendants, or simply people with a particular surname.

There is a useful article on 'Finding People' by Phil Bradley in issue 20 of *Ariadne* at **<www.ariadne.ac.uk/issue20/search-engines/>**, which evaluates sites for locating people and e-mail addresses.

Phone numbers and addresses

The UK phone directories are on-line at **<www.bt.com/directory-enquiries/dq_home.jsp>** and this will give you an address, postcode and phone number. 192.com at **<www.192.com>** provides more extensive searching, including electoral rolls. This is a commercial service, though the initial free registration allows you to conduct 10 searches. A list of UK dialling codes can be found at **<www.brainstorm.co.uk/utils/std-codes. html>**.

The internet is particularly useful for foreign phone numbers, since only a small number of major reference libraries in the UK have a full set of international directories. Yahoo has many links to national phone directories. One way to locate these is to go directly to the relevant reference page for the country, e.g for Ireland **<dir.yahoo.com/Regional/ Countries/Ireland/Reference/>** will provide links to various reference resources including phone books.

Ancestry has European telephone listings at **<www.ancestry.com/search/ rectype/directories/eurotel/main.htm>** which cover Austria, Belgium, Denmark, France, Germany, Italy, Luxembourg, the Netherlands, Spain and the United Kingdom. However, the numbers here are not entirely up to date; for example, they still show 0171 and 0181 as the dialling codes for London numbers.

The Telephone Directories on the Web site at **<www.teldir.com/eng/>** has 'links to Yellow Pages, White Pages, Business Directories, Email Addresses and Fax Listings from over 170 countries all around the world'. International dialling codes are at **<kropla.com/dialcode.htm>**.

E-mail addresses

Finding e-mail addresses is not straightforward. For a start, there is no single authoritative directory of e-mail addresses in the way that the phone book is for phone numbers. There are simply too many e-mail addresses and they are changing all the time. Also, there is no single place to register them. However, there are a number of directories of e-mail addresses on the Web.

Yahoo has a 'People Search' at **<people.yahoo.com>** with a UK/Ireland version at **<ukie.people.yahoo.com>**. The Yahoo directory has links to many sites providing general or specific e-mail address searches at **<uk.dir.yahoo.com/Reference/Phone_Numbers_and_Addresses/Email_Ad dresses/Individuals/>**. One of the best-known e-mail directories is Bigfoot at **<www.bigfoot.com>**. There is also the Internet Address Finder at **<www.iaf.net>**. Cyndi's List has a 'Finding People' page at **<www. CyndisList.com/finding.htm>**.

One point to bear in mind is that it is easy to add an e-mail address to a database by extracting it from a message sent to a mailing list or newsgroup, or if it is provided on a web page. However, it is quite impossible for a database to know when the address ceases to be valid (perhaps because the person concerned has changed their internet provider), so the databases are full of old, no longer valid e-mail addresses as well as current ones. (The Internet Address Finder usefully gives 'last updated' information.) Except for fairly unusual names, you will find multiple entries, and since e-mail addresses often give no clue to the geographical location of the person it may be hard to identify the one you are looking for. Also, people posting messages to newsgroups often give fake e-mail addresses to prevent spam (i.e. unsolicited bulk mail), though these should be easy to spot if you are familiar with the way e-mail addresses are constructed.

Another way to find an e-mail address is simply to use a standard search engine to look for the relevant name, but success will depend on the person concerned having a web page, and the search could be time consuming.

If you want to make it easy for people to find your e-mail address some of the services mentioned above (Yahoo People and Internet Address

Finder, for example), allow you to submit your details. Alternatively, you could create a web page with your contact details and submit its URL to a few of the major search engines (see Chapter 12).

Adoption and child migration

While the resources discussed so far can be useful for tracing people when you know their names they may be of little use in the case of adoption or child migration, and you may need to go to sites specifically devoted to these issues.

The FamilyRecords portal has brief information on UK adoption records at <www.familyrecords.gov.uk/adoptionmain.htm> and more detailed information, including details of the Adoption Contact Register, is available on the ONS site at <www.statistics.gov.uk/nsbase/registration/adoptions.asp>. The FFHS has a leaflet 'Tracing The Birth Parents Of Adopted Persons In England And Wales' (relevant to the period since 1927) at <www.ffhs.org.uk/General/Help/Adopted.htm>.

The Salvation Army offers a Family Tracing Service. The home page for this is at <www.salvationarmy.org.uk/familytracing/> and there is an FAQ at <www.salvationarmy.org.uk/faqs/familytracing.html>. Searching in Ireland has a page for Irish-born adoptees at <www.netreach.net/~steed/search.html>. The newsgroup alt.adoption is for all issues relating to adoption.

Cyndi's List has a page devoted to Adoption resources at <www.cyndislist.com/adoption.htm>, and John Fuller has an extensive list of mailing lists relating to adoption at <www.rootsweb.com/~jfuller/gen_mail_adoption.html>.

The Department of Health has information on child emigration at <www.doh.gov.uk/childinf.htm> and links to organizations that provide information and support for child migrants. The Child Migrants Trust has some brief historical background at <www.nottscc.gov.uk/child_migrants/HISTORY/Index.htm>, while the 'Young Immigrants to Canada' page on Marjorie Kohli's site <www.ist.uwaterloo.ca/~marj/genealogy/homeadd.html> has information and links relating to child emigration to Canada up to 1939.

7 Social Groups

Chapter 4 covered the major sources of primary genealogical data on-line which, because they are common to all our ancestors, are likely to be of use to every family historian. However, our ancestors did much more than be born and buried, or be discovered living in a certain place by the census enumerator, and there is a great variety in terms of occupation, religious persuasion and geographical mobility. The aim of this chapter is to cover some of the more important of these social groupings. While Chapter 4 is intended to be reasonably comprehensive, this chapter cannot mention more than a handful of the many web sites devoted to these topics. Unlike the sites mentioned in Chapter 4, the material discussed here is mostly general historical information, but there are still a number of sites which include small data extracts for particular groups of people.

Churches and denominations

Records relating to parish registers are covered in Chapter 4 (p. 42 ff). However, most of the available material relates to the established Church, though FamilySearch does include some Catholic and Nonconformist registers. Beyond the sources mentioned in Chapter 4 you should not, on the whole, expect to find parish register material on-line. Nonetheless, there is some useful information on the Web about churches and religious denominations, though this is not, to be sure, any substitute for the specialist books on the subject.

John Fuller has a page for mailing lists relating to individual churches and denominations at **<www.rootsweb.com/~jfuller/gen_mail_religions.html>**.

Churches
The main site for all UK churches is Church Net at **<www.churchnet.org.uk>**. It has a list of all denominations represented in the UK at **<www.churchnet.org.uk/ukchurches/>** and links to relevant web sites, whether for a denomination as a whole or for an individual congregation. The official web sites for the national churches of the UK are:

- Church of England **<www.cofe.anglican.org>**
- Church in Wales **<www.churchinwales.org.uk>**
- Church of Ireland **<www.ireland.anglican.org>**

- Church of Scotland <www.churchofscotland.org.uk>
- Scottish Episcopal Church <scotland.anglican.org>

You can expect these to provide information about individual parishes, usually organized by diocese or accessible via a search facility such as the C of E's 'church-search' at <www.church-search.com>.

Many individuals have placed pictures of local churches on-line, and these are discussed under 'Photographs' in Chapter 8, p. 107.

Roman Catholic Church
The official web sites for the Roman Catholic Church in the UK are:

- England and Wales <www.tasc.ac.uk/cc/>
- Scotland <www.catholic-scotland.org.uk>

The PRO has a leaflet on 'Catholic Recusants' at <catalogue.pro.gov.uk/leaflets/ri2173.htm>, which gives a guide to the relevant official records. The Catholic Record Society at <www.catholic-history.org.uk/crs/> is the main publishing body for Catholic records, while the Catholic Central Library has a guide to its collections at <www.catholic-library.org.uk>. The Catholic Archives Society has a web site at <www.catholic-history.org.uk/catharch/>.

Information about the Catholic Family History Society will be found at <www.catholic-history.org.uk/cfhs/index.htm>, and the Catholic History site at <www.catholic-history.org.uk> also hosts three regional Catholic FHS web sites.

The Local Catholic Church History and Genealogy Research Guide and Worldwide Directory at <home.att.net/~Local_Catholic/> is a comprehensive research guide to Catholic records. It has details of individual churches and links to on-line information, with very thorough pages for the UK and Ireland. The Fianna web site has a guide to Roman Catholic records in Ireland at <www.rootsweb.com/~fianna/county/parishes.html> taken from Brian Mitchell's *A Guide to Irish Parish Registers*.

Cyndi's List has over 100 links to Catholic resources at <www.CyndisList.com/catholic.htm>.

Nonconformist churches
The ChurchNet site mentioned above has links to the web sites of the Nonconformist Churches of Britain. The Spartacus Internet Encyclopaedia has a brief history of the most important religious groups at <www.spartacus.schoolnet.co.uk/religion.htm>, with links to details of individual reformers and reform movements. Cyndi's List has pages devoted to Baptist, Huguenot, Methodist, Presbyterian and Quaker materials (listed

under the heading 'Religion and Churches' on the main page), and links to many other relevant resources at **<www.CyndisList.com/religion.htm>**. Many of the denominational mailing lists at **<www.rootsweb.com/ ~jfuller/gen_mail_religions.html>** are for dissenting groups. (Huguenot immigration is covered on p. 96.)

The following is just a selection of the Nonconformist material on the Web:

- Protestant Nonconformity in Scotland **<www.genuki.org.uk/big/ sct/noncon1.html>**: an article by Sherry Irvine, CGRS, FSA
- Quaker Family History Society **<www.qfhs.mcmail.com>**: has details of Quaker records and their location, with a page for each county
- Methodist Ministers and Probationers, 1870s–1936 **<www.geocities. com/Heartland/Pointe/4320/m_1.html>**
- Baptist, Methodist, Presbyterian and Quaker Records in Ireland **<www.rootsweb.com/~fianna/county/churches.html>**

Dr Williams's Library, the main repository of English and Welsh Nonconformist registers, is not on-line, though there is brief information at **<www1.rhbnc.ac.uk/hellenic-institute/Drwilliams's.html>**

Occupations

Occupational records have on the whole not formed part of the official state records discussed in Chapter 4, so they do not feature strongly in the major on-line data collections. The PRO's 'Pathways to the Past' (see p. 6) includes material on occupations, under the title 'People at Work', with pages devoted to apprentices, the police, customs and excise officers, coastguards and the legal profession. The PRO has leaflets on the following occupations and professions for which there are state records:

- Royal Warrant Holders and Household Servants
- Attorneys and Solicitors
- Tax and Revenue Collectors
- Metropolitan Police
- Royal Irish Constabulary
- Teachers
- Nurses
- Railway Staff

The largest set of occupational records on-line is the apprenticeship material on the English Origins site at **<www.englishorigins.com>**: the London City Apprenticeship Abstracts 1568–1850 (already on-line) and the Apprentices of Great Britain 1710–1774 (in preparation). The site has additional information about apprenticeship records and a list of City Livery Companies at **<www.englishorigins.com/lonapps-details.html>**.

Genuki has an 'Occupations' page at **<www.genuki.org.uk/big/ eng/Occupations.html>** with a number of links for particular occupations, and links to all the PRO leaflets mentioned. Cyndi's List has a page of resources relating to occupations at **<www.CyndisList.com/occupatn. htm>** with separate sections devoted to Actors and Entertainers, Fishermen and Mariners, Medicine, Mining, Police, Railroad.

Ron Taylor's census index site (see p. 41) has a collection of Occupations Census Indexes for 1851 which cover apprentices, policemen, servants, physicians, doctors, nurses, sailors, Royal Navy, soldiers, travellers and clergy at **<rontay.digiweb.com/visit/occupy/>**.

The Modern Records Centre at the University of Warwick holds records relating to 'labour history, industrial relations and industrial politics'. While it has not put any records on-line, there are genealogical guides to the records of carvers, compositors, gilders, house decorators, painters, picture-frame makers, printing workers, quarrymen, railwaymen and stonemasons at **<cal.csv.warwick.ac.uk/services/library/mrc/mrcgene.shtml>**.

There are many sites devoted to individual occupations, sometimes with just historical information, sometimes with a database of names. Examples of the latter are the Database of Sugar Bakers and Sugar Refiners at **<www.mawer.clara.net/intro.html>** and the Biographical Database of British Chemists at **<www5.open.ac.uk/Arts/chemists/>**. The Coalmining History Resource Centre at **<www.cmhrc.pwp.blueyonder.co.uk>** has lists of mines at various dates, transcripts of an 1842 report on child labour in the mines, and a database of mining deaths with 90,000 names.

There are an increasing number of mailing lists devoted to occupations. These are listed at **<www.rootsweb.com/~jfuller/gen_mail_occ.html>** and include, for example, CANAL-PEOPLE, CHURCHMEN-UK, CIRCUS-FOLK, COALMINERS, Itinerantroots, Mariners, POLICE-UK, RAILWAY-UK, SCOTTISH-MINING, THEATRICAL-ANCESTORS, VIOLIN-MAKERS. There is also a general OCCUPATIONS list.

Resources relating to the merchant navy are discussed along with those for the Royal Navy, on p. 89.

Trade directories, discussed on p. 51, are an important source of occupational information.

Occupational terms
Brief explanations of past occupations are provided in John Hitchcock's 'Ranks, Professions, Occupations and Trades' page at **<www.gendocs. demon.co.uk/trades.html>** and John Lacombe's 'A List of Occupations' at **<cpcug.org/user/jlacombe/terms.html>**. These are very similar and cover about 1,600 occupational terms.

For the period before parish registers Olive Tree's list of 'Medieval And Obsolete English Trade And Professional Terms' at **<olivetreegenealogy.**

com/misc/occupations.shtml#med> may be useful, especially since it includes medieval Latin terms for many occupations, and some older English spellings.

The most comprehensive listing of occupational terms, with something like 30,000 entries and descriptions, is the Open University's *Dictionary of Occupational Terms*. However, this is available only on CD-ROM and is not on-line.

Crime

Whether crime is regarded as an occupation or an alternative to an occupation, its records form a significant part of our social history. The official records of crime are those of the courts and the prison system, and these will be found in the PRO, which has a number of leaflets devoted to the subject, including:

- Outlawry in Medieval and Early Modern England
- Criminal Trials, Old Bailey and the Central Criminal Court
- Criminal Trials at the Assizes
- Convicts and Prisoners 1100–1986

All of these are on-line at **<www.pro.gov.uk/leaflets/Riindex.asp>**. The PRO also has material on 'Ancestors and the Law' in its 'Pathways to the Past' section (see p. 6).

Cyndi's List has a page devoted to 'Prisons, Prisoners & Outlaws' at **<www.cyndislist.com/prisons.htm>**. Genuki lists relevant resources under the headings Court Proceedings and Correctional Institutions on national and county pages. There is a PRISONS-UK mailing list, details of which will be found at **<www.rootsweb.com/~jfuller/gen_mail_occ.html>**. More specific resources include Jeff Alvey's page on 'Newgate Prison' at **<www.fred.net/jefalvey/newgate.html>** which has a list of names taken from an 1896 book on the subject. The same site lists some of the executions in England from 1606 at **<www.fred.net/jefalvey/execute. html>**.

A major on-line resource planned for the end of 2002 is the University of Sheffield's Lottery funded project to put the Old Bailey Proceedings, i.e. accounts of criminal trials, 1670–1834 on-line. (There are brief details at **<www.nof-digitise.org>**.)

There are many resources on-line relating to convict transportation to the colonies, and these are discussed under Emigration on pp. 91–5.

The armed forces

There are two official sites for information on the armed forces and their records: the PRO and the Ministry of Defence (MoD). The PRO provides an extensive series of leaflets to help you understand how the records are organized and how to locate and understand them. These can be found at <www.pro.gov.uk/leaflets/Riindex.asp>. And the 'Pathways to the Past' pages have a section devoted to the army and navy at <www.pro.gov.uk/pathways/FamilyHistory/gallery3/>.

The MoD site at <www.mod.uk>, while mainly devoted to the present-day forces, has detailed pages on the location of recent service records, and provides many contact addresses. Each branch of the services has its own web site within the MoD's internet domain: <www.royal-navy.mod.uk>, <www.army.mod.uk> and <www.raf.mod.uk>. Beyond these central bodies, there are the individual regiments, ships, squadrons and other units, many of which have their own web pages with historical information. The easiest way to find these is from the site for the relevant arm of the services, which has links to its constituent bodies.

The PRO and MoD sites do not offer information about individuals, and at present the only major collection of on-line data relating to service personnel is the Debt of Honour Register at <www.cwgc.org>, discussed in Chapter 4 (p. 47), which lists the Commonwealth war dead from the two world wars. However, there are other small collections of data at some of the sites for individual branches of the services. The PRO has not announced any project to make military records available on-line, but given their importance for family historians this material is a good candidate for digitization in the near future.

Beyond the official sites, there are many others, some of which have good small datasets. The most comprehensive collection relating to the whole of the armed forces is the History of the British Armed Forces site at <british-forces.com>. In addition to sections on the main branches of the services, there is material on Commonwealth forces, a glossary of abbreviations, an index of engagements going back to the Spanish Armada, sections on individual conflicts including substantial material on the world wars, and details of many medals, orders and decorations. There is relatively little biographical information on the site.

The Scots at War site at <www-saw.arts.ed.ac.uk> concentrates mainly on the 20th century. It has a Commemorative Roll of Honour with service and biographical information on Scottish servicemen, and detailed genealogical help pages which will be of interest to anyone with Commonwealth military ancestors.

Genuki has pages devoted to Military Records at <www.genuki.org.uk/big/MilitaryRecords.html> and Military History at <www.genuki.org.uk/big/MilitaryHistory.html>. Cyndi's List has a page devoted to UK Military at <www.CyndisList.com/miluk.htm>, which covers all branches of the services, while her 'Military Resources Worldwide' page at <www.CyndisList.com/milres.htm> has more general material.

If you need to identify medals, good starting points are MedalNet at <www.medal.net> which is devoted to Commonwealth medals, and The International Electronic Phaleristic Encyclopedia (IEPE) at <haynese.

winthrop.edu/iepe.html>, which has links to sites for British medals. There are also sites devoted to the holders of gallantry medals, particularly the Victoria Cross, for which lists of recipients can be found at <www.chapter-one.com/vc/> and <www2.prestel.co.uk/stewart/vcross.htm>. There is a site devoted to the George Medal at <www.btinternet.com/~stephen.stratford/george_medal.htm>. The PRO has a leaflet on medals and their records at <catalogue.pro.gov.uk/leaflets/ri2120.htm>.

The Imperial War Museum at <www.iwm.org.uk> has a family history section at <www.iwm.org.uk/lambeth/famhist.htm>, and links to many military museums. The Canadian Forces College has a worldwide list of military museums at <www.cfcsc.dnd.ca:80/links/milhist/mus.html>, while the MoD has a comprehensive listing of British military museums at <www.army.mod.uk/ceremonialandheritage/museums_main.htm>.

There are a number of mailing lists devoted to particular wars, including GREATWAR, WORLDWAR2 and WW20-ROOTS-L, details of which will be found at <www.rootsweb.com/~jfuller/gen_mail_wars.html>.

The Royal Navy

The official Royal Navy site at <www.royal-navy.mod.uk> has separate sections for ships, the Fleet Air Arm, submarines, the Royal Marines and naval establishments. Historical information is in a section called 'RN profile' at <www.royal-navy.mod.uk/static/pages/168.html>.

Although the merchant navy is not an arm of the state, it has long been subject to government regulation and many maritime ancestors will have served in both the Royal Navy and the merchant fleet. Information about the records of merchant seamen will be found among the PRO's leaflets at <www.pro.gov.uk/leaflets/Riindex.asp> and in 'Pathways to the Past' at <www.pro.gov.uk/pathways/FamilyHistory/gallery3/seaman.htm>. Bob Sanders has good material on 'Tracing British seamen and their ships' at <www.angelfire.com/de/BobSanders/Site.html>. Genuki has a page of merchant marine links at <www.genuki.org.uk/big/MerchantMarine.html>, while the Royal Navy is included in the Military Records and Military History pages mentioned above.

A general gateway to maritime resources on the Web is the National Maritime Museum's Port site at <www.port.nmm.ac.uk>. In addition to a search facility, there is an option to browse by subject or historical period. The site offers a detailed description of each resource it links to.

The MARINERS mailing list is for all those whose ancestors pursued maritime occupations. The list has a web site at <www.mariners-L.freeserve.co.uk> with sections devoted to individual countries, as well as more general topics such as wars at sea, and shipping companies. The site has instructions on how to join the mailing list.

The army [4]

In addition to the detailed information about army records in the PRO leaflets mentioned above, there is basic information about locating records in the PRO for individual soldiers at **<www.pro.gov.uk/research/ easysearch/Army.htm>**. GENUKI has a page devoted to British Military History at **<www.genuki.org.uk/big/MilitaryHistory.html>**, and an article by Jay Hall on 'British Military Records for the 18th and 19th Centuries' at **<www.genuki.org.uk/big/MilitaryRecords.html>**. The FFHS provides some basic information in the on-line version of its leaflet 'In search of your Soldier Ancestors' at **<www.ffhs.org.uk/General/Help/Soldier.htm>**; and there is a useful article by Fawne Stratford-Devai devoted to 'British Military Records Part 1: The Army' in *The Global Gazette* at **<globalgazette.net/gazfd/gazfd44.htm>**.

The crucial piece of information about any ancestor in the army is the regiment or unit he served in. A useful area of the army site at the MoD is that devoted to the organizational structure of the army, at **<www. army.mod.uk/unitsandorgs/>**, which has links to the web pages for the individual regiments. However, over the centuries, regiments have not been very stable in either composition or naming and you are likely to need historical information about the particular period when an ancestor was in uniform. The official pages for each regiment on the MoD site give a brief history and a list of engagements, but the essential web site for regimental history is T. F. Mills' Land Forces of Britain, the Empire and Commonwealth site at **<www.regiments.org>**. The site not only provides detailed background information on the regimental system at **<regiments.org/ milhist/uk/bargts.htm>**, but also lists the regiments in the army in particular years since the 18th century. For an overview of regimental name changes and amalgamations, see Cathy Day's listing of 'Lineages of all British Army Infantry Regiments' at **<www.ozemail.com/~clday/ regiments.htm>**. Barney Tyrwhitt-Drake has a convenient list of the important 1881 name changes at **<www.tdrake.demon.co.uk/ infantry.htm>**. The Scots at War site has a list of Scottish regiments at **<www-saw.arts.ed.ac.uk/army/regiments/>** and has pages devoted to each one. There is a britregiments mailing list, details of which will be found at **<www.rootsweb.com/~jfuller/gen_mail_wars.html>**.

If you want to know what uniform an ancestor wore, or are trying to identify a photograph, the illustrations from two booklets by Arthur H. Bowling, on the uniforms of British Infantry Regiments 1660–1914 and Scottish Regiments 1660–1914, are on-line at **<geocities.com/Pentagon/ Barracks/3050/buframe.html>**. The Military Images site at **<www.**

---

[4] The material in this section is based on my article on 'Military genealogy on the internet' in the April 2001 issue of the PRO's *Ancestors* magazine, which should be consulted for additional sites.

capefam.freeserve.co.uk/militaryimages.htm> has several thousand military photographs on-line, mainly from the First World War.

The Royal Air Force

The official RAF site is at <www.raf.mod.uk>, with a list of units and stations at <www.raf.mod.uk/stations/>. The 'Histories' section at <www.raf.mod.uk/history/histories.html> offers historical material on individual squadrons and stations, with images of squadron badges and details of battle honours and aircraft. If you have an ancestor who took part in the Battle of Britain, you will want to look at the operational diaries at <www.raf.mod.uk/bob1940/bobhome.html>. The 'Links' page at <www.raf.mod.uk/links/> has links to the web sites of individual squadrons and stations. The MoD site has (non-electronic) contact details for RAF Personnel records at <www.mod.uk/index.php3?page=125>.

Colonies, emigration and immigration

Former British colonies are genealogically important for British and Irish family history for three reasons: they have been the destination of emigrants from the British Isles (both voluntary and otherwise), the source of much immigration, and a place of residence and work for many British soldiers, merchants and others. There have, of course, been other sources of immigration and these are discussed towards the end of this section.

There is not space here to deal with internet resources relating to the individual countries, or to records unrelated to immigration or emigration, but good places to start are Cyndi's List at <www.cyndislist.com>, which has individual pages for all the countries or regions, and the Genweb site for the country at <worldgenweb.org> (see p. 22).

Genuki has links relating to both emigration and immigration at <www.genuki.org.uk/big/Emigration.html>.

Resources relating to child migration are covered in 'Adoption and child migration' on p. 82.

General information

For details of the official British records of emigration, the PRO's 'Emigration' leaflet is the definitive on-line guide at <catalogue.pro.gov.uk/leaflets/ri2272.htm>. For convict transportation, there are leaflets relating to North America and the West Indies at <catalogue.pro.gov.uk/leaflets/ri2234.htm>, and to Australia at <catalogue.pro.gov.uk/leaflets/ri2235.htm>.

Key records for emigration from the British Isles are passenger lists, and there are a number of sites with information about surviving passenger lists, or with data transcribed from them. Cyndi's List has a 'Passenger Ships' page at <www.CyndisList.com/ships.htm>. Among other information, this has links to many passenger lists and lists of ship arrivals.

The Immigrant Ships Transcribers Guild at <istg.rootsweb.com> has transcribed over 3,500 passenger lists and is adding more all the time. These can be searched by date, by port of departure, port of arrival, passenger name or captain's name. In addition to its own material, the Guild's 'Compass' web site at **<istg.rootsweb.com/newcompass/pcindex. html>** has an enormous collection of links to passenger-list sites on-line. For Irish emigration, the ScotlandsClans site has many links at **<www.scotlandsclans.com/irshiplists.htm>**. There are a number of mailing lists for immigrant ships, but the most general is TheShipsList, details of which are at **<www.rootsweb.com/~jfuller/gen_mail_emi.html>**. This page also has details of other lists relating to emigration and immigration.

The PRO has information about official records in leaflets devoted to 'Immigration' at **<catalogue.pro.gov.uk/leaflets/ri2156.htm>** and 'Naturalisation' at **<catalogue.pro.gov.uk/leaflets/ri2257.htm>**.

There is a Museum of Immigration at Spitalfields in London which has a web site at **<www.19princeletstreet.org.uk>**.

North America

The American colonies were the first dumping ground for convicts, and the PRO leaflet 'Transportation to America and the West Indies, 1615–1776' at **<catalogue.pro.gov.uk/leaflets/ri2234.htm>** gives details of the records. More general information about colonies on the other side of the Atlantic will be found in 'The American and West Indian Colonies Before 1782' at **<catalogue.pro.gov.uk/leaflets/ri2105.htm>**. For post-colonial emigration to the US, see 'Emigrants to North America After 1776' at **<catalogue. pro.gov.uk/leaflets/ri2107.htm>**. The US National Archives and Records Administration has a leaflet on 'Immigration Records' at **<www.nara.gov/ genealogy/immigration/immigrat.html>**, and one on 'Naturalization Records' at **<www.nara.gov/genealogy/natural.html>**. For other links relating to emigration to North America, the best starting point is the 'Immigration and Naturalization' page on Cyndi's List at **<www. CyndisList.com/immigrat.htm>**.

US sites of course have a wealth of data relating to immigrants. Ancestry.com, for example, has databases of Immigrants to New England 1620-33, Irish Quaker Immigration into Pennsylvania, New England Founders, New England Immigrants, 1700–75, New England Irish Pioneers and Scots-Irish in Virginia (most of these databases require a subscription to Ancestry). Ancestry.com is discussed more fully on p. 54. For the late 19th and early 20th centuries, the American Family Immigration History Center at **<www.ellisislandrecords.org>** has a searchable database of passengers who entered America through Ellis Island between 1892 and 1924.

There are many sites devoted to individual groups of settlers, for example the *Mayflower* Passenger List at **<members.aol.com/calebj/ passenger.html>**. The immigration page on Cyndi's List is the easiest way to find such sites. For historical background on 19th-century Irish emigration, see the *Belfast Telegraph's* 'Exodus' site at <**www.belfasttelegraph.co.uk/emigration/**>. The 'Immigration And Ships Passenger Lists Research Guide' at <**home.att.net/~arnielang/shipgide.html**> offers help and guidance on researching ancestors who emigrated to the USA.

There is less material on-line for Canada. Marjorie Kohli's 'Immigrants to Canada' site at <**www.ist.uwaterloo.ca/~marj/genealogy/thevoyage.html**> has an extensive collection of material, and links to many related resources. The National Archives of Canada has information on 'Immigration Records' at <**www.archives.ca/02/02020204_e.html**>, covering both border entry and passenger lists. There is a pilot on-line database for a selection of the records (only for surnames beginning with C in the years 1925–35). The inGeneas site at <**www.inGeneas.com**> also has a database of passenger lists and immigration records; the National Archives of Canada Miscellaneous Immigration Index is free; the index to other material can be searched free, but there is a charge for record transcriptions.

The West Indies

The Open Directory's African-British page at <**dmoz.org/Society/Ethnicity/African/African_British/**> is a good starting point for Web resources relating to African and Afro-Caribbean immigration into Britain, though the listing does not specialize in genealogical sources.

The BBC web site has material relating to its *Windrush* season at <**www.bbc.co.uk/education/archive/windrush/**>, while there is a longer historical perspective in Channel 4's 'Untold' Black History Season web site at <**www.channel4.com/untold/**>. Specifically genealogical material, with a host of useful links, will be found on the web site for Channel 4's *Extraordinary Ancestors* series, particularly the pages on West Indian, African and African-American immigration. All this material is linked from the 'Tracing an ancestor who was an immigrant' page at <**www.channel4.com/nextstep/geno/geno3.html**>. The site has links for resources relating to the individual islands. For links to Caribbean data extracts, visit the archive of the Caribbean GenWeb Project at <**www.rootsweb.com/~caribgw/cgw_archive/**>.

A more general project which may be of interest, though it is academic in focus and does not have specifically genealogical information, is CASBAH at <**www.casbah.ac.uk**>. This aims to 'identify and map national research resources for Caribbean Studies and the history of Black and Asian people in Britain'. The database of material is due to be made available on-line in May 2002.

There are two Caribbean surname lists (see Chapter 5, p. 73): the Caribbean Surnames Index, CARSURDEX, at <**www.candoo.com/surnames/index.html**>; and the West Indies Surname Interests List, maintained by Vaughan Royal. This is accessible only via e-mail, and details are given at <**www.rootsweb.com/~jfuller/gen_email.html**>.

There is a newsgroup for discussion of Caribbean ancestry, soc.genealogy.west-indies, which is gatewayed with the CARIBBEAN mailing list (see **<www.rootsweb.com/~jfuller/gen_mail_country-gen. html>**). Details of other West Indies mailing lists will be found at **<www.rootsweb.com/~jfuller/gen_mail_country-wes.html>**. The GEN-AFRICAN-L mailing list, gatewayed with the soc.genealogy.african newsgroup, also covers Afro-Caribbean genealogy (see **<www.rootsweb. com/~jfuller/gen_mail_african.html>**).

Cyndi's List has an extensive collection of links for slavery at **<www.cyndislist.com/african.htm#Slavery>**, though most of these relate to the US.

For convict transportation to the West Indies, see the PRO leaflets mentioned under 'North America' above.

India

For official records of British colonial activity in India, the India Office Library, part of the British Library's Oriental and India Office Collections, is the main repository, and the British Library web site includes material about these records at **<www.bl.uk/collections/oriental/records/>**.

The best starting point for genealogical research into British India is Cathy Day's Family History In India site at **<members.ozemail.com.au/ ~clday/>**, which provides a comprehensive guide for 'people tracing their British, European and Anglo-Indian family history in India, Burma, Pakistan and Bangladesh.' It has extensive material relating to the British army in India and many small data extracts. The Families in British India Society has a web site at **<www.links.org/FIBIS/>**.

If your ancestors had some connection with the East India Company, you will find suitable links on some of the maritime resources discussed under 'The Royal Navy' on p. 89, in addition to the India Office material mentioned above.

There are currently two relevant mailing lists, BANGLADESH and INDIA. Details will be found at **<www.rootsweb.com/~jfuller/gen_mail.html>**.

Links for other Asian countries will be found on the 'Extraordinary Ancestors' site at **<www.channel4.com/nextstep/geno/geno3e.html>** and on WorldGenWeb at **<worldgenweb.org>**.

Australasia

There are extensive materials on-line relating both to convict transportation to Australia, and to later free emigration to Australia and New Zealand. A good starting point is the 'Australia and New Zealand' page on Cyndi's List at **<www.CyndisList.com/austnz.htm>**. Another worthwhile site is the Australian Family History Compendium, which has a list of on-line sources at **<www.cohsoft.com.au/afhc/netrecs.html>**. For information on the official records held by the British state, see the PRO's on-line leaflets.

Convict lists for the first, second and third fleets will be found on Patricia Downes' site at <www.pcug.org.au/~pdownes/>. The National Archives of Ireland has an on-line database of Transportation Records 1788–1868 at <www.nationalarchives.ie/search01.html>. In addition to the passenger-list sites mentioned above, links to on-line passenger lists for Australasia will be found at <www.users.on.net/proformat/auspass.html>.

Australian government agencies have much information relating to convict and free settlers on-line. The National Archives of Australia web site at <www.naa.gov.au> has a family history section, which includes material on immigration at <www.naa.gov.au/The_Collection/ Family_History/immigrants.html>. The Victoria Public Record Office has an on-line database of Immigration to Victoria 1852–1889 at <www.vic.gov.au/prov/UNASSISTED1.asp>. The Archives Office of Tasmania, at <www.archives.tas.gov.au>, has a Tasmanian Family Link Database with about 500,000 entries and an Index to Naturalisation Applications for 1835–1905. New South Wales has all 19th-century civil registration indexes on-line at <www.bdm.nsw.gov.au> and Assisted Immigrants Indexes at <www.records.nsw.gov.au/publications/immigration/ introduction.htm>, though the full records are not on-line. Comprehensive links to Australian Archives are on the Archives of Australia site at <www.archivenet.gov.au>.

There are dozens of mailing lists for Australian and New Zealand genealogy, all listed at <www.rootsweb.com/~jfuller/gen_mail_country-aus.html> and <www.rootsweb.com/~jfuller/gen_mail_country-nez. html>. Those of most general interest are: AUS-CONVICTS, AUS-IRISH, AUS-MILITARY, AUSTRALIA, NEW-ZEALAND, TRANS-CRIPTIONS-AUS and TRANSCRIPTIONS-NZ. But there are also lists for individual states, regions and even towns. The newsgroup soc.genealogy.australia+nz is gatewayed with the GENANZ mailing list.

Jews

There are many sites devoted to Jewish genealogy, though not many are specifically concerned with British Jewry. The JewishGen site at <www.jewishgen.org> is a very comprehensive site with a number of resources relevant to Jewish ancestry in the British Isles. These include an article on researching Jewish ancestry at <www.jewishgen.org/ infofiles/ukgen.txt>, and the London Jews Database <www.jewishgen.org/ databases/londweb.htm>, which has about 9,000 names, compiled principally from London trade directories. The Jewish genealogical magazine *Avotaynu* has a 'Five-minute Guide to Jewish Genealogical Research' at <www.avotaynu.com/jewish_genealogy.htm>. The PRO has a leaflet 'Anglo Jewish History: Sources in the PRO, 18th–20th Centuries' on-line at <catalogue.pro.gov.uk/leaflets/ri2183.htm>. As usual, Cyndi's List has a good collection of links at <www.CyndisList.com/jewish.htm>.

The Jewish Genealogical Society of Great Britain's web site, at <www.

jgsgb.ort.org>, has a substantial collection of links to Jewish material in Britain and worldwide. *Avotaynu* has a Consolidated Jewish Surname Index at **<www.avotaynu.com/csi/csi-home.html>**. There is a varied collection of material relating to London Jews on Jeffrey Maynard's site at **<www.jeffreymaynard.com>**. The Channel 4 web site has a page relating to Jewish genealogy on its *Extraordinary Ancestors* pages, at **<www. channel4.com/nextstep/geno/geno3a.html>**.

The newsgroup soc.genealogy.jewish is devoted to Jewish genealogy. This group is gatewayed with the JEWISHGEN mailing list and John Fuller lists another three dozen mailing lists for Jewish genealogy at **<www.rootsweb.com/~jfuller/gen_mail_jewish.html>**. Most are specific to particular geographical areas, and JEWISHGEN and JEWISH-ROOTS are the only general interest lists.

The JewishGen Family Finder (JGFF) at **<www.jewishgen.org/jgff/>** is a 'database of ancestral towns and surnames currently being researched by Jewish genealogists worldwide', with over 65,000 surnames submitted by 45,000 Jewish genealogists.

Huguenots

Cyndi's List has a list of Huguenot resources at **<www.CyndisList.com/ huguenot.htm>**, while for historical background there is a Huguenot timeline at **<www.kopower.com/~jimchstn/timeline.htm>**. There is a Huguenots-Walloons-Europe and a general Huguenots mailing list, both hosted at RootsWeb (subscription details at **<www.rootsweb. com/~jfuller/gen_mail_religions.html>**). The former has its own web site at **<www.island.net/~andreav/>** and has a good collection of links and its own surnames list. The Huguenot Surnames Index at **<www.aftc.com.au/ Huguenot_Index/huguenot_index.html>** will enable you to make contact with others researching particular Huguenot families.

Information about the Huguenot Library, housed at University College London, will be found at **<www.ucl.ac.uk/Library/huguenot.htm>**, and information on the French Protestant Church of London is on the Institute of Historical Research site at **<ihr.sas.ac.uk/ihr/associnstits/huguenots.mnu. html>**.

Gypsies

There are two starting points on the Web for gypsy ancestry. The Romany & Traveller Family History Society site at **<website.lineone.net/~rtfhs/>**, apart from society information (including a list of contents for recent issues of its magazine), has a page on 'Was Your Ancestor a Gypsy?'. This lists typical gypsy surnames, forenames and occupations. The site also has a good collection of links to other gypsy material on the Web.

The Gypsy Collections at the University of Liverpool site at **<sca.lib.liv.ac.uk/ collections/gypsy/intro.htm>** has information about, and photographs of, British gypsy families as well as a collection of links to other gypsy sites.

Extracts from the 1881 census for travellers will be found at <**www.users.globalnet.co.uk/~paulln/docs/census6.htm**>. This is part of a site devoted to 'Circus, Theatre and Music Hall families research resources', which has much material relating to itinerants. The home page is <**www.users.globalnet.co.uk/~paulln/**>.

Part of Kent County Council's Lottery-funded genealogy project is to include 'a traveller archive for the largest ethnic community in Kent' with a range of sources, manuscript, oral and photographic. This is due to go live by the end of 2002.

Directories of gypsy material can be found in the Open Directory at <**dmoz.org/Society/Ethnicity/Romani/**> and there is more specifically genealogical material on Cyndi's List at <**www.cyndislist.com/peoples. htm#Gypsies**> on a page titled 'Unique Peoples & Cultures'.

There is a UK-ROMANI mailing list for British gypsy family history, details of which will be found at <**www.rootsweb.com/~jfuller/ gen_mail_country-unk.html**>.

Royal and notable families

The Web has a wide range of resources relating to the genealogy of royal houses and the nobility, as well as to famous people and families. For initial orientation, Genuki's page on 'Kings and Queens of England and Scotland (and some of the people around them)' at <**www.genuki.org.uk/ big/royalty/**> provides a list of Monarchs since the Conquest, Kings of England, Kings of Scotland, Queens and a selection of the most notable Queens, Kings, Archbishops, Bishops, Dukes, Earls, Knights, Lords, Eminent Men, Popes and Princes. There is also a detailed table of the Archbishops of Canterbury and York, and the Bishops of London, Durham, St David's and Armagh, from AD 200 to the present day at <**www.genuki.org.uk/big/eng/History/Archbishops.html**>.

Cyndi's List has a page with over 150 links relating to Royalty and Nobility at <**www.CyndisList.com/royalty.htm**>.

The best place for genealogical information on English royalty is the Brian Tompsett's Directory of Royal Genealogical Data at <**www.dcs.hull. ac.uk/public/genealogy/royal/catalog.html**>, which contains 'the genealogy of the British Royal family and those linked to it via blood or marriage relationships.' The site provides much information on other royal families, and includes details of all English peerages at <**www.dcs.hull. ac.uk/public/genealogy/royal/peerage.html**>. It can be searched by name, by date, or by title. Another massive database devoted to European nobility will be found on the WW-Person site at <**www8.informatik.uni- erlangen.de/html/ww-person.html**>.

The official web site of the royal family is at <**www.royal.gov.uk**> which, among other things, offers family trees of the royal houses from the ninth-century kingdom of Wessex to the present day in PDF format at <www.royal.gov.uk/history/trees.htm>.

Royal and noble titles for many languages and countries are explained in the 'Glossary of European Noble, Princely, Royal, and Imperial Titles' at <www.heraldica.org/topics/odegard/titlefaq.htm>.

Genuki has part of *The English Peerage* (1790) on-line at <www.genuki.org.uk/big/eng/History/Barons/>, with information on a number of barons and viscounts of the period.

Alongside royalty and nobility, you can almost certainly find information on the Web on any other genealogically notable group of people. Thus there are sites devoted to the sons of Noah (<www.geocities. com/Tokyo/4241/geneadm2.html>), the *Mayflower* pilgrims (<members. aol.com/calebj/mayflower.html>) and even the *Bounty* mutineers (<www. lareau.org/genweb.html>).

Mark Humphrys has a site devoted to the Royal Descents of Famous People at <www.compapp.dcu.ie/~humphrys/FamTree/Royal/ famous.descents.html>, while Ulf Berggren provides genealogical information on many notable people from Winston Churchill to Donald Duck (really!) at <www.stacken.kth.se/~ulfb/genealogy.html>. The ancestry of the US presidents will be found on a number of sites, and <www.rootsweb.com/~rwguide/presidents/> provides an Ahnentafel listing for each of them.

Chris Gaunt has a listing of sites relating to the genealogy of famous people at <www-personal.umich.edu/~cgaunt/famous.html>. There are also the mailing lists GEN-ROYAL and SCT-ROYAL (details at <www.rootsweb.com/~jfuller/gen_mail_occ.html>).

Clans

Information on Scottish clans will be found among the surname materials discussed in Chapter 6, but there are also some general sites devoted to clans. The Scottish Tourist Board offers some general information about clans at <www.visitscotland.com/faqs/detail_faq.asp?ID=76>, while the ScotlandsClans site at <www.scotlandsclans.com> has links to sites for individual clans, as well as a message board and a mailing list. Another mailing list is CLANS, details of which can be found at <www.rootsweb. com/~jfuller/gen_mail_country-unk.html>, and there is also a newsgroup, alt.scottish.clans (see p. 129). The Gathering of the Clans site at <www.tartans.com> has pages devoted to individual clans (with a brief history, badge, motto, tartan, etc.) and a 'Clan Finder' at <www.tartans. com/cgi-bin/clans.cgi> which matches surnames to clans.

Heraldry

Heraldry is intimately connected with royal and noble families, and there is quite a lot of material relating to it on the Web. The authoritative source of information about heraldry in England and Wales is the web site of the

College of Arms at **<www.college-of-arms.gov.uk>**. Its FAQ page deals with frequently asked questions about coats of arms. The Institute of Heraldic and Genealogical Studies (IHGS) has a web site at **<www.ihgs.ac. uk>**. The SoG has a leaflet on 'The Right to Arms' at **<www.sog.org.uk/ leaflets/arms.html>**.

The Heraldry on the Internet site at **<www.digiserve.com/heraldry/>** is a specialist site with a substantial collection of links to other on-line heraldry resources, and Cyndi's List has a page of heraldry links at **<www.CyndisList.com/heraldry.htm>**. The British Heraldic Archive at **<www.kwtelecom.com/heraldry/>** has a number of articles on heraldry, as does the British Heraldry site at **<www.heraldica.org/topics/britain/>**. The Heraldry Society will be found at **<www.kwtelecom.com/heraldry/ hersoc/index.html>**.

For the meaning of terms used in heraldry, an on-line version of Pimbley's 1905 *Dictionary of Heraldry* is at **<www.digiserve.com/ heraldry/pimbley.htm>**, while there is an on-line version of James Parker's *A Glossary of Terms used in Heraldry* (1894) at **<www04.u-page. so-net.ne.jp/ta2/saitou/ie401/>**. Heraldic terms will also be found in the 'Knighthood, Chivalry & Tournament Glossary of Terms' at **<www.chronique.com/Library/Glossaries/glossary-KCT/glssindx.htm>**. Accounts of the British orders of chivalry will be found at **<www.kwtelecom.com/chivalry/britords.html>**. A substantial article on Scots heraldry can be found at **<www.kwtelecom.com/heraldry/ scother1.html>**.

8 Geography

Maps and gazetteers are essential reference tools for family historians and while the internet cannot offer the wealth of maps available in reference libraries and record offices, let alone the British Library Map Library (web site at <www.bl.uk/collections/maps/>), there are nonetheless many useful resources on-line. Good starting points for on-line maps and gazetteers are the 'Maps, Gazetteers & Geographical Information' page on Cyndi's List <www.CyndisList.com/maps.htm> and the Genuki county pages.

Gazetteers

The definitive gazetteer for the present-day UK is that provided by the Ordnance Survey (OS) at <www.ordsvy.gov.uk/products/Landranger/lrmsearch.cfm> which has a database of all places listed on the Landranger series of maps. The search leads to a diagrammatic map of the area in which the chosen place is located, and links to a 500 × 636 pixel graphic

Places within 5 miles of Barrow-in-Furness , OS Gridref SD190690

SD190690 Barrow-in-Furness, Lancashire which encompasses the area containing:

    SD190690 Hindpool
    ~ 1 miles SW SD180680 Vickerstown
    ~ 1 miles NW SD180700 North Scale
    ~ 2 miles W SD170690 North Walney

~ 2 miles SSW SD180670 Walney, Lancashire
~ 4 miles ENE SD240700 Dendron, Lancashire
~ 4 miles ESE SD240660 Rampside, Lancashire
~ 4 miles NE SD230740 Dalton-in-Furness, Lancashire
~ 5 miles E SD260690 Newbiggin
~ 5 miles ENE SD260730 Little Urswick

Figure 8.1 The Genuki Gazetteer entry for Barrow-in-Furness <www.genuki.org.uk/big/eng/Gazetteers.html>

⇧Parish search   GENUKI Contents

Parishes/churches within 5 miles of SD190690

The following entries were found:

Miles	Place	Dedication	County	Denomination	Founded	Closed	Gridref
1.4	Walney	St Mary the Virgin	Lancashire	Parish	1856		SD180670
0.0	Barrow in Furness	Register Office	Lancashire		1837		SD190690
0.0	Barrow-in-Furness	St Patrick	Lancashire	Roman Catholic	1877		SD190690
0.0	Barrow in Furness	St Mary	Lancashire	Roman Catholic	1865		SD190690
3.2	Dendron	St Mathew	Lancashire	Parish	1803		SD240700
4.0	Dalton-in-Furness	Our Lady of the Rosary	Lancashire	Roman Catholic	1878		SD230740
4.0	Dalton-in-Furness	St Mary	Lancashire	Parish	1689		SD230740
5.8	Urswick	St Mary and St Michael	Lancashire	Parish	1634		SD270740
5.3	Ireleth	St Peter	Lancashire	Parish	1714		SD220770

Figure 8.2 The Genuki Parish Locator <www.genuki.org.uk/big/parloc/search.html>

of the whole Landranger map. This is not large enough to see any detail, but sufficient to get an idea of the geography of the area. (See 'Present-day maps', below, for more information about the maps on the OS site.)

Genuki has two gazetteers. The first can be found at **<www.genuki.org. uk/big/eng/Gazetteers.html>**. This page provides a search field for a gazetteer which will tell you the county and OS grid reference of a place, and also provides a list of other places within a chosen distance. If there is a Genuki page for the parish a link is provided, and there will also be a link to the relevant Genuki county. A more specialized facility is Genuki's Parish Locator at **<www.genuki.org.uk/big/parloc/search.html>**. Rather than listing places, this lists churches and register offices (see Figure 8.2). Genuki also has a database of places mentioned in the 1891 census at **<www.genuki.org.uk/big/census_place.html>** (England and Wales only).

Two university geography departments have useful gazetteers. Queen Mary and Westfield College, London, has an on-line gazetteer at **<www.geog. qmw.ac.uk/gbhgis/gaz/start.html>** based on the parishes in the 1911 census; and the University of Edinburgh has a project to provide an on-line gazetteer of Scotland, details of which can be found at **<www.geo.ed.ac.uk/scotgaz/>**. An interesting feature of the search on the latter site is that you can specify what sort of thing you are looking for, from Airport, Archaeological Site, Bank or Shoal, down to Waterfall and Whirlpool.

The National Archives in Ireland has a searchable index of documents in its OS collection at **<www.nationalarchives.ie/cgi-bin/ naigenform02?index=OS>**, which includes lists of towns and parishes, and thus effectively acts as a gazetteer. For Northern Ireland, PRONI has a geographical index at **<proni.nics.gov.uk/geogindx.htm>**, as well as lists of parishes and townlands in Northern Ireland at **<proni.nics.**

gov.uk/geogindx/parishes/> and <proni.nics.gov.uk/geogindx/townland/ townland.htm> respectively. Sean Ruad has a searchable database of townlands, parishes and baronies at <www.seanruad.com>.

Other on-line gazetteers include the Gazetteer of British Place Names at <www.gazetteer.co.uk> maintained by the Association of British Counties, and county record offices may also provide resources for their local area. For example, Greater Manchester County Record Office has a 'Greater Manchester Gazetteer' at <www.gmcro.co.uk/gazframe.htm>.

Going beyond the UK, probably the most important single gazetteer site on the Web is the Getty Thesaurus of Geographic Names browser at <shiva.pub.getty.edu/tgn_browser/>, which covers the whole world. Even for the UK this is useful, since it includes geographical, and some historical, information (see Figure 8.3).

Present-day maps

The OS web site at <www.ordsvy.gov.uk> is the obvious starting point for any information about the mapping of the present-day British Isles. In addition to details of the full range of OS maps available for purchase, the site's Get-a-map facility at <www.ordsvy.gov.uk/getamap/getamap_ index.htm> allows you to call up a map (derived from the 1:50,000 and 1:250,000 series) centred on a particular place. You can search by place name, postcode, or OS grid reference. Alternatively, you can just click on the map of the UK and gradually zoom in to your chosen area. The maps are free for personal use (including limited use on personal web sites). There is also an option to go to the 19th-century OS maps discussed in 'Historical maps', below.

There are two main commercial sites that provide free UK maps. The Streetmap site at <www.streetmap.co.uk> allows searches by street (London only), postcode, place name, OS grid, Landranger grid,

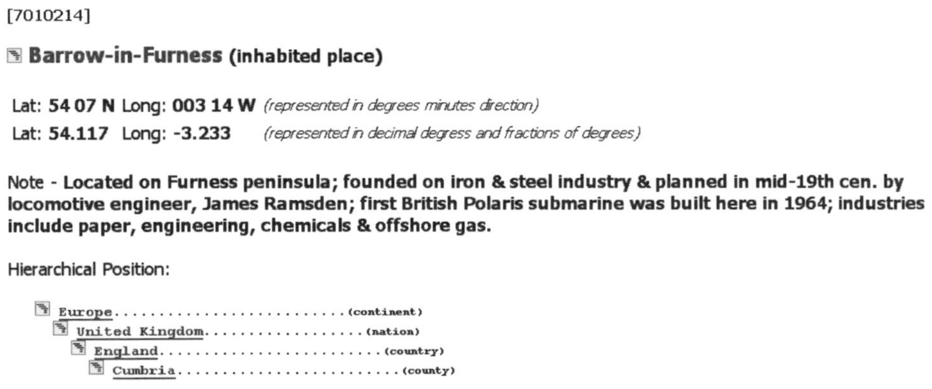

[7010214]

▨ **Barrow-in-Furness (inhabited place)**

Lat: **54 07 N** Long: **003 14 W** *(represented in degrees minutes direction)*
Lat: **54.117** Long: **-3.233** *(represented in decimal degress and fractions of degrees)*

Note - **Located on Furness peninsula; founded on iron & steel industry & planned in mid-19th cen. by locomotive engineer, James Ramsden; first British Polaris submarine was built here in 1964; industries include paper, engineering, chemicals & offshore gas.**

Hierarchical Position:

```
▨ Europe........................(continent)
  ▨ United Kingdom................(nation)
    ▨ England......................(country)
      ▨ Cumbria....................(county)
```

Figure 8.3 The Getty Thesaurus of Geographic Names <shiva.pub.getty.edu/tgn_browser/>

latitude/longitude, or telephone code. The resulting default display shows maps at a resolution of 200 × 200 pixels for a 1 km square and is thus more detailed than the maps on the OS site, with an option to zoom in to double that scale. Although you can search on street names only for London, most other places have them marked on the largest scale maps. Multimap at **<uk.multimap.com>** offers similar facilities: the largest scale (1:10,000) gives an image at 700 × 410 pixels in size with 330 pixels for a 1 km square, and you can search by place, address or postcode. Genuki has instructions on 'How to find a present day house, street or place in the U.K. (or to find only the Post Code)' by using the Multimap site at **<www.genuki.org.uk/big/ModernLocations.html>**.

Both Streetmap and Multimap provide aerial photographs, often at quite a high level of detail, for cities and some other parts of the country. Microsoft's Terraserver at **<www.terraserver.com>** has aerial photographs of several parts of the UK, with high-resolution images of London. Obviously these photographs are of limited use for some purposes – for example, identifying streets by name – but can be useful for features like field boundaries (which are marked on the 6 in. OS maps but are not shown on the present-day maps available on-line) or the sizes of gardens. The Terraserver has an overview page showing the areas of the country covered; with Streetmap and Multimap, availability of an aerial photograph is indicated by an icon on each map page.

Historical maps

There are quite a lot of historical maps available on the Web, though many that are of interest to historians have insufficient local detail to be of use to genealogists. In general, the best places to look for links to on-line maps of counties or towns are Genuki's county pages, though it is also worth looking at county record office web sites. The Guildhall Library, for instance, has an extensive collection of maps and views of London on-line at **<collage.nhil.com/collagedev/categories/places-Streets.html>**.

However, the single most useful map resource for the genealogist is the complete collection of 19th-century 6 in. OS maps (1:10,560 scale) for the whole of England, Wales and Scotland, dating from 1846 to 1899. The site is located at **<www.old-maps.co.uk>** and provides two versions of the maps, each with its own strengths and weaknesses.

The original version of the site, now at **<www.old-maps.co.uk/oldSite/>**, simply provides a scan of the 6 in. series, with each sheet divided into 16 individual graphic files (in GIF format) of 2,666 × 1,784 pixels (equivalent to 36 × 24 in.). This means that you cannot view the whole map on screen at once, and have to scroll around. (The gazetteer provides a list of places in each county which links to the relevant map; it also indicates which quarter of the map a place is in.) Arrows at the top of the page allow you to move to an adjacent map, except where the adjacent sheet is for a different county. Because of the high resolution, all the detail on the maps is clearly visible, though some of the smaller text can be hard to read, and one or two of the original maps used for scanning seem to have been rather faint. Alternatively you can download the image and use a graphics program to zoom in or print out either the whole image or part of it. The file sizes vary, with those for densely populated areas up to 400k while more rural areas will be under 100k.

The new version of the site, at <www.old-maps.co.uk>, makes it much easier to locate an individual place – there is not only a county gazetteer with a list of towns and villages, but also a search facility to locate a place by place name, address, postcode, or OS grid reference. This takes you to a map centred on the place in question and there are five levels of zoom. You cannot go directly to an adjacent map, but clicking on any part of a map will recentre it on that point, which means that the edge of one map can become the centre of the next. The map area on the screen is approximately 500 × 270 pixels, and the highest level of zoom gives the same level of detail as the maps on the old site. It does not seem to be possible to download the images from this site, though you can of course make screen shots. So this version of the site makes it much easier to locate places, but is less useful if you want to save a map.

A more general resource on historical maps will be found on the Institute of Historical Research web site at <ihr.sas.ac.uk/maps/>, which includes a collection of links to web map resources for Europe at <ihr.sas.ac.uk/maps/webimages.html#europe>.

The National Library of Scotland offers 'Highlights of the Map Collection' at <www.nls.uk/digitallibrary/map/>. Details of its project to

Figure 8.4 Scarborough Old Harbour at the highest zoom level on the Old-maps site at <www.old-maps.co.uk>

digitize Timothy Pont's 16th-century maps of Scotland will be found at <**www.nls.uk/digitallibrary/map/pont.htm**>. The University of Wisconsin-Madison has some historical maps of Ireland, including a Poor Law map, at <**history.wisc.edu/archdeacon/famine/**>.

Another source for historical maps on-line may be the sites of commercial map-dealers. For example, Heritage Publishing at <**www.chycor.co.uk/heritage-publishing/index.htm**> has scans of some of John Speed's 1610 maps of the British counties. David Hulse Associates have got a wide selection of historic maps on-line at <**www.antique-maps-books.com/Maps/UK/UK_page_maps.htm**>. It is well worth using a search engine to locate sites which have the phrase 'antique maps' and the town or county of your choice.

It is not possible here to give detailed coverage of historical maps of individual counties and areas – these are best found by looking at the relevant Genuki county page or by visiting the Genmaps site at <**freepages.genealogy.rootsweb.com/~genmaps/**>, which has an extensive collection of historical maps and links to many others, organized by county. But perhaps it is worth mentioning Charles Booth's famous 1889 Map of London Poverty on the LSE's Charles Booth site at <**booth.lse.ac.uk**>, and Greenwood's 1827 map of London at <**www.bathspa.ac.uk/greenwood/home.html**>.

Map collections

For guides to map collections, the British Cartographic Society's 'A Directory of UK Map Collections' at <**www.cartography.org.uk/Pages/Publicat/Ukdir/UKDirect.html**> is a very comprehensive starting point.

The catalogues of the archives and libraries mentioned in Chapter 5 include their map holdings. The PRO has a leaflet 'Maps in the Public Record Office' at <**catalogue.pro.gov.uk/leaflets/ri2179.htm**>. The British Library web site has detailed information on its map collections at <**www.bl.uk/collections/maps/collections.html**>. The National Library of Scotland Map Library has a web page at <**www.nls.uk/collections/maps/**>. The National Library of Wales has material on its Map Collection at <**www.llgc.org.uk/dm/dm0067.htm**>. PRONI's map holdings are described at <**proni.nics.gov.uk/records/maps.htm**>.

Streets and street names

The Streetmap and Multimap sites mentioned above show street names for the present day. If you are looking for a street that no longer exists, or has been renamed, many of the historical maps available on the Web are at too large a scale to indicate street names. However, for major cities, especially London, you may well be able to locate a particular street on-line. The best starting point for a particular city will be the relevant Genuki county page.

The Bolles Collection London Map Browser at <**www.perseus.tufts. edu/cgi-bin/city-view.pl**> has digitized copies of a dozen maps of London from the 17th to the 19th century. There is an optional overlay of the modern street pattern and the ability to identify streets and major buildings by location or name (see Figure 8.5).

Gendocs has a 'Victorian London A-Z Street Index' at <**www.gendocs. demon.co.uk/lon-str.html**> which gives the registration districts for over 60,000 streets. The 'Lost London Street Index' at <**members.aol.com/ WHall95037/london.html**> lists over 3,500 streets that have undergone a name change or have disappeared altogether over the last 200 years.

The counties

All towns and villages in the British Isles have a place in the administrative geography of the constituent counties, and this has not necessarily remained constant over the last few hundred years. Genuki provides a

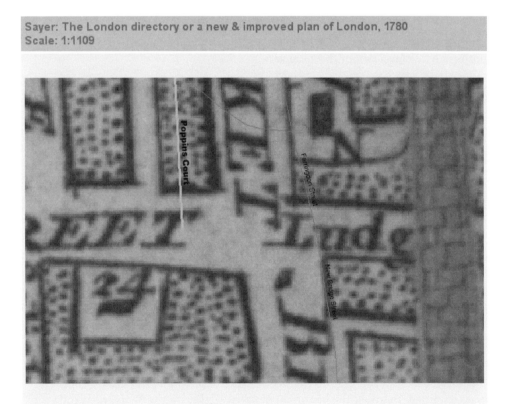

Sayer: The London directory or a new & improved plan of London, 1780
Scale: 1:1109

Figure 8.5 Ludgate Circus in Sayer's 1780 map of London. Poppins Court is marked and named, even though not indicated on the original map (Bolles Collection London Map Browser at <www.perseus.tufts.edu/cgi-bin/ city-view.pl>)

general overview of Administrative Regions and, as well as pages for the individual counties, has material on 'Local Government Changes in the United Kingdom' at **<www.genuki.org.uk/big/Regions/UKchanges.html>** with detailed tables for England, Wales, Scotland and Northern Ireland. The situation in the Republic of Ireland is more straightforward as the pre-independence counties remain.

Genuki has maps of the counties of England, Wales and Scotland at **<www.genuki.org.uk/big/Britain.html>** and of Ireland at **<www.genuki. org.uk/big/Ireland.html>**. Each Genuki county page also has a description of the county, usually drawn from a 19th-century directory or similar source.

If you are from outside the UK and are not familiar with the counties and other administrative divisions you will find Jim Fisher's page 'British Counties, Parishes, etc. for Genealogists' at **<homepages.nildram.co.uk/ ~jimella/counties.htm>** useful.

Where counties have changed their boundaries over the years, the individual Genuki county pages will provide relevant details. The creation of Greater London and demise of Middlesex in 1965 is dealt with at **<www.gold.ac.uk/genuki/LND/parishes.html>**, which lists the changes that gave rise to the metropolitan boroughs in 1888, and the current London boroughs. The major reorganization of 1974 saw the creation of new counties and boroughs. The Department of Transport, Local Government and the Regions has comprehensive information on the current structure of local government, and proposed changes, under the heading 'Structure and History of Local Government' at **<www.local.doe.gov.uk/struct/reorg.htm>**.

It is important to bear in mind that genealogists almost always refer to pre-1974 counties and any genealogical material on the internet is likely to reflect that. This is why there are no pages on Genuki for Tyne and Wear or the present-day Welsh counties. Counties are often referred to by three-letter abbreviations, the Chapman County Codes, e.g. SFK for Suffolk. A list of these can be found on Genuki at **<www.genuki.org.uk/big/ Regions/Codes.html>**.

Photographs

Photographs of villages and parish churches on the Web are of particular value to those who live far away from the homes of their ancestors. Many places are too small to be found depicted in books other than those held in county record offices or major national libraries. But the Web (along with the scanner or digital camera) has made it easy for genealogists to post pictures of their local area. For example, there are Bedfordshire Church photographs at **<met.open.ac.uk/group/kaq/beds/church.htm>**, and Ettrick Graphics provides an Old Scottish Borders Photo Archive at **<www.ettrickgraphics.co.uk/bordersindex.htm>**. *Richard's Church Album* at **<www.thirdman-webmaster.co.uk/indexframe1.html>** currently contains pictures of around 1,000 churches in all parts of England. Guy Etchells has a collection of links to UK church photographs on his Worldwide Cemetery Page at **<gye.future.easyspace.com>**. The best way to find such sites is to go to the relevant Genuki county page.

A site with old photographs of the whole country is the Francis Frith Collection at **<www.francisfrith.com>**. Frith was a Victorian photographer whose company photographed over 7,000 towns and villages in Britain, from 1860 until the closure of the company in 1969. The site is a commercial one selling prints, but it has thumbnails (under 300×200 pixels) of all the pictures in the collection, which can be located by search or via a listing for each (present-day) county.

For modern photographs of historical buildings, look at the National Monuments Register's Images of England site at **<www.imagesofengland. org.uk>**. This is intended to be 'an internet home for England's listed buildings' with good-quality photographs and descriptions of every listed building in the country, though the project is not complete at the time of writing. Search facilities include search by county or town, building type, period or person (an architect or other individual associated with a building). Thumbnail images link to full-size images with descriptions.

9 Historical Background

While genealogists are concerned mainly with individual ancestors, both their lives and the documents that record them cannot be understood without a broader historical appreciation of the times in which they lived. The aim of this chapter is to look at some of the general historical material on the internet that is likely to be of use to family historians.

Local and social history

There is no single good starting point for looking at local and social history on the internet though, as usual, Genuki's county pages will link to materials for individual counties.

Local History Magazine has a collection of links at **<www.local-history. co.uk/links/>**, and its 'Useful links to historical sites' page will point you to the web sites of local history societies, university departments and individuals who are publishing local history material on the Web.

County record office web sites can offer good on-line resources for local history. Good examples of how local authorities and record offices are using the Web to provide historical information can be seen in the Powys Digital History Project at **<history.powys.org.uk>** or the Knowsley (Lancs) Local History site at **<history.knowsley.gov.uk>**. The City of Liverpool has begun an on-line project at **<www.liverpool2007.org.uk>** as a 'gateway to Liverpool's historical past', and I think we can expect many more such initiatives in future.

Although the Web provides material on any aspect of social history you care to name, from slavery to education, it is difficult to know what you can expect to find on a given topic in terms of quality and coverage. In view of the large number of possible subjects which come under 'social history', and the very general application of these headings (education, poverty, etc.), using a search engine to locate them can be quite time consuming. However, if you know any terms that refer only to historical material (1840 Education Act, Poor Law, etc.) this may make searching easier. Also, local history sites are likely to include some material on social history and local museums, and may provide useful links to non-local material.

For more recent local and social history, local newspapers are an important source, and newspaper resources are discussed on p. 50.

Where aspects of social history are bound up with the state, you can expect to find some guidance on official sites. The PRO, for example, has leaflets on Education, Enclosures, Lunacy and Lunatic Asylums, Outlawry, and the Poor Law, among other subjects. Of course, the PRO holds extensive records relating to crime and has many leaflets on the courts and prisons on-line at **<www.pro.gov.uk/leaflets/Riindex.asp>**.

A comprehensive guide to social history sites is beyond the scope of this book, but the following examples may give a taste of some of the resources on the internet.

Professor George P. Landow's Victorian Web includes an overview of Victorian Social History at **<landow.stg.brown.edu/victorian/history/ sochistov.html>** with a considerable amount of contemporary documentation. This site, incidentally, was one of the first to use the Web to make linked historical materials available.

The Workhouses site at **<www.workhouses.org.uk>** provides a comprehensive introduction to the workhouse and the laws relating to it, along with lists of workhouses in England, Wales and Scotland, and a guide to workhouse records (see Figure 9.1).

The Gendocs site has a list of 'Workhouses, Hospitals, Lunatic Asylums, Prisons, Barracks, Orphan Asylums, Convents, and other Principal Charitable Institutions' in London in 1861 at **<www.gendocs.demon. co.uk/institute.html>**.

The Powys Digital History project mentioned above has sections

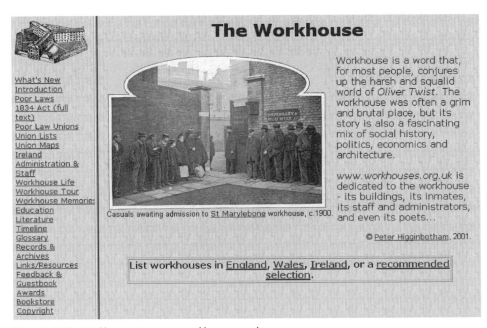

Figure 9.1 The Workhouses site <www.workhouses.org.uk>

devoted to crime and punishment, education and schools, religion in Wales, and care of the poor, at **<history.powys.org.uk/history/intro/ themes.html>**, which make use of original documents and photographs.

Finally, the Spartacus Educational site at **<www.spartacus.schoolnet. co.uk>** is a model of what can be done with historical material on the Web. It has information on many topics in social history since the mid-18th century, such as child labour, the railways, the textile industry and female emancipation. The site contains both general information and historical documents. The pages devoted to the textile industry, for example, at **<www.spartacus.schoolnet.co.uk/Textiles.htm>**, contain general information on the machinery, the various occupations within the industry and the nature of daily life in the textile factory, but also include biographical material on individual inventors, entrepreneurs and factory workers, the latter taken from interviews before a House of Commons Committee in 1832.

There are many examples of small data extracts for local areas, best found via the Genuki county pages. They include:

- Tithe Titles for Kelsall, Cheshire **<www.the-dicksons.org/Kelsall/ kelsall/tithespg.htm>**
- Tithe Book of Bolton with Goldthorpe, 1839 **<www.genuki.org.uk/ big/eng/YKS/WRY/Boltonupondearne/TitheBook/>**
- Sittingbourne Land Tax 1780 **<home.thezone.net/~mrawson/landtax1. html>**
- Lay Subsidy transcriptions for Lincolnshire (1332) and Rutland (1296/7) **<www.le.ac.uk/elh/pot/intro/intro3a.html>**

Surnames

A regular topic on mailing lists and newsgroups is the origin of surnames. When talking about surnames, though, the term 'origins' has two distinct meanings: how the name came about linguistically (its etymology); and where it originated geographically (its home). Unfortunately there is little reliable information on the Web relating to the first of these. The definitive sources for British surname etymologies are the modern printed surname dictionaries, which are not available on-line. If you are lucky you may find a surname site that quotes and gives references for the relevant dictionary entries for your particular surname, but in the absence of source references you should treat etymological information on genealogy web sites as unreliable. Even where sources are given, you should be cautious – some of the older surname dictionaries quoted are the work of amateurs rather than scholars.

The most reliable site I am aware of is the Surname Origins Index at **<www.sonic.net/~csawyer/surnames.html>**. This has a growing number of surname etymologies, and for many it gives references to reputable surname dictionaries. Another good site for surname etymology, though with less detailed information, is that of the Family Chronicle, whose Surname Origin List at **<www.familychronicle.com/surname.htm>** gives a brief explanation of the origins of many British surnames. It also provides a classification of names as patronymic, geographical, occupational, or nickname. Cyndi's List has a page devoted to surnames in general at **<www.CyndisList.com/surn-gen.htm>**.

There is no single on-line source to help you to decide whether surname X is in fact a variant of surname Y, but if someone has registered the surname with the Guild of One-Name Studies (see p. 75), that person would be useful to contact. Looking at the geographical distribution in a major database such as FamilySearch at **<www.familysearch.org>** can sometimes be helpful, though you should be cautious about drawing etymological inferences from distributional information in this sort of database.[5]

There is a mailing list devoted to discussion of surname etymology, SURNAME-ORIGINS-L, details of which can be found at **<members. tripod.com/~Genealogy_Infocenter/surname-origins.html>**.

A site devoted not to surname origins but to surname distribution is Philip Dance's Modern British Surnames site at **<homepages. newnet.co.uk/dance/webpjd/>**, designed as a guide to the resources for the study of surname frequency and distribution. The site also includes discussion of the various approaches to surname origins. A site covering local names is Graham Thomas' Gloucestershire Names and their Occurrence at **<www.grahamthomas.com/glocnames.html>**.

Understanding old documents

If the queries on genealogy mailing lists are anything to go by, one of the main things genealogists need help with is making sense of old documents, whether it is a census entry or a 16th-century will. In some cases it's just a matter of deciphering the handwriting, in others it is understanding the meaning of obsolete words, and in older documents the two problems often occur together. While the internet hardly provides a substitute for the specialist books on these subjects, there are quite a few resources on-line to help with these problems.

Handwriting
As the mistakes in census transcriptions show, even fairly modern handwriting can sometimes be problematic to read, and once you get back beyond the 19th century the difficulties become ever greater.

The University of Leicester has materials relating to an MA in Palaeography on-line at **<www.le.ac.uk/elh/pot/medfram.html>**, though

---

[5] See my article 'What surname distribution can't tell us', on-line at **<www.spub. co.uk/surnames.pdf>**.

the materials, from the 12th and 13th centuries, are earlier than most of those used by genealogists. There is also a non-frame home page for this site at **<orb.rhodes.edu/textbooks/palindex.html>**.

The Scottish Archive Network site has materials on Scottish hand-writing for the period 1500–1750 at **<www.scan.org.uk/researchrtools/ handwriting/scottishhandwriting.htm>**, which will be useful not only to those needing to read Scottish records.

Andrew Booth's Two Torches at Keighly site has downloadable TrueType fonts of 16th- and 17th-century handwriting at **<www.booth1. demon.co.uk>**, with a page in Adobe Acrobat format showing the different forms for all the characters at **<www.booth1.demon.co.uk/Characters. pdf>**. The documents reproduced on the site provide a good test of reading skills.

Dates and calendars

There are a number of useful resources on the Web to help you make sense of the dates and calendars used in older genealogical sources.

There are two particular types of dating which are generally unfamiliar to modern readers. The first is the dating of documents, particularly legal ones, by regnal years, i.e. the number of years since the accession of the reigning monarch (so 1 January 2002 is 1 January 49 Eliz. II). The Regnal Year Calculator at **<www.albion.edu/english/calendar/regnal.htm>** will convert regnal years for the period from the Norman Conquest to George I. Saints' days are also frequently encountered in early documents, and the On-line Calendar of Saints' Days at **<members.tripod.com/~gunhouse/ calendar/home.htm>** should enable you to decode these. The Catholic Encyclopedia's 'Dates And Dating' page at **<www.newadvent.org/cathen/ 04636c.htm>** is also useful.

In September 1752 Britain switched from the old Julian calendar to the Gregorian. For information on this change see Mike Spathaky's article 'Old Style And New Style Dates And The Change To The Gregorian Calendar' at **<www.genfair.com/dates.htm>**. Steven Gibbs has a con-version routine for the Julian and Gregorian calendars at **<www.guernsey. net/~sgibbs/roman.html>**, which may be useful if you are consulting records from countries which switched either earlier (most of Europe) or later (Russia) than the UK.

To find out what day a particular date fell on, consult Genuki's Perpetual Calendar at **<www.genuki.org.uk/big/easter/>**, which also gives the dates of Easter. The years 1550 to 2049 are covered.

Chris Phillips provides a comprehensive guide to chronology and dating at **<www.medievalgenealogy.org.uk/guide/chron.shtml>**, as part of a site devoted to medieval genealogy.

Latin

For medieval genealogy and for legal records up to the 1730s, you will often encounter texts written in Latin. Even in English texts Latin phrases or, worse, abbreviations for them are not uncommon. Latin has also, of course, been much used for inscriptions.

General help in reading Latin documents will be found at <www.italiangenealogy.com/toolbox/latin.htm>, while there are Latin dictionaries at **<humanum.arts.cuhk.edu.hk/Lexis/Latin/>** and **<www.nd. edu/~archives/latgramm.htm>**. The latter also provides a grammar and links to other useful resources. Be warned, however, that these cover classical Latin and not the Latin of medieval and early modern Britain. Lynn H. Nelson's 'Latin Word List' at **<kufacts.cc.ukans.edu/ftp/ pub/history/latin_language/latwords.html>** seems to be based on the Vulgate and will therefore be of use for Christian Latin terms. There is a list of 'Hard Little Words: Prepositions, Adverbs, Conjunctions (With Some Definitions of Medieval Usage)' at **<www.georgetown.edu/ irvinemj/classics203/resources/latin.lex>**.

These sites will not include feudal land-tenure terms, and are not going to enable you to translate a medieval charter, but they can certainly help with Latin words and phrases embedded in English prose.

Latin abbreviations are often used, particularly in set phrases, and the FAQ for the soc.genealogy.medieval newsgroup has a list of some of those commonly found in genealogical documents at **<users.erols.com/wrei/ faqs/medieval.html>**.

Technical terms

Genealogists encounter technical terms from many specialist areas, and have the additional difficulty that it may not be apparent whether a term is specialized or in fact obsolete. Useful places to turn when you encounter this sort of problem are the rather inappropriately named OLD-ENGLISH mailing list, which is for 'anyone who is deciphering old English documents to discuss interpretations of handwriting and word meanings' or the OLD-WORDS mailing list 'for the discussion of old words, phrases, names, abbreviations, and antique jargon useful to genealogy'. Details of how to subscribe to these lists are at **<www.rootsweb.com/~jfuller/ gen_mail_general.html>**. You can also browse or search the archives for them at **<archiver.rootsweb.com/o.html>**. Bear in mind that the contributors to the lists have widely varying expertise, and you will need to evaluate carefully any advice you receive. However, the companion web site for the OLD-ENGLISH list at **<homepages.rootsweb.com/~oel/>** has an excellent collection of material, as well as some useful links at **<homepages.rootsweb.com/~oel/links.html>**.

Old terms for occupations are discussed on p. 86.

Legal

Even where they are not written in Latin many early modern texts, particularly those relating to property, contain technical legal terms that are likely to mean little to the non-specialist, but which may be crucial to the understanding of an ancestor's property holdings or transactions. A useful list of Legal Terms in Land Records will be found at <www.ultranet.com/~deeds/legal.htm>, while the equivalent but distinct terminology for Scotland is explained at <www.hmce.gov.uk/notices/742-3.htm>. These are both guides to present-day usage, but in view of the archaic nature of landholding records this should not be a hindrance. A more specifically historical glossary is provided on the Scottish Archive Network site at <www.scan.org.uk/researchrtools/glossary.htm>.

Medical

Death certificates of the last century, and earlier references to cause of death, often include terms that are unfamiliar. Some can be found in one of the on-line dictionaries of contemporary medicine, such as MedTerms at <www.medterms.com> or Dr Graham Dark's 'On-line Medical Dictionary' at <www.graylab.ac.uk/omd/index.html>. But for comprehensive coverage of archaic medical terms, Paul Smith's Archaic Medical Terms site at <www.paul_smith.doctors.org.uk/amt1.htm> is the best place to go. Cyndi's List has a 'Medical & Medicine' page at <www.CyndisList.com/medical.htm>.

Measurements

Leicester University's Palaeography course materials, mentioned on p. 112, include a number of useful lists covering terms likely to be found in old legal documents: land measurement terms, the Latin equivalents of English coinage, and Roman numerals.

Steven Gibbs' site, mentioned on p. 113, has facilities for converting to and from Roman numerals at <www.guernsey.net/~sgibbs/roman.html>.

Details of old units of measurement (though not areal measurements) can be found at <www.shaunf.dircon.co.uk/shaun/metrology/english.html>, while both linear and areal measures are covered by <www.headley1.demon.co.uk/histdate/measures.htm>. There is a comprehensive Dictionary of Measures at <www.unc.edu/~rowlett/units/> which includes a useful article on English Customary measures at <www.unc.edu/~rowlett/units/custom.html>. Cyndi's List has a page devoted to Weights and Measures at <www.CyndisList.com/weights.htm>.

Medieval

There are a number of general guides to medieval terms, including NetSERF's Hypertext Medieval Glossary at <netserf.cua.edu/glossary/home.htm>, The Glossary Of Medieval Terms at <cal.bemidji.msus.edu/History/mcmanus/ma_gloss.html>, and The Guide To Medieval Terms at

<orb.rhodes.edu/Medieval_Terms.html>. Resources for the terminology of heraldry are discussed on p. 98.

Value of money

A very frequent question on genealogy mailing lists is the present-day equivalent of sums of money in wills, tax rolls and the like. There is a very detailed analysis of the historical value of sterling in a House of Commons Research Paper 'Inflation: the Value of the Pound 1750–1998', which is available on-line in PDF format at **<www.parliament.uk/commons/lib/research/rp99/rp99-020.pdf>**. For a longer time span, there are two tables covering the period from the 13th century to the present day at **<www.headley1.demon.co.uk/histdate/moneyval.htm>**.

Alan Stanier's 'Relative Value of Sums of Money' page at **<privatewww. essex.ac.uk/~alan/family/N-Money.html>** has statistics relating to wages for various types of worker (mainly craftsmen and labourers) from 1264, but also for domestic servants and professionals for the 18th and 19th centuries (see Figure 9.2).

The Economic History Services' site has a page on 'The Purchasing power of the pound' at **<eh.net/ehresources/howmuch/poundq.php>**,

1859 - 1861

Average Yearly Wages paid to Domestics

Source: *Beeton, 1859-61*

THE FOLLOWING TABLE OF THE AVERAGE YEARLY WAGES paid to domestics, with the various members of the household placed in the order in which they are usually ranked, will serve as a guide to regulate the expenditure of an establishment:-

	When not found in Livery.	When found in Livery.
The House Steward	£40 to £80	-
The Valet	25 to 50	£20 to £30
The Butler	25 to 50	-
The Cook	20 to 40	-
The Gardener	20 to 40	-
The Footman	20 to 40	15 to 25
The Under Butler	15 to 30	15 to 25
The Coachman	-	20 to 35
The Groom	15 to 30	12 to 20
The Under Footman	-	12 to 20
The Page or Footboy	8 to 18	6 to 14
The Stableboy	6 to 12	-

Figure 9.2 Wages for domestic servants <privatewww.essex.ac.uk/~alan/family/N-Money.html>

which enables you to find the modern equivalent of an amount in pounds, shillings and pence in a particular year. This is part of a 'How much is that?' section at <eh.net/hmit/> which also has information on UK and US inflation rates since the 1660s and the pound–dollar conversion rate for the last 200 years. If you are too young to remember the pre-decimal system of pounds, shillings and pence, then 'What's A Guinea?' at <www. deadline.demon.co.uk/wilkie/coins.htm> will enlighten you.

Photographs

The Web provides an ideal medium for publishing photographs whether individually or in collections. It costs more or less nothing to scan a photograph and make it available on the Web whereas the cost of putting more than the odd photograph in a published family history is a regrettable disincentive to making the pictorial past more widely accessible. While you are not particularly likely to come across a photograph of your great-great-grandmother on the Web (unless she was, say, Queen Victoria), there are an increasing number of modern photographs of places and scans of 19th-century photographs. There are a number of sites devoted to military photographs, which may help you identify an ancestor's uniform or a medal, discussed on p. 88. Photographs of places are discussed on p. 107, and aerial photographs of modern Britain on p. 103.

If you are looking for help with the dating of old photographs, the BBC web site for the *Blood Ties* programme has a brief 'Guide to Victorian Studio Photographs' at **<www.bbc.co.uk/history/programmes/blood/victor_photo_1.shtml>**. Andrew J. Morris' site 19th Century Photography for genealogists at <www.ajmorris.com/roots/photo/photo.htm> is a more detailed account of various photographic processes and techniques (though the details about costume and the design of card mounts for photographs relate specifically to the US).

There is also help on the Web if you are interested in preserving and restoring old photographs, for example the article by David L. Mishkin 'Restoring Damaged Photographs' at **<www.genealogy.com/10_restr. html>**.

Finally, there is a mailing list, VINTAGE-PHOTOS, is devoted to 'the discussion and sharing of information regarding vintage photos including, but not restricted to, proper storage, preservation, restoration, ageing and dating, restoration software, photo types and materials used, restoration assistance, and scanning options'. Information on how to join the list will be found at **<www.rootsweb.com/~jfuller/gen_mail_general. html#VINTAGE-PHOTOS>**.

Cyndi's List has a page devoted to links for 'Photographs and Memories' at **<www.cyndislist.com/photos.htm>**.

10 Discussion Forums

One of the most useful aspects of the internet for anyone researching their family history is that is very easy to 'meet' other genealogists on-line to discuss matters of common interest, to exchange information and to find help and advice. The specific issues of locating other people with interests in the same surnames and families are dealt with in Chapter 6.

Mailing lists

Electronic mailing lists provide a way for groups of people to conduct on-line discussions via e-mail. They are simply a logical extension of your electronic address book – instead of each member of a group having to keep track of the e-mail addresses of everyone else, this list of e-mail addresses is managed by a computer called a list server, which also allows people to add themselves to the list, or remove themselves from it, without having to contact everyone else.

You join a list by sending an e-mail message to a list server. Thereafter you receive a copy of every message sent to the list by other list members; likewise, any message you send to the list gets circulated to all the other subscribers.

What lists are there?

The first genealogical mailing list, ROOTS-L, goes back to a period long before the internet was available to the general public – its first message was posted in December 1987. There are now over 20,000 mailing lists devoted to genealogy.

A large proportion of the genealogy lists are hosted by RootsWeb, and details of these will be found at **<lists.rootsweb.com>**. Another site that hosts many genealogy lists is Yahoo Groups at **<groups.yahoo.com>**. Most of the groups hosted here are listed under the Family & Home | Genealogy category, though there are many others for particular countries and areas, which can be found by using the search facility.

In spite of the large number of lists, it is a simple matter to find those which might be of interest to you. John Fuller and Chris Gaunt's Genealogical Resources on the Internet site has a comprehensive listing of genealogy mailing lists at **<www.rootsweb.com/~jfuller/gen_mail.html>**, subdivided into the following categories:

- Countries other than USA
- USA
- Surnames
- Adoption
- African-Ancestored
- Cemeteries/Monuments/
  Obituaries
- Computing/internet Resources
- Genealogical Material/Services
- General Information/Discussion
- Jewish

- LDS
- Native American
- Occupations
- Religions/Churches (other than
  Jewish/LDS)
- Ships/Trails
- Societies
- Software
- Vital Records (census, BDM)
- Wars/Military
- Uncategorized

The 'uncategorized' lists include a number devoted to topics of general interest, such as the Blacksheep, GENEALOGY-DNA, GEN-MEDIEVAL and TRANSLATIONS lists.

The mailing lists most likely to be of use to UK family historians are the county-based lists (including some which cover a group of adjacent counties), and these can be most easily found on Genuki's mailing list page at <www.genuki.org.uk/indexes/MailingLists.html>. In addition to the county lists, there are quite a number of general lists covering particular topics in relation either to the entirety of the British Isles, or to some constituent of it. The advantage of the Genuki listing is that it includes lists which, although of interest to UK genealogists, are not categorized under the UK by John Fuller or RootsWeb – notably war-related lists such as the AMERICAN-REVOLUTION, BOER-WAR or WARBRIDES lists hosted by RootsWeb. John Fuller has a listing of specifically UK lists at <www.rootsweb.com/~jfuller/gen_mail_country-unk.html>. In spite of its 'United Kingdom' title, this page includes a number of Irish lists, though there is a more comprehensive listing for Ireland at <www.rootsweb.com/~jfuller/gen_mail_country-ire.html>.

If you want to find mailing lists on topics other than genealogy, the International Federation of Library Associations and Institutions provides some useful links on its 'Internet Mailing Lists Guides and Resources' page at <www.ifla.org/I/training/listserv/lists.htm>. Also, since many mailing lists have either a web page of their own or at least a listing somewhere on the Web, a search engine can be used to locate them.

List archives

Many genealogy mailing lists, including almost all the lists hosted by RootsWeb, have an archive of past messages. The RootsWeb list archives can be found at <archiver.rootsweb.com>. Not all list archives are open to non-members of the relevant list, but where a list has open membership it would be very rare to have a closed archive.

The archives have two main purposes. First, they allow you to have a look at the nature of the discussion that takes place on the list and judge whether it would be worth your while joining – in particular, an archive will give you some idea of the level of traffic on the list, i.e. how many messages a day are posted. Second, they provide a basis for searching, whether by the list server's own search facility, or by a general search engine such as those discussed in Chapter 11. This means that you can take advantage of information posted to a mailing list without joining it.

Joining a list

In order to join a list you need to send an e-mail message to the list server, the computer that manages the list, instructing it to add you to the list of subscribers. The text of the e-mail message must contain nothing but the correct command.

Although the basic principles for joining a list are more or less universal, there are a small number of different list systems and each has its own particular features.

Many lists are run on 'listserv' systems (the name of the software that manages the lists). To join one of them you need to send a message to listserv@*the-name-of-the-list-server*, and the text of the e-mail message should start with the word **SUB** (short for 'subscribe'), followed by the name of the list and then your first and last names. So to join WW20-ROOTS-L, a list for the discussion of genealogy in all 20th-century wars, you would send the following message (supposing your name was John Smith):

> **To: listserv@listserv.indiana.edu**
> **SUB WW20-ROOTS-L John Smith**

You need to specify the list name because this particular list server could be managing many different lists.

On other systems such as RootsWeb, however, there may be a separate subscription e-mail address for each list. This is typically formed by adding the word *request* to the list name. So to join the GENBRIT-L list, for example, you send your joining command to GENBRIT-L-request@rootsweb.com and the text of the message itself only needs to say *subscribe*:

> **To: GENBRIT-L-request@rootsweb.com**
> **subscribe**

Yahoo Groups uses a similar system – to join the yorkshiregentopics group, you would need to send the following message:

> **To: yorkshiregentopics-subscribe@yahoogroups.com**

You should not need to worry about which to use. Any site with details of mailing lists, such as Genealogy Resources on the Internet, should give explicit instructions on how to join any lists mentioned. As you can see from Figure 10.1, on Yahoo Groups the home page for each group gives subscription instructions.

Because these messages are processed by a computer, you should send *only* the commands – there is no point in sending a message to an automatic system saying, 'Hello, my name is . . . and I would like to join the list, please.' Also, it is a good idea to remove any signature at the end of your e-mail message, so that the list server does not attempt to treat it as a set of commands.

Incidentally, do not be worried by the word 'subscription'. It does not mean you are committing yourself to paying for anything, it just means that your name is being added to the list of members.

If you have more than one e-mail address you need to make sure that you send your joining message from the one you want messages sent to. Most mailing lists will reject an e-mail message from an address it does not have in its subscriber list.

Some lists have web pages with an on-line form for joining. In this case you simply type your e-mail address in the box. There is a similar system for the mailing lists at Yahoo Groups, though here you have to register (free) before you can join any of its lists. Once you have signed in, you can click on the subscribe button for any list and it will bring up a page such as the one in Figure 10.2 for the yorkshiregentopics list, where you can select your subscription options and join the list.

When you join a list you will normally get a welcome message. You should make sure you keep this, as it will give you important information

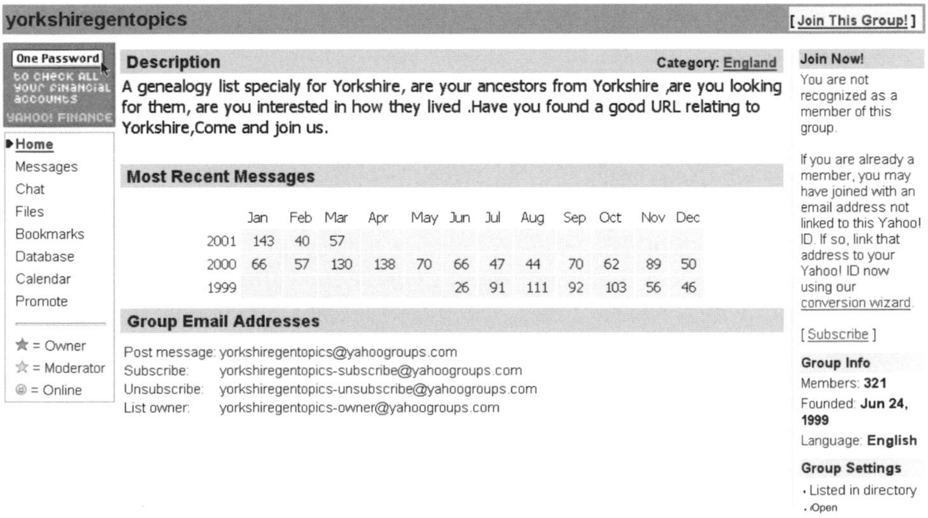

Figure 10.1 Home page for the yorkshiregentopics group on Yahoo

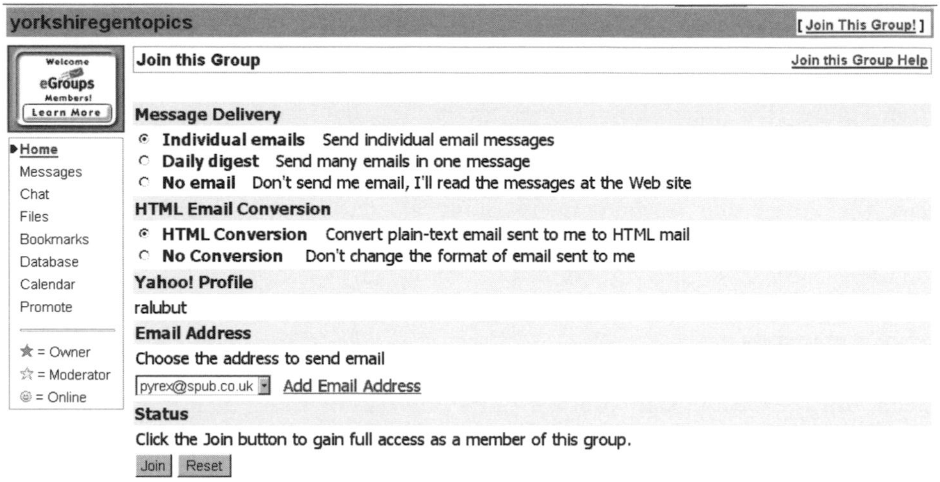

Figure 10.2 Subscribing to a list on Yahoo Groups

about the list and the e-mail addresses to use. There are few things more embarrassing on-line than having to send a message to everyone on a mailing list asking how to unsubscribe because you have lost the welcome message which contains the instructions.

There are some circumstances in which you will not be able to join a list by one of the methods discussed here: some lists are 'closed', which means that they are not open to all comers. This is typically the case for mailing lists run by societies for their own members. In this case, instead of sending an e-mail to the list server you will probably need to contact the person who manages the list, providing your society membership number, so that he or she can check that you are entitled to join the list and then add you.

Closed mailing lists are also often used for the management of genealogical projects. In such cases those involved in the project are usually added to a list as soon as they join the project and no outsiders are admitted. Closed lists can also allow geographically remote committee members of a society to keep in touch, as with the trustees of Genuki, who conduct all affairs via a closed mailing list.

Subscription options

Many mailing lists have two ways in which you can receive messages. The standard way is what is called 'mail mode', where every individual message to the list is forwarded to you as soon as it is received. However, some older mail systems were not able to cope with the potentially very large number of incoming messages, so lists also offered a 'digest mode', in which a bunch of messages to the list are combined into a single larger message, thus reducing the number of messages arriving in the subscriber's mailbox. Even though few of us nowadays are likely to encounter this sort of technical problem, some people do not like to receive the dozens of mail

Address	What It's For
The list server	Automatic control of your subscription to the list. Messages sent to this address are not read by a human, and can only consist of specific commands.
The list itself	This is the address to be used for contributions to the discussion. Anything sent to this address is copied to all the list members. A common beginner's mistake is to send a message meant for the list server to the list address; hundreds, or even thousands, of people receive your 'unsubscribe' message.
The list owner/administrator	This is for contacting the person in charge of the list. For most lists it should only be needed if there is some problem with the list server (e.g. it won't respond to your messages), or something the automated server can't deal with that requires human intervention (e.g. abusive messages). For closed lists, you will probably need to use this address rather than the list-server address in order to subscribe.

Table 10.1 Mailing List Addresses

messages per day that can come from a busy list, and prefer to receive the messages as a digest.

However, there are also disadvantages to this. For a start, you need to look through each digest to see the subjects of the messages it contains, whereas individual messages with subject lines of no interest to you can quickly be deleted unread. Also, if you want to reply to a message contained within a digest your e-mail software will automatically include the subject line of the *digest*, not just the message within the digest you are replying to, with the result that others on the list will not be able to tell from your subject line which earlier message you are responding to. If your e-mail software automatically quotes the original message in reply, then you will need to delete almost all of the quoted digest if you are not to irritate other list members with an unnecessarily long message, most of which will be irrelevant (see Netiquette, p. 137).

There are a number of different ways of arranging to receive a list in digest form. With the lists on RootsWeb there is a different subscription address, containing -D- instead of -L-, so subscription messages for the digest form of GENBRIT list go to **GENBRIT-D-request@rootsweb. com.** On listserv systems, once you have joined a list you should send a message with the text **set LISTNAME digest** to change to digest mode, and **set LISTNAME nodigest** to switch back to mail mode. On lists with a Web subscription form, you may be able to choose between mail and digest on the form, as you can see in Figure 10.2.

Text formatting

E-mail software generally allows you to send messages in a number of different formats, and normally you do not need to worry about exactly how your mail software is formatting them. When you start sending messages to mailing lists, however, you may find that this is an issue you need to consider. The reason for this is that some mailing lists will not accept certain types of formatting, and even if they do, some recipients of your formatted messages may have difficulties.

The standard format for an e-mail message is plain text. This can be handled by any list server and any e-mail software. However, most modern e-mail software will let you send formatted text with particular fonts and font sizes, colour, italics and so on, i.e. something much more like what you produce with your word processor, and some software even uses this as the default. The way it does this is to include an e-mail attachment containing the message in RTF format (created and used by word processors) or HTML format (used for web pages).

You may feel that this is exactly how you want your e-mail messages to look. But if someone is using e-mail software that can't make sense of this format they may have trouble with your message. They may even receive what looks like a blank message with an attachment, and many people are, rightly, wary of opening an attachment which could contain a virus, particularly if it's attached to a suspicious-looking blank message. The only way they will be able to read your message is by saving the attachment as a file and then opening it with the relevant piece of software, and no one will thank you for sending a message requiring all that extra work. Indeed, people using text-based e-mail on some systems, such as UNIX, may not even have access to software for reading such files.

Also, messages with formatting are inevitably larger than plain text messages, so people have to spend more time on-line to download them, which, while trivial for an individual message, could be significant for someone who is a member of a few busy lists. All things considered, there is really no good reason for using formatted text in mailing-list messages.

Different lists and list systems deal with this problem in a variety of ways. As you can see from Figure 10.2, Yahoo Groups allows you to choose whether you receive messages from the list as HMTL or as plain text. RootsWeb does not permit the use of HTML or RTF formatting at all, and will not allow messages with formatted text to get through.

If you need to find out how to turn off the formatting features of your e-mail software, RootsWeb has a useful page on 'How to Turn Off HTML or RTF in Various E-mail Software Programs' at **<helpdesk.rootsweb.com/ help/html-off.html>**. The page shows you how to do this for all the most popular e-mail software, but even if it does not include the software you use, it should give you an idea of what to look for in your own e-mail package.

The only formatting feature that can be really useful in an e-mail message is the ability to highlight words to be stressed, and the traditional way of doing this in a plain text message is to put *asterisks* round the relevant word. One thing *not* to do, in genealogy mailing lists anyway, is put words in upper case – this is traditionally reserved for indicating surnames.

Filtering

If you do not want to subscribe to mailing lists in digest mode, you can still avoid cluttering up your inbox with incoming messages from mailing lists. Most modern e-mail software has a facility for *filtering* messages, i.e. for moving them automatically from your incoming mailbox to another mailbox when it spots certain pieces of text in the header of the message. You will need to consult the on-line help for your e-mail software in order to see exactly how to do it, but Figure 10.3 shows a filter in Eudora 4.3 which will move all mail received from the GENBRIT mailing list into a dedicated mailbox called genbrit (in Eudora, filters are created via the **Tools | Filters** menu). This does not reduce the number of messages you receive, but it keeps your list mail separate from your personal mail and you can look at it when it suits you.

Other uses of mailing lists

Although in general mailing lists allow all members to send messages, and messages are forwarded to all members, there are two types of list that work differently.

Some lists are not used for discussion at all, but only for announcements. Typically, this sort of list is used by an organization to publish an e-mail newsletter. It differs from a normal list in that you will not be able to send messages, only receive the announcements. The electronic newsletters mentioned in Chapter 13 are in fact mailing lists of this type.

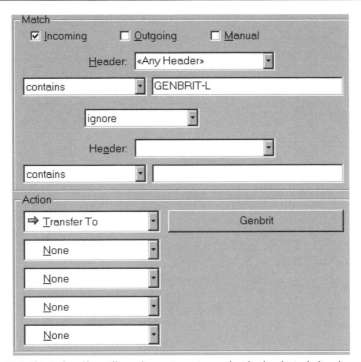

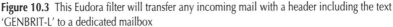

Figure 10.3 This Eudora filter will transfer any incoming mail with a header including the text 'GENBRIT-L' to a dedicated mailbox

Normally, mailing lists allow only members of the list to send messages to it, and messages from non-members are rejected. But there are a few lists that accept messages from non-members, for example to allow people to submit information to a project. In a case like this you will not be able to join the list yourself but will be able to send messages to it. Genuki uses a system like this for users to report errors or submit additional information, which is automatically circulated via a mailing list to all Genuki county maintainers. In fact, from the non-members' point of view this is just a special e-mail address, and the fact that it is actually a list may not even be apparent.

Newsgroups

While mailing lists are very useful, they do have some disadvantages. Join a couple of big mailing lists or a few smaller ones and the number of e-mails you get in a day will rise drastically. Particularly if you have a slow internet connection, you may feel you do not want to spend ages downloading messages when a good proportion of them may not be relevant to your interests.

An alternative type of forum for discussion and questions is the newsgroup. Newsgroups work in a completely different way from mailing lists, and have the great advantage that you do not have to join anything and end up downloading every single message.

Whereas a mailing list is like an on-line club – you really need to be a member to get the best from it – newsgroups are more like electronic notice-boards, where anyone can post a message and everyone can read it. What is good about newsgroups is that you can dip in and out of them as you like. However, there is also the disadvantage that you may miss something useful, because you have to remember to go and look at the messages. They do not automatically come to you.

News servers

Unlike mailing lists, which are simply a particular way of using e-mail, news is actually a quite separate internet facility which requires special software and which depends on a network of servers around the world called news servers. The way it works is that when you post a message to a newsgroup, the message is uploaded to your local news server, which passes your message on to all the neighbouring news servers, which in turn pass it on until your message has reached every news server on the internet. This means that anyone with access to a news server will be able to read your message. It also means that the news service as a whole never breaks down, though it might be locally unavailable. This is quite different from a mailing list, whose operation is completely suspended if the particular server that hosts it is out of action, as happens, for example, when RootsWeb closes down its servers for maintenance.

Most subscription ISPs provide a news server for their subscribers, though many of the free providers do not. If your ISP does not provide a news server, you will need to use one of the Web-based news archives discussed below.

Newsreading software

In order to look at newsgroups you need a piece of software called a newsreader, or you need to use a web browser or e-mail package that has newsreading facilities. There are several shareware newsreaders and a number of freeware ones available. Forté's Free Agent is a popular freeware newsreader for Windows, while Newswatcher is a freeware Macintosh newsreader. These can be downloaded from <easynet.tucows. com/news95.html> and <easynet.mac.tucows.com/newsmac.html> respectively, which also list a variety of other shareware and freeware packages.

However, if you have Netscape Navigator or Internet Explorer installed on your computer you will be able to access your ISP's news server without additional software. In Netscape, there is a Newsgroups option on the Communicator menu (up to version 4.75), and via Mail in version 6 or later.[6] Outlook Express can be set up to read news.

---

[6] See Netscape's instructions at <help.netscape.com/kb/consumer/19960627-3.html>.

Newsgroup hierarchies

Newsgroups are organized in a particular way, which you need to understand in order to use them. Each mailing list name is guaranteed to be unique because each is hosted on a particular list server, and the people managing the list server make sure that names are distinct and give some indication of the topic the list is devoted to. Newsgroups are a single global system and they are named in such a way that you can easily see what topic a newsgroup covers. Groups devoted to related topics have similar names. Newsgroup names are built up of two or more parts, separated by a dot. The first part of the name indicates the general subject area and each additional part indicates a narrower subject area. Each subject area, or subdivision of one, is called a 'hierarchy'.

Most of the genealogy newsgroups are in the soc. hierarchy, which is for social and cultural topics. Their names start soc.genealogy (as opposed to soc.history, soc.culture, etc.), followed by a specific genealogical subject area, for example soc.genealogy.computing or soc.genealogy.ireland. There are many other hierarchies, but the oldest and most important are alt, comp, news, misc, rec, and sci (see Figure 10.4, the home page for Google's news archive at **<groups.google.com>**).

Genealogy newsgroups

There are a number of groups dedicated to the genealogy of particular countries, regions or ethnic groups:

- soc.genealogy.african
- soc.genealogy.australia+nz
- soc.genealogy.benelux

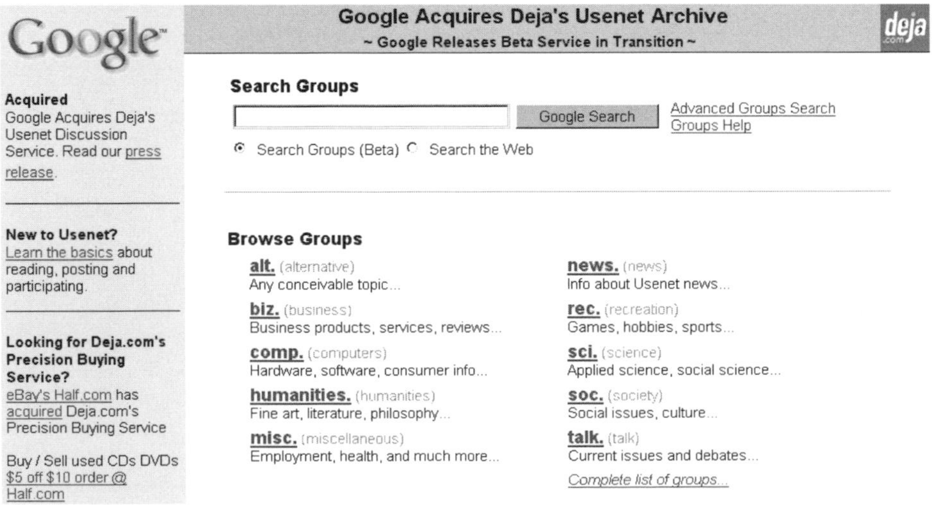

Figure 10.4 Google's news service <groups.google.com>

- soc.genealogy.britain
- soc.genealogy.french
- soc.genealogy.german
- soc.genealogy.hispanic
- soc.genealogy.ireland
- soc.genealogy.italian
- soc.genealogy.jewish
- soc.genealogy.nordic
- soc.genealogy.slavic
- soc.genealogy.west-indies
- alt.scottish.clans
- wales.genealogy
- wales.genealogy.general

These are the best groups for discussion of genealogical sources and issues relating to the individual countries etc.

There are a few non-geographical groups devoted to general topics:

- alt.genealogy
- soc.genealogy.computing (for anything relating to genealogy software and electronic data)
- soc.genealogy.marketplace (for announcements of commercial services or anything for sale – commercial activity is generally frowned upon in the other genealogy newsgroups)
- soc.genealogy.medieval
- soc.genealogy.methods (for discussion of the techniques and methods of genealogy)
- soc.genealogy.misc

There are a number of groups specifically intended not for general discussion but for the posting of surname interests:

- soc.genealogy.surnames
- soc.genealogy.surnames.britain
- soc.genealogy.surnames.canada
- soc.genealogy.surnames.german
- soc.genealogy.surnames.global
- soc.genealogy.surnames.ireland
- soc.genealogy.surnames.misc
- soc.genealogy.surnames.usa

There is another range of newsgroups devoted to individual surnames. These are in the alt.family-name and alt-family-names hierarchies, for example alt.family-names.anderson, alt.family-names.lloyd. At the time of writing there are about 150 of these, but they are in practice of doubtful value – they are very little used and have few messages of interest to genealogists. In addition, not all news servers carry these groups so their distribution is more restricted than that of other newsgroups. Only the main group alt.family-names seems to be of any use. For specific surnames, a mailing list is much more likely to be useful.

All the groups listed so far are English-language groups, but there are also non-English groups which may be of interest if you have ancestors from another European country. Obviously, the discussion is mostly in the local language, but if you post in English you may well get a response.

- dk.historie.genealogi (Danish)
- fr.rec.genealogie (French)
- fr.comp.applications.genealogie (French, for genealogy software)
- de.sci.genealogie (German)
- no.slekt (Norwegian)
- no.slekt.etterlysning (Norwegian)
- no.slekt.programmer (Norwegian, for genealogy software)
- se.hobby.genealogi (Swedish)

If you have ancestors from other non-English-speaking countries, you may be able to get some help by posting in an appropriate group in the soc.culture hierarchy – these groups, such as soc.culture.brazil and soc.culture.netherlands, have discussion in English on the country concerned. They may be useful for getting general information about a country, but you should not expect to find specifically genealogical expertise.

Finally, there are two groups for heraldry, alt.heraldry.sca and rec.heraldry, and a group for adoption, alt.adoption, which may be of use in genealogical research.

Newsgroup charters

Every newsgroup has a charter which explains what topics it is intended to cover and what needs it is meant to meet. Charters for all the main genealogy newsgroups can be found at **<homepages.rootsweb.com/~socgen/>**, and this page has other useful information about these newsgroups. The charter for soc.genealogy.ireland is given on the next page as an a example – note the prohibition on things like posting photographs and political discussion.

Reading news

Once you have set up your newsreading software there are several different stages in reading news. The very first thing you need to do is get your newsreader to download the list of all the newsgroups that are available on your news server. This can take a good few minutes as there are over 50,000 groups, but it only needs to be done once. Thereafter your software

CHARTER: soc.genealogy.ireland

Soc.genealogy.ireland is an unmoderated group for genealogy and family history discussion among people researching ancestors, family members, or others who have a genealogical connection to any people in any part of Northern Ireland and The Republic of Ireland.

The group is open to anyone with an interest in genealogy in any of the populations in or from this area, including, but not limited to: people who live, lived, or may have lived there; emigrants; immigrants; and their descendants.

The scope of the group reflects the language, history, migrations, and the realities of researching public records and genealogical data archives, and includes questions of local customs and history, or of regional or national history which affected the lives of these people and which are difficult to research in the present. Posts may be in any language but those seeking replies from a wide spectrum of readers (or at all) would be well advised to post in English.

The focus of the group is on the genealogy of individuals, as members of ethnic groups, and as part of migration patterns. Postings on topics unrelated to genealogy, especially relating to current political or religious topics are not acceptable.

Postings concerning general surnames searches are not welcome and should be directed to the soc.genealogy.surnames.ireland newsgroup. Postings containing MIME attachments, graphics, binary or GEDCOM files, and program listings are also not acceptable.

will only need to download the names of any new groups each time it connects to the server. Note that at this stage no messages have been downloaded, just the names of the groups.

With a list of groups in your newsreader, you need to decide which ones to read. Newsreaders generally allow you two ways of selecting a newsgroup to read. You can either 'subscribe' to it or you can just select it. Subscribing simply means that your newsreader keeps a permanent note that you want to look at the group – it does not mean you are 'joining' the group as you are when you subscribe to a mailing list. The advantage of subscribing is that you don't need to select the group again each time you use your newsreader.

Once you have selected or subscribed to a group, the next stage is to download the message headers – this is not the contents of the messages themselves but simply the details of the messages: who they're from, their subject lines, their date of posting, their size. You have still not downloaded any actual messages, and the idea of downloading the headers is that you can see which messages are likely to be of interest and look at only those. This is the advantage of a newsgroup over a mailing list: you

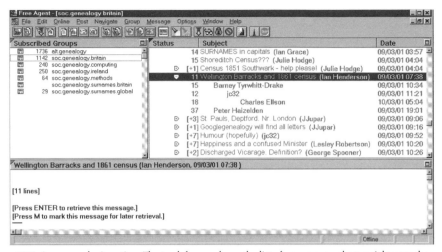

Figure 10.5 A newsreader in action. The top left pane shows the list of newsgroups, the top right pane the message headers. Clicking on the highlighted message will download it into the bottom pane

don't get a copy of every message, just the ones you decide you want to read. If it is the first time you have looked at a group, or there are a lot of new messages, you will probably be offered an option to download either all the headers or just some of them.

Exactly how you view messages depends on your software. Netscape will automatically download and display any message your cursor rests on, while in Free Agent you have to double click on a message to display it. Another possibility is to mark all the messages you want to read and then download them in one go. If you do this, you can then disconnect from the internet and read the messages off-line, keeping down your connection time and costs. If you regularly want to download all the messages from selected newsgroups you can use your newsreading software in off-line mode, or get a dedicated 'off-line reader'. However, almost all genealogy groups are also available in mailing list format (see 'Mailing list gateways', below), and this is probably a more convenient way to ensure you get all the messages.

Posting messages

One advantage of newsgroups over mailing lists is that you don't need e-mail facilities to read the messages, nor a permanent e-mail address. Your newsreader will post your message straight to the news server and, although it may ask you to configure the software with an e-mail address, you do not need to enter an authentic working e-mail address at all. This means newsgroups are ideal for the occasional internet user and anyone who has not got their own computer and internet connection.

It also means that it is possible to send messages to newsgroups anonymously (which is not to say the computer you are using could not be traced if it were worth someone's time and trouble).

Mailing list gateways

There is another way to access some newsgroups without a news server: RootsWeb acts as a gateway that makes most of the main genealogy groups available in mailing list format. This is much more convenient if you want to make sure you don't miss any of the messages in a group. Also, because the mailing lists are available in digest form, this can be a good way of reducing the number of individual messages. Table 10.2 shows each newsgroup and its equivalent mailing list. Full details of the individual lists and how to join them can be found on RootsWeb at <www.rootsweb.com>. There is also, of course, an archive of the mailing list messages at <archiver.rootsweb.com>.

Table 10.2 Genealogy newsgroups and their equivalent mailing lists

Newsgroup	Gatewayed Mailing List
alt.genealogy	ALT-GENEALOGY
fr.comp.applications.genealogie	GEN-FF-LOG
fr.rec.genealogie	GEN-FF
soc.genealogy.african	GEN-AFRICAN
soc.genealogy.australia+nz	GENANZ
soc.genealogy.benelux	GEN-BENELUX & GENBNL-L
soc.genealogy.britain	GENBRIT
soc.genealogy.computing	GENCMP
soc.genealogy.french	GEN-FR
soc.genealogy.german	GEN-DE
soc.genealogy.hispanic	GEN-HISPANIC
soc.genealogy.ireland	GENIRE
soc.genealogy.italian	GEN-ITALIAN
soc.genealogy.jewish	JEWISHGEN
soc.genealogy.marketplace	GEN-MARKET
soc.genealogy.medieval	GEN-MEDIEVAL
soc.genealogy.methods	GENMTD
soc.genealogy.misc	GENMSC
soc.genealogy.nordic	GEN-NORDIC
soc.genealogy.slavic	GEN-SLAVIC
soc.genealogy.surnames.britain	SURNAMES-BRITAIN
soc.genealogy.surnames.canada	SURNAMES-CANADA
soc.genealogy.surnames.german	SURNAMES-GERMAN
soc.genealogy.surnames.global	SURNAMES
soc.genealogy.surnames.ireland	SURNAMES-IRELAND
soc.genealogy.surnames.misc	SURNAMES-MISC
soc.genealogy.surnames.usa	SURNAMES-USA
soc.genealogy.west-indies	CARIBBEAN

Newsgroup archives

If your ISP does not provide a news server, you can still read newsgroups and post messages to them by using one of the web sites devoted to newsgroups. If you just want to look at past messages but not to post messages yourself, Yahoo has a searchable archive at **<search.yahoo.com/search/options/>**. A more comprehensive site is provided by Google at **<groups.google.com>**.

You might think that this sort of service makes dedicated newsreading software and news servers redundant, but in fact there is a big disadvantage to Web-based news services: they are much slower to access. Because the connection to your ISP's news server is a very short one, a newsreader will respond very quickly to your commands, whereas it will take Google, based in the US, much longer to respond to a keypress from the UK, and the screen will have to be redrawn every time, which slows things down even further. This means that unless you are only an occasional user of news, or do not have access to a news server, using a newsreader will generally be better for normal newsreading.

However, even if you use a newsreader, there are still circumstances when a news archive will be useful. The most important factor is that news servers do not keep messages for ever. Because they have limited disk space, the only way they can make room for gigabytes of new messages every day is to delete older messages which then become unavailable on the server. Exactly how quickly messages 'scroll off' a news server varies, and partly depends on how busy a particular newsgroup is, but on the whole you should not expect to find messages more than a month old on a server. For older messages, you will need to look at a newsgroup archive. For the genealogy newsgroups the archive of the equivalent mailing list at RootsWeb can be used.

If you want to search for a particular topic across all the newsgroups, this can only be done in a news archive. Your newsreader may have facilities for searching, but these will be restricted to headers and messages you have already downloaded, and there is no way to use a newsreader to search all the messages on the server in the way that an archive's search facility can.

Finally, you may find that your news server does not carry all the genealogy groups, in which case you will need to go to an archive.

Web forums

A third type of discussion group is the Web-based forum. These work in very much the same way as Google's Web-based news service: a web site acts as a bulletin or message board where people can post messages for others to read. As with newsgroups, this does not clutter up your mailbox and does not require any long-term commitment. And, of course, it does not require you to install or configure software. However, as with

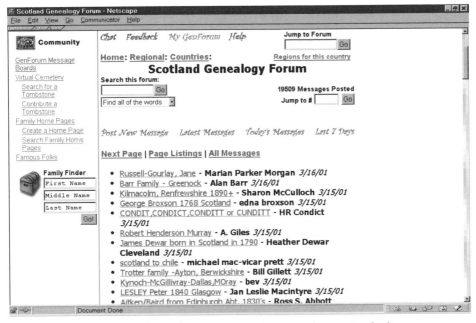

Figure 10.6 GenForum's Scotland Genealogy Forum at <genforum.genealogy.com/scotland/>

Google's news service, these forums can be very slow to use, in comparison with using a newsreader to access a local news server, and as there is no way to select a whole group of messages for reading you have to look separately at every single message of interest, each of which is delivered to you as a separate web page.

Unfortunately, there is no comprehensive list of such discussion forums, as many ISPs provide a facility for their subscribers to set up Web-based discussion groups, and a number of companies, such as Yahoo Groups (see p. 120) or Smartgroups at **<www.smartgroups.com>**, provide such facilities for all comers.

One of the major sites providing discussion forum facilities for genealogy is GenForum at **<genforum.genealogy.com>**. There are forums for over 100 countries, each US state, about 30 devoted to general topics (e.g. emigration, Jewish genealogy, marriage records) and about 20 devoted to computers and genealogy software. There are also over 20,000 forums relating to individual surnames.

Another site that provides a large number of genealogy forums is RootsWeb via its GenConnect site at **<genconnect.rootsweb.com>**, with over 120,000 genealogy 'message boards'. GenConnect has forums for all parts of the UK and Ireland. There is a message board for each county for general queries, and, in addition, for most counties there are boards relating to bible records, biographies, deeds, obituaries, pensions and wills. There are also boards for:

- Most other countries
- Many of the individual counties in each US state
- Thousands of individual surnames
- A small number of individual ethnic or religious groups

To assist in finding messages relating to individual surnames, there is a global search facility. There is an extensive FAQ about GenConnect's facilities at **<genconnect.rootsweb.com/HINTS/userfaqs.html>**.

FamilyHistory.com at **<www.familyhistory.com>** has over 130,000 message boards. The majority are devoted to individual surnames, but there are about 500 geographical boards and over 300 devoted to particular genealogical topics.

As you can see from Figure 10.2, Yahoo Groups allows you to read messages on the Web rather than receiving them as e-mail.

Forums on other providers can be found by using a search engine, and any forum relating specifically to UK genealogy should be found on the relevant county page on Genuki.

Frequently Asked Questions (FAQ)

Once you have been on a mailing list or looking at a newsgroup for some time, you will realize that certain questions come up again and again. Needless to say, regular members of a list don't relish the thought of repeatedly taking the time to answer these questions, so most newsgroups and general-interest mailing lists (i.e. those not dedicated to particular surnames) have what is called an FAQ, a file of frequently asked questions. The FAQ for a newsgroup is normally posted to the group once a month, but practice varies in mailing lists. Many newsgroup FAQs are also archived on the Web – those for the genealogy newsgroups can be found at **<www.woodgate.org/FAQs/>**.

If you are thinking of asking a question in a particular newsgroup for the first time, it's a good idea to consult the FAQ for the group. This will give you a guide as to what are considered appropriate or inappropriate issues to discuss and answers some of the most obvious questions.

By way of example, here is a list of the topics covered in the FAQ for soc.genealogy.britain:

- Is there such a thing as an Email Virus?
- What is a 'cockney'?
- What is Britain, and how is it sub-divided?
- What is an IRC? Snail mail to and from the UK.
- Is there a list of old Occupations online that can tell me what a French Polisher does? A Cordwainer? A Whitesmith, etc?
- What county is (...) in? Is there a Gazetteer of UK placenames online?
- What is the IGI? Is it going online? Can I buy it on CD-ROM?

- What are the actual dates the UK Census was taken?
- Is the UK census online?
- What do full-age/fa/ofa/bofa/minor/mi/do/DO mean in Public Records, etc?
- Is there a list of Causes of Death online? My gggf died of 'Asthenia'.
- What is Jno short for?
- What naming conventions are there?
- Is there a coat of arms for SMITH family (or other surname?)
- Why are parent details missing from the certificate?
- Where does the term Black Irish originate?
- Are 'World Books of (Your Surname)' worth buying?
- Posting Guidelines
- Where do I find other FAQs?
- What is the charter of this group?

The last three questions are to do with the customs of the particular newsgroup, and the remainder concern basic information for those new to British genealogy, including topics commonly raised by people living outside the UK.

Particularly if you are going to post information about your surname interests to one of the soc.genealogy.surnames groups, you should make sure you read the relevant FAQ, because there are fairly strict guidelines about appropriate formats for postings to these groups, which, unlike most groups, are not intended for general discussion.

The FAQs for all the main newsgroups can be found at <www.faqs. org>.

Netiquette

Mailing lists and newsgroups are essentially social institutions and, like face-to-face social institutions, they have a set of largely unwritten rules about what counts as acceptable or unacceptable behaviour. While individual newsgroups and mailing lists may spell some of these out in an FAQ, most of these rules are common to all on-line discussion groups and are often referred to collectively as 'netiquette'.

Of course, no one can stop you making inappropriate postings to a newsgroup, but breaking the rules will not make you popular: those who repeatedly breach them are likely to be on the receiving end of rebukes, and some people may configure their newsreading software to ignore messages from such miscreants. A mailing list is very likely to make some of these rules explicit conditions for its use, and list owners usually exclude those who persistently ignore them. Even though people are pretty tolerant of mistakes from beginners, it is worth reading the FAQ for a newsgroup or mailing list, and the welcome message from a mailing list.

The culture of newsgroups is rather different from that of mailing lists.

The main reason for this is that whereas every mailing list has an owner, no one is in charge of a newsgroup. In fact, newsgroups are one of the few social institutions that are genuinely anarchic. The only control is that the operator of each news server decides which groups to take and which to ignore. This means that if people 'misbehave' in a newsgroup, there is no one to appeal to.

Some mailing lists and a very small number of newsgroups are 'moderated'. In some cases this means that the messages pass through some sort of editorial control before being posted publicly; in others it means those who post inappropriate messages will be reprimanded and possibly, in the case of a list, forcibly unsubscribed.

Advice on 'Basic newsgroup and mailing list Netiquette' will be found at **<www.woodgate.org/FAQs/netiquette.html>**. The complete text of Virginia Shea's book *Netiquette* is on-line at **<www.albion.com/ netiquette/book/>**.

Good manners

Manners can be a problem in on-line discussion forums. The absence of the normal cues we expect in face-to-face interaction seems to make people less restrained (i.e. less polite), and such groups can contain a very diverse mix of individuals, both socially and geographically. This means you cannot rely on instincts developed in the off-line world to guide your behaviour.

- Make sure that any messages you send are relevant to the topic of the list or group. Some will tolerate the occasional off-topic message, some will not. If the list owner or others in a newsgroup ask you to discontinue a topic, you should do so.
- Be very wary of using humour and irony, particularly if you are new to a group or list. Even those who share your language may not share your cultural norms. You can use a smiley ;-) to signal a joke.
- Don't be rude to others, no matter how ignorant or rude they may seem. An apparently stupid question about, say, English counties may be perfectly reasonable if it comes from someone who has limited familiarity with the history and geography of the British Isles or who is not a native speaker of English.
- Never send an angry message as an immediate response to another message. Allow yourself time to cool down, because once you have sent the message you cannot cancel it when you have second thoughts.
- Avoid politics and religion, except where strictly relevant to a genealogical issue.
- Messages which are all in upper case are very difficult to read. If you post a message all in upper case, people will tell you 'DON'T SHOUT!'. Reserve upper case for highlighting surnames.
- If you are going to criticize, try and be positive and constructive. Much

of what is on the internet for genealogists is the result of volunteer projects and individuals giving up their free time. While it is, of course, legitimate to subject any genealogical material or project to criticism, criticizing individuals in the public forum of a newsgroup because they have not done something the way you would have done it is not going to improve the genealogical world. Criticizing commercial services is another matter but, even so, there is no need to be rude.

- Messages which advertise goods or services are out of place in most mailing lists and all genealogy newsgroups except **<soc.genealogy. marketplace>**. They can actually be counter-productive, as people tend to take a dim view of self-promoting commercial postings. However, it is perfectly legitimate to make recommendations about books or software, as long as you are not the author or retailer. Advertising a personal, non-commercial web site or any sort of free service is OK as long as it is not done too frequently.

- If you are using one of the twinned newsgroup/mailing lists described above, bear in mind that mailing list messages will reach all members very shortly after the original mailing, but news messages may take some time to make their way around the world. This means that newsgroup users sometimes appear slightly out of touch with the discussion, but that is an artefact of the technology, not a personal failing.

- Don't pass on virus warnings to a list, as almost all virus warnings are hoaxes. If you think one is not a hoax (check at sites like Vmyths **<www.Vmyths.com>**), mail it to the list owner, and he or she can then post it to the list if it seems to be genuine, i.e. it comes from an authoritative computer security source.

- Don't post messages containing other people's data or data from CD-ROMs. This is more than bad manners, it's probably copyright infringment.

- Don't forward to a list a message sent to you personally unless you have the original sender's permission or it is obvious from the content that it is meant for wider dissemination.

These last two points are discussed in more detail under 'Copyright and Privacy' (p. 194).

Appropriate replies
One of the basic rules of on-line discussion is that any reply to a previous message should be 'appropriate'.

- Don't post a reply to the list or group if your answer is going to be of interest only to the sender of the original message – e-mail that person directly. So if someone asks how to locate particular records, any reply is likely to be of interest to all; an offer to lend a microfiche reader is only of interest to the person who posted a message asking for one.

- Don't quote the entirety of a previous message in a reply, particularly if your reply comes right at the bottom – just quote the relevant part.
- If you receive a mailing list as a digest, not only are you going to need to edit out most of the original text in your reply, you will also need to change the subject to something more appropriate. If you don't, people will not know what your message relates to and most will not even look at it.

Asking questions

While discussion groups contain much discussion, they also provide places for people to post queries and receive help and advice. One of the reasons that the internet is so useful for family historians is that it provides a huge pool of experience and expertise. In fact much of the discussion in genealogy groups arises out of particular queries. If you are asking a mailing list or newsgroup for help or advice, there are a number of things to bear in mind to ensure you get the help want.

1. **Post your query in the right place**
   There is little point in posting a Scottish query to a Channel Islands mailing list, or asking about a surname in <**soc.genealogy.computing**>. For very general queries, newsgroups and their equivalent mailing lists are probably the best places to ask: *any* question relating to British genealogy is within the scope of soc.genealogy.britain, for example. To be sure, check the group's charter (see p. 130). Do not post the same query to a lot of groups or mailing lists.

2. **Give an explicit subject line**
   One of the most important things in any message asking for assistance is making sure people who could assist you notice the message. This applies particularly in a newsgroup or a busy mailing list with many messages a day.
   - Make sure your subject line is explicit and helpful. If you use subject lines like 'genealogy' or 'problem' in a genealogy newsgroup or mailing list, few people will even bother to look at your message.
   - Put any surnames you are enquiring about in upper case in your subject line. This makes it easy for people who are scanning a list of message headers to notice the surname. Ideally, do this in the body of your message, too.

3. **Don't have unreasonable expectations**
   Some of the more experienced and active members of discussion groups devote considerable time to answering queries from relative beginners, but it is important not to abuse this willingness by having unreasonable expectations of what people will do for you.
   - Don't ask a question that is covered in the FAQ if there is one.
   - Don't expect people to give you factual information that you can

easily look up in a standard reference book or find on-line for yourself. If you ask, 'Is the Family Records Centre open on Saturdays?' it means you cannot be bothered to use a search engine to find its web site (and were not paying attention in Chapter 5), and are expecting other people to take the time to provide you with the information. If you are a genealogist living in Britain, you really ought to have a good atlas of the country, so a question like 'Where is Newport Pagnell?' should only come from non-UK residents, though questions requiring detailed local knowledge ('Where is such and such a building?') are entirely reasonable on the county mailing lists.

- Don't expect other list members to teach you the basics of genealogical research. You really need to have a good book on the subject, and should look at the tutorial material discussed in the Introduction (p. 6).
- If you are looking for help with computer software problems (whether specifically genealogical or not), consider looking at the web site or discussion forum of the software supplier before asking on a non-technical mailing list or newsgroup.
- On the other hand, any request for advice and recommendations is fair enough – the pooling of expertise in a discussion group makes it one of the most sensible places to raise such questions.

Starting your own discussion group

There are many sites that allow you to start your own discussion group. As mentioned above, you may find that your own ISP provides facilities to set one up in your Web space. Alternatively, you could look at using Yahoo Groups at **<groups.yahoo.com>** or Smartgroups at **<www.smartgroups. com>**. The advantage of using well-known services like these is that people will be much more likely to come across your group.

RootsWeb hosts an enormous number of genealogical mailing lists and is a good place to create a new one. Details of how to request a new mailing list will be found at **<resources.rootsweb.com/adopt/>**. There is detailed coverage of mailing list administration at **<helpdesk.rootsweb. com/help/listutil.html>**.

Bear in mind that maintaining a mailing list or discussion group could end up requiring a significant amount of your time if it becomes popular. Unless a list is small, it is certainly much better for it to be maintained by more than one person so that responsibilities can be shared. On the other hand, a mailing list for a particular surname is not likely to generate nearly as much mail as one on a general topic. RootsWeb provides detailed information about the responsibilities of list owners on their system, and other sites that provide discussion forums will do the same.

Starting a new newsgroup is another matter entirely. Generally, a newsgroup can only be set up after the publication of a Request For Discussion (RFD) which outlines the group's proposed purpose (and why existing groups do not meet the same needs), which is then followed by a discussion period. Ultimately a Call For Votes (CFV) is published and all interested can vote for or against the creation of the new group. Clearly, this is not something you could do, as an individual, on the spur of the moment. However, you can set up a newsgroup under the alt. hierarchy without the formal procedure for other groups, though this is not something for the technologically faint-hearted. Given the ease of setting up a mailing list or a Web-based discussion forum, it is difficult to see a good reason for setting up a new genealogy newsgroup except by the accepted consensual method.

Which discussion group?

Which mailing lists or newsgroups you read will, of course, depend on your genealogical interests. The main general group for British genealogy is soc.genealogy.britain and its associated mailing list. If you are not already familiar with mailing lists, you may not want it to be the first one you join – you could be a bit overwhelmed with the 50-plus messages per day arriving in your mailbox, and may prefer to look at the newsgroup rather than the mailing list. Also, it can be a rather boisterous group.

If you know where your ancestors came from, it may be more useful to join one of the county mailing lists (see **<www.genuki.org.uk/indexes/ MailingLists.html>**). There are fewer messages, and more of the postings are likely to be relevant. You will certainly have a better chance of encountering people with whom you share surname interests, not to mention common ancestors. Other useful lists are those for special interests, such as coalminers or the Boer War.

You might think that the best thing to do is join the lists for your surnames of interest, and there are thousands of lists and web-based forums devoted to individual surnames. However, they differ widely in their level of usefulness. Some have very few subscribers and very few messages, while, particularly in the case of reasonably common English surnames, you may well find lists dominated by US subscribers with mainly post-colonial interests. But with a reasonably rare surname in your family tree, particularly if it is also geographically limited, it is very likely that some other subscribers on a surname list will share your interests. Whereas the relevant county mailing list is certain to be useful, with surname lists it's more a matter of luck.

The simplest way to see whether any discussion forum is going to be worth joining is to look at the archives for the list to see the kind of topics that are discussed. This also has the advantage that you can get a rough idea of how many messages a month you would be letting yourself in for. You could also simply join a group and 'lurk', i.e. receive and read the messages without contributing yourself.

11 Search Engines

One of the most obvious features of the internet that makes it good for genealogical, or indeed any research is that it is very large, and the amount of material available is rapidly increasing. The size of the Web is probably close to 2,000 million pages, and that does not include any data held in on-line databases.[7] However, as the internet grows, this has the contrary effect of making it harder to locate specific material. Of course, it is not difficult to find the web sites of major institutions, but much of the genealogical material on the Web is published by individuals and small organizations and can be harder to find. Also, there is no foolproof way to locate material, and a failed search does not necessarily mean there is no relevant material on-line.

A search engine is a web site that combines an index to the Web and a facility to search the index. Although many people do not recognize any difference between directories, gateways and portals on the one hand, and search engines on the other, they are in fact very different beasts (which is why they are treated separately in this book) and have quite different strengths and weaknesses, shown in Table 11.1.

These differences mean that directories, and particularly gateways and portals, are likely to be good for finding the sites of organizations, but much less well suited to discovering sub-pages on individual topics. Even those with substantial links to personal web sites and surname resources probably don't include more than a fraction of those discoverable via a search engine.

Sometimes it is essential to search for words contained in a page; sometimes it is actually unhelpful. If you were trying to find the opening times of the Family Records Centre, it would be very irritating to retrieve thousands of web pages which mention the Family Records Centre, let alone all those that include the words *family* or *records* or *centre* – for information like opening hours a gateway is ideal. But if you are looking for pages which mention the name of one of your ancestors, there is little point in using a directory or gateway. You have to use a search engine.

---

[7] A study conducted by Steve Lawrence and C. Lee Giles in early 1999, 'Accessibility of information on the web' in *Nature*, 8 July 1999, pp. 107–109 (summary at <wwwmetrics.com>) found 800 million publicly accessible web pages.

Table 11.1 Comparison of directories, etc., with search engines

DIRECTORIES, GATEWAYS AND PORTALS	SEARCH ENGINES
Directories and gateways list web *sites* according to general subject matter.	Search engines list individual *pages* according to the words on the page.
Directories are constructed and maintained by intelligent humans. In the case of genealogy gateways you can assume they actually have some expertise in genealogy.	Search engines rely on indexes created automatically by 'robots', software programs that roam the internet looking for new or changed web pages.
Directories, and particularly specialist gateways for genealogy, categorize genealogy web sites intelligently.	While some search engines know about related terms, they work at the level of individual words.
Directories are selective (even a comprehensive gateway like Genuki only links to sites it regards as useful).	Search engines index everything they come across.
Directories, offering a ready-made selection, require no skill on the part of the user.	The number of results returned by a search engine can easily run into six or seven figures, and success is highly dependent on the searcher's ability to formulate the search in appropriate terms.
Gateways often annotate links to give some idea of the scope or importance of a site.	A search engine may be able to rank search results in order of relevance to the search terms, but will generally attach no more importance to the web site of an individual genealogist than to that of a major national institution.

Using a search engine

There are many different search engines. The main ones, i.e. the largest and most popular, are listed in Table 11.2.

Table 11.2 The main search engines

AltaVista	<www.altavista.com> also: <av.com>
FAST Search (all the Web)	<www.alltheweb.com>
Google	<www.google.com>
Hotbot	<www.hotbot.lycos.com>
Lycos	<www.lycos.com>
NorthernLight	<www.northernlight.com>
WebTop	<www.webtop.com>

There are UK versions of AltaVista at **<www.altavista.co.uk>**, of Lycos at **<www.lycos.co.uk>** and of Hotbot at **<www.hotbot.lycos.co.uk>**. For a comprehensive set of links to search engines, see Yahoo's listing for Search Engines & Directories at **<dir.yahoo.com/Computers_and_internet/ internet/World_Wide_Web/Searching_the_Web/Search_Engines_and_ Directories/>**.

In spite of the more or less subtle differences between them, all search engines work in basically the same way. They offer you a box to type in the 'search terms' or 'keywords' you want to search for, and a button to click on to start the search. The example from FAST Search shown in Figure 11.1 is typical. Once you've clicked on the Search button, the search engine will come back with a page containing a list of web sites (see Figure 11.2), each with a brief description culled from the page itself, and you can click on any of the items listed to go to the relevant web page. Search engines differ in exactly how they expect you to formulate your search, how they rank the results, how much you can customize display of the results, and so on, but these basics are common to all.

Most search engines will report the total number of matching web pages found, so-called 'hits', and if there is more than a pageful (typically 10 or 20), it will provide links to subsequent pages of hits.

Figure 11.1 The FAST Search home page <www.alltheweb.com>

Formulating your search

Your success in searching depends only in part on your choice of search engine (see p. 152), but is greatly dependent on your skill in formulating your search terms. There are actually several different types of search offered by several engines.

AND/OR

The most important distinction is that between an OR search and an AND search.

- An OR search treats your search words as alternatives and will retrieve from its index all pages with any of the search words. This can be useful if there are spelling variants of a surname.
- An AND search will find only pages on which all the words occur (the search in Figure 11.2 is an AND search).

The reason this distinction is important is that each search engine will have one of these as its default option, but it may not be obvious which.

AltaVista, for example, assumes you want to do an OR search. You might think that entering the keywords [Tonbridge genealogy] would give

All the Web, All the Time™

fast :::

Search for | all of the words ▼ | genealogy Cheshire | **FAST Search**

Help   Customize   Advanced Search

14084 documents found - 0.4653 seconds search time

Search Restrictions: Offensive content reduction = On

1 CHESHIRE
GENUKI The GENUKI pages for Cheshire have moved to a new address: http://www.fhsc.org.uk/genuki/chs/
Please update your bookmarks accordingly.
http://www.users.zetnet.co.uk/blangston/genuki/chs.htm

2 Cheshire and Chester Archives and Local Studies - What's New
Includes details of location and opening times; types of records held and how to access them; facilities including research consultant; useful links and wills index
http://www.cheshire.gov.uk/recoff/

3 The Family History Society of Cheshire
now in its 30th year, with almost 2000 members, in the UK and all over the world
http://www.users.zetnet.co.uk/blangston/fhsc/

4 Southern Cross Connect - the Internet Connection Site for Senior Australians
execution hanging gallows coastguard, 1749, Westminster Pollbook, Australian, genealogy, Eureka, convicts prisoners, WWII, kias pows convicts transportation Liverpool Cromwell Australia liobians...
http://www.southernx.com.au/

5 UK Genealogy - Researching in Cheshire?

Figure 11.2 The first few hits from a search for 'genealogy' and 'Cheshire' in FAST Search

fewer results than just entering [Tonbridge], but this is not so in AltaVista, which finds 11,785 results for [Tonbridge] alone, but 4,036,491 for both terms.[8] Compare this with Google, which assumes you want to do an AND search and gives 26,000 hits for [Tonbridge], but only 675 for both words.

In a search engine which has an OR search as its default, you will always get more results as you add words; if the default is an AND search, more keywords should produce fewer hits. Of the major search engines, AltaVista, Excite and Infoseek all have an OR search as their default.

Whatever the default, however, all search engines offer you both types of search – you just need to know how to formulate them. In fact, most will allow you to use the words AND and OR in your searches to do this (they usually *must* be in upper case). So a search for [Tonbridge OR genealogy] on Google brings 1,470,000 hits; a search for [Tonbridge AND genealogy] on AltaVista gives 576 hits.[9]

Boolean searches

AND and OR are just the most commonly used parts of a general technique for formulating a search called Boolean logic.[10] Some search engines allow you to enter much more complex Boolean expressions. For example, if you were looking for pages containing genealogical information on the surname Robinson in either Devon or Cornwall, you would be unable to formulate it using the standard search facilities in AltaVista or FastSearch, since these do not let you combine the two types of search. You would need to go to a page such as AltaVista's advanced search and enter, say,

> [Robinson AND (genealogy OR "family history") AND (Devon OR Cornwall) AND (cobbler OR cordwainer)].

Inclusion/exclusion

Another technique for running an AND search is to prefix your search terms with a + sign, indicating that the term *must* be in the pages retrieved. So a search for [+Tonbridge +genealogy] on AltaVista's main search page will produce the same results as [Tonbridge AND genealogy] on the

---

[8] In this chapter I have put search terms between square brackets. To run the search in a search engine, type in the text between the brackets *exactly*. Note that the figures given for the number of hits have indicative status only. They were correct when I tried out these searches, but the indexes used by search engines grow daily, so you will not get identical results. However, the differences between the various *types* of search and formulation should be of the same order.

[9] Searches including the operators AND/OR can only be carried out on AltaVista's advanced search page.

[10] This topic can be handled only briefly here. For more information on using Boolean expressions for searching, look at the help pages of the search engines or the Complete Planet tutorial at **<www.completeplanet.com/Tutorials/Search/part4.asp>**.

advanced search page, or on a search engine like NorthernLight which defaults to an AND search.

A counterpart is the − sign, which can be prefixed to words which *must not* be present on the pages retrieved, thus allowing you to exclude certain words. The normal use of this is to exclude unwanted pages when searching on a word that has several meanings or distinct uses, e.g. [+Bath −wash] would be a way to ensure that your enquiry about a town in Somerset was not diluted by material on cleanliness. There is one very common problem when searching for geographical information which this technique can help to alleviate: names of cities and counties are used as names for ships, regiments, families and the like; also, when British emigrants settled in the colonies they frequently reused British place names. This means that many searches which include place names will retrieve a good number of irrelevant pages.

If you do a search on [Gloucester], for example, you will soon discover that there is a Gloucester county in Virginia and in New Brunswick, a town of Gloucester in New South Wales and Massachusetts (not far from the town of Essex), and you probably do not want all of these included in your results if you are looking for ancestors who lived along the Severn. Then there is HMS Gloucester, the Duke of Gloucester, pubs called the Gloucester Arms and so on. Likewise, if you're searching on [York], you do not really want to retrieve all the pages that mention New York.

Obviously it would be rather tedious to do this for every possibility, but you could easily exclude those which an initial search shows are the most common, e.g. [+Gloucester −Virginia], [+York −"New York"].

Another case where this technique would be useful is if you are searching for a surname which also happens to be that of a well-known person: [+Gallagher −Oasis] or [+Blair −Tony] will reduce the number of unwanted results you will get if you are searching for the surnames Gallagher or Blair.

Unfortunately, if you are searching for a surname which is also a place name, e.g. Kent or York, there is no simple way to exclude web pages with the place name, though on p. 151 I suggest a technique for restricting your hits to personal genealogy web sites.

Phrases and names

Another important issue when using a search engine is how to group words together into a phrase: most search engines require you to use inverted commas to identify a phrase, which is particularly useful for two-part place names, e.g. ["North Shields"] or ["High Wycombe"], or if you want to search on forename and surname. Search engines faced with, say, [Thomas Walker] may well retrieve all the pages with both [Thomas] and [Walker], whereas ["Thomas Walker"] will find only those where [Thomas] occurs next to [Walker].

Some search engines will in fact recognize two-part place names and easily recognizable forename+surname combinations without requiring inverted commas. You can easily see if this is the case by trying a search for phrases like [High Wycombe] or [Queen Victoria]. They may not, however, be very good where the names are also words in everyday use. A search on AltaVista for [John Smith] (no inverted commas, no + signs) produces 71,000 hits, and a search for ["John Smith"] produces the same 71,000. On the other hand [+Mark +Hills] retrieves 7,630, but ["Mark Hills"] only 71 hits. So AltaVista knows that John Smith is a name but not that Mark Hills is. Unfortunately, there is only one way to find out whether a search engine recognizes a particular place name or personal name as a phrase – try it!

Some search engines let you search for phrases by selecting this option from a menu, sometimes as an alternative to using inverted commas, sometimes as the only way of selecting a phrase. However, this option is of little use unless *all* your search words combine to form a single phrase.

Case

It can also be important to use initial capital letters on names. If you enter a lower case letter in your keyword, search engines will include instances where that letter is upper case. If you make a letter upper case, most search engines will ignore examples of the word where that letter is lower case. So, for example, [+mark +hills] finds over 10,000 pages on AltaVista, not just the 7,630 it found for [+Mark +Hills]. This probably will not matter much where a word is only found in names, e.g. Wycombe or London, but a search for the Walker family from Reading will be hampered by entering [+walker +reading]. However, not all search engines do this – Google is one of those that does not, for example.

Truncation and wild cards

Another issue is how to deal with surname variants. It is, of course, possible to list the variants in an OR search, but there may be an easier way in some search engines. AltaVista, Hotbot and NorthernLight all permit the use of truncated word forms, indicated by an asterisk, so, for example, [Burrow*] would find Burrow, Burrowes and Burrows. Some search engines permit the asterisk to be used as a 'wild card' anywhere within the word, so [B*rrow*] would also find Barrow, Borrow, Barrows, Borrows, etc.

Natural language searching

Some search engines claim to offer natural language searching, i.e. you type in your query not as a terse series of keywords, but as a properly formulated question. This might make you feel marginally less intimidated by the technology, but it will do nothing to improve your search results. All the search engine does is strip out the small, common words and search on the remainder. The lack of intelligence in this feature is nicely shown by

AltaVista's attempt to promote it: they offered sample queries to try out, one of which was [What is the time in Okinawa?]. This query produced dozens of pages about the USS Hospital Ship Okinawa, each of which had a line at the bottom giving the date and time it was last updated. Supposing you are looking for London probate records. You might type in [where can I find wills for London?] in NorthernLight, but you will get over three million hits, with none at the top of the list looking remotely relevant. You would be much better off giving a bit more thought to your query and submitting [London AND "probate records"]. Indeed, if you are looking for information on the holdings of repositories you will probably be better off using the Genuki search engine discussed on p. 158.

Search tips

Apart from taking care to formulate your query, there are a number of other things to bear in mind if your searching is going to be successful and not too time consuming.

The first is not to assume that your initial search will find what you want and produce a manageable list of results. Look on it as an initial diagnostic run, so you can refine the formulation of your search. If you are looking for an organization, you may be successful first time, but if you are looking for material on a particular subject be prepared to reformulate your results on the basis of the initial results.

The second is that the better you know the particular search engine you are using, the better results you will get. Look at the options it offers, and look at the Help or Tips pages. Although I have highlighted the main features of the most widely used search engines, each has its idiosyncrasies. And while it is quite easy to find what it will do, sometimes the only way to find out what it *will not* do is to see what is missing from the Help pages. It is also worth trying out some different types of query, just so you get a feel for how many results to expect and how they are sorted.

If you carry out searches on your particular surnames on a regular basis, it can be worth adding the URL of the results pages to your bookmarks (Netscape) or favorites (Internet Explorer). This will allow you to run the same query again directly from your bookmarks/favorites without re-entering the search terms. This works because, in most search engines, the browser submits the search terms as an appendage to the URL, so, for example, when you search Google for [Robinson AND Exeter], the browser sends the URL <www.google.com/search?q=Robinson+Exeter& btnG=Google+Search>, which is then shown as the address of the first page of results.

There is one simple browser technique which will save you time when using a search engine. Once you have got a list of search results that you want to look at, open each site found in a new window so that the original list of search results remains open (on Windows a right-mouse click over the link will achieve this with Netscape and Internet Explorer; on the Macintosh shift+click). Otherwise, each time you want to go back to your results the search engine will run the search all over again. Another useful trick for a long page of results is to save it to your hard disk so that you can explore the hits at your leisure later.

Limitations

It is important to bear in mind some of the limitations of search engines. First, no search engine indexes the whole of the Web. The study by Lawrence and Giles mentioned at the start of this chapter found that even the best search engines did not index more than 25 per cent of the estimated totality of the Web, and not even their combined coverage captured half the Web. This means that just because you cannot find a resource when using a search engine, it does not mean it is not there – a search engine is not a library catalogue. Second, do not expect all results to be relevant. Even a fairly precisely formulated query may get some irrelevant results, and web pages which have long lists of names and places will inevitably produce some unwanted matches. For example, a surname interest list which contains a Robinson from Lancashire and some other surname from Devon would appear among the results for a search on [+Robinson +Devon]. Particularly if you do not include terms like ["genealogy"] or ["family history"], or something that occurs more frequently on genealogy sites than elsewhere – (["monumental inscriptions"] or ["parish register"], for example) – you will get many irrelevant results. And, of course, searching for a fairly common surname may retrieve numerous genealogical pages that are nothing to do with your own line.

There are ways to cut down on irrelevant results if you are looking for a particular family. The more precise your geographical information the better: if you know your Robinsons came from Exeter, search not for [Robinson AND Devon] but for [Robinson AND Exeter AND Devon]. (Keep Devon in – you do not want Exeter College, HMS Exeter, Exeter in New Hampshire, etc.) If you search on both surnames of a married couple, even if they are individually quite common, you are much more likely to get relevant results, for example [Robinson AND Armstrong AND Exeter AND Devon AND genealogy]. If you use full names, all the better – even ["John Smith" AND "Ann Williams"] only finds 75 pages on AltaVista; if you add [AND Yorkshire], it comes down to 10!

You will still tend to retrieve a few surname listing pages, but there is little that can be done about that, unless you use a search engine such as Lycos or AltaVista which has a special NEAR operator which will find two search terms within 25 words of each other.

Another important problem in finding surname material on the internet is that much of it is available not in permanent web pages, but in databases. The only way to find the information is to go to the site with the database and carry out a search. This material cannot be retrieved by search engines, and the individual items of data have no place in directories either. This means that the material discussed in Chapter 4 will not show up in search engine results. The same is true for much of the material covered in Chapter 6.

Choosing a search engine

One of the most fundamental differences between search engines is the size of the index used. Especially when searching for personal sites relating to the genealogy of particular families and surnames, this should probably be the main criterion for using one search engine rather than another. Since search engines are constantly striving to improve their performance and coverage, there can be no guarantee that what is the most comprehensive search engine at the time of writing will still hold that position when you are reading this. Search Engine Watch at <www.searchenginewatch.com> keeps up-to-date information about the size of the main search engines at <www.searchenginewatch.com/reports/sizes.html>. Figure 11.3 shows the sizes of the main search engines as given by Search Engine Watch in April 2001. (The exact figures should be treated with some caution as they are based on self-reporting by the search engines and have not been independently audited.)

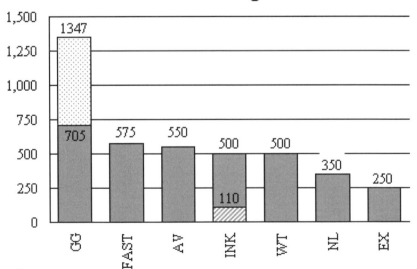

Figure 11.3 Coverage of main search engines (April 2001) according to Search Engine Watch <www. searchenginewatch.com/reports/sizes.html>. KEY: GG=Google, FAST=FAST, AV=AltaVista, INK=Inktomi, WT=WebTop.com, NL=NorthernLight, EX=Excite. Reprinted with permission from **<www. internet.com>**. Copyright 2001 INT Media Group, Incorporated. All rights reserved. Datamation and internet.com are the exclusive trademarks of INT Media Group, Incorporated.

Which is the best search engine depends on a number of factors, not simply on the size of the index. One of these is what you are looking for. There are several different aims you might have when using search engines. You might be trying locate a particular site that you know must exist – you only need one result and you will know it when you see it. This is usually a search for a particular organization's web site, or some particular resource that you've heard of but can't remember the location of.

Alternatively, you may be trying to find any site which might have information on a particular surname, or even a particular ancestor. The difference between this and the previous search is that there is no way of telling in advance what your search will turn up, and probably the search results will include a certain number, perhaps even a lot, of irrelevant sites. Another difference is that in the first case, you almost certainly have some idea of what the site, or least some its pages, might be called.

This can be important because some search engines let you restrict your search to the words in the titles of web pages. For example, NorthernLight retrieves 457 items in a search for ["Historical Manuscripts Commission"] in the page title, but 36,867 for the phrase itself. Even in search engines without this option it is very likely that pages with the search phrase in the page title will be shown high up in the listing order, as in the Google search in Figure 11.4. Such a site is amongst the easiest things to find on a search engine, and it may even be quicker than navigating the hierarchy of one of the gateways where you know the information must be given. It also means that, for this sort of enquiry, the differences between the search engines are generally not very significant.

When it comes to looking for personal genealogy pages of those interested in the same families as you, or even pages with extracts from

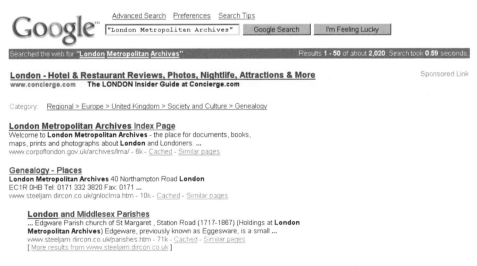

Figure 11.4 Google search results for "London Metropolitan Archives" <www.google.com>

primary sources which include a name you are researching, the size of the index is a major issue in the choice of search engine. A rough and ready way to get an idea of how many personal genealogy sites are listed on a search engine is to search for the phrase "surname list" – many of the software packages that can create a web site from a genealogy database (see Chapter 12) will create a page with this as a title or heading. The results will also include, of course, some non-personal sites such as the county surname lists, but the phrase will not be common on non-genealogy sites.

Another important point to consider is the range of search features a particular search engine offers. If you want to carry out more precise searches, you will need to use one that has more advanced facilities. While Google may have the largest index of any of these search engines, which makes it justifiably popular, its lack of facilities to execute some of the searches I have used as examples makes it less valuable for more complex searches.

A final consideration is how the results are ranked, since obviously you would like the most relevant results ranked first. As mentioned above, many search engines will give priority to pages with the search terms in the title of the page, and some will give a numerical estimate of their relevance (as a percentage). Some search engines rank results by 'link popularity', i.e. the number of other sites that make links to a page. Google is the engine most noted for this feature, but according to Search Engine Watch, AltaVista, Excite, FAST and NorthernLight also use it. This is good if you want the home page of a site to rank higher than sub-pages, but for surname searches on personal sites, this is a positive disadvantage since these will automatically rank lower than well-linked commercial sites which happen to have the same surname on them.

There are useful comparative tables of search engine features on Ian Winship's 'Web search service features' page at <www.unn.ac.uk/central/isd/features.htm> and in Infopeople's 'Search tools Chart' at <www.infopeople.org/search/chart.html>. For evaluation of the different search engines, see the links on the 'Evaluation Of Internet Searching And Search Engines' page at <www.umanitoba.ca/academic_support/libraries/units/engineering/evaluate.html>. Sheila Webber has a 'Reviews of search engines' page at <www.dis.strath.ac.uk/business/search.html>, which also has many useful links. Search Engine Watch at <www.searchenginewatch.com> is a site devoted entirely to information about search engines.

Meta-search engines

One technique for overcoming the fact that no search engine indexes the whole of the Web is to carry out the same search on several different search engines. To do this by hand would, of course, be immensely time-consuming, not to mention tedious, but there are two ways of making the task easier.

One is to use an 'all-in-one' search page, which allows you to submit a search to many different search engines. An example of this is Proteus

Internet Search at **<www.thrall.org/proteus.html>**, where you type your search terms in the Find box and then select which search engine to submit them to (see Figure 11.5). Proteus keeps a record of your searches in any one session, so you can easily rerun them. You can also choose to have the search results displayed in a new window so that you do not keep having to click on the Back button. Cyndi's List has a small all-in-one search facility on its Search Engines page at **<www.CyndisList.com/search. htm#Forms>**. Here you have to enter your search terms in a different box for each search engine, but you can easily do that by cutting and pasting. Yahoo has a list of All-in-One Search sites. Its URL is 142 characters long, so it is best located by going to **<www.yahoo.com>** and running a search for "All-in-One Search".

Even more labour-saving are meta-search engines. In these you enter your search only once and it is then automatically submitted to a range of search engines. One of the most popular is DogPile **<www.dogpile.com>**, which automatically submits a query to the following search engines: AltaVista, Direct Hit, DogPile Open Directory, FindWhat, Google, GoTo, Infoseek, Kanoodle, LookSmart, Lycos, RealNames, Sprinks from About, Web Catalog, and Yahoo. It submits your query to each search engine in turn, pausing when it has given you a page of 10 results. You can in fact customize the order in which it goes to the search engines. However, you have no control on how your keywords are submitted to the individual engines.

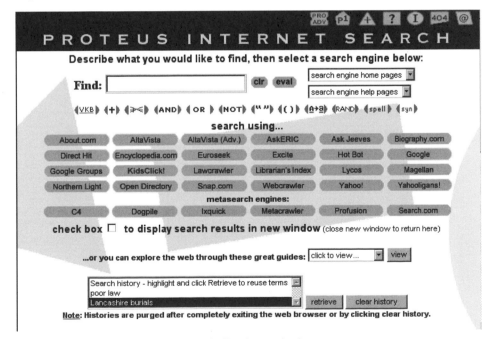

Figure 11.5 Proteus Internet Search at <www.thrall.org|proteus.html>

Another well-known meta-search engine is MetaCrawler at <www.metacrawler.com>. This has more sophisticated input options (you can specify AND, OR or phrase search). Since it does all the searches before giving you the results, it can also allow you to choose the order in which they are presented (sorted by relevance, by site or by search engine). Figure 11.6 shows the entry of a search for Boyd's Marriage Index in MetaCrawler and Figure 11.7 shows the first few results.

It might seem that these types of search facility make visiting the individual search engines redundant, and they might well do so for certain types of search. But there are important limitations. First, if you look at the list of search engines used by DogPile, for example, the absence of some of the largest (Fast Search, NorthernLight, WebTop) is disconcerting. Second,

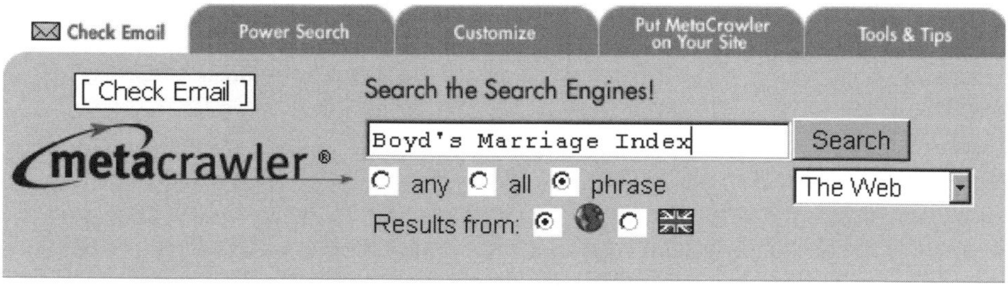

Figure 11.6 MetaCrawler search for [Boyd's Marriage Index] at <www.metacrawler.com>

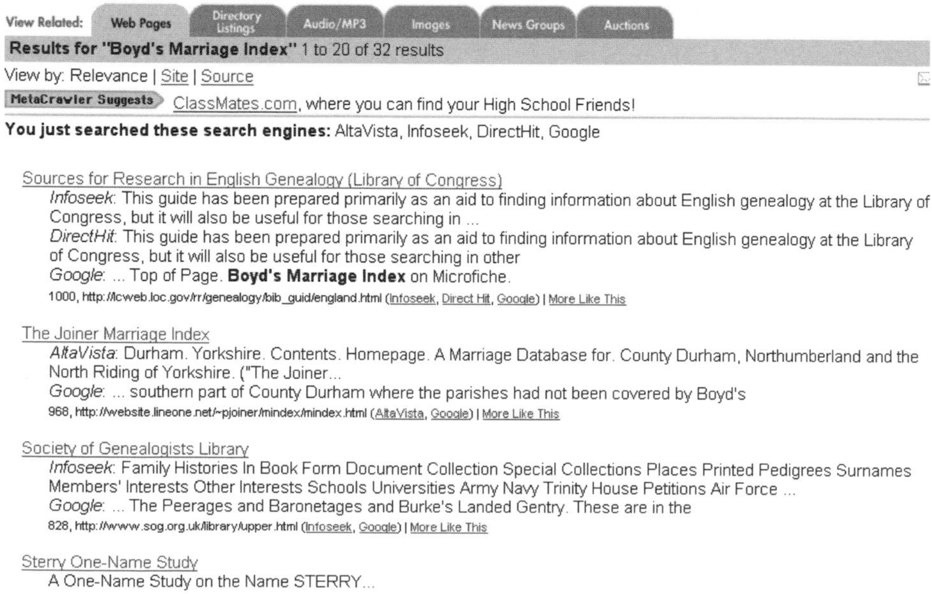

Figure 11.7 Search results for [Boyd's Marriage Index] on MetaCrawler at <www.metacrawler.com>. For each hit, MetaCrawler tells you which search engines it was found on

while you can do an AND search or a phrase search by this method, anything more complex is going to fall down because of the different facilities offered by the different engines. Also, it is important to recognize that meta-search engines give *fewer* results for many searches than the individual search engines do – for example, 'Boyd's Marriage Index' on Google gives 341 hits, most of which MetaCrawler has ignored. This is because meta-search engines typically select the first few results. Also, a meta-search engine may retrieve no results at all from a search engine which is slow to respond and is timed out. However, MetaCrawler is good in that it gives you control over these facilities on its 'power search' page at <www.metacrawler.com/index_power.html>.

For these reasons, meta-search engines are not appropriate for all types of search. They are best when you are looking for a particular site, or want to find the most popular sites devoted to a particular subject. They are poor for locating pages devoted to particular pedigrees or surnames.

There is a useful guide to meta-search engines by Jian Liu at <www.indiana.edu/~librcsd/search/meta.html>, with descriptions of 13 of them and a general discussion of their advantages and disadvantages.

Search software

A similar tool for searching is a 'searchbot', sometimes also called an 'intelligent agent'. Rather than being a web site which you must go to in order to carry out a search, a searchbot is a piece of software that runs on your own computer, allowing you to formulate searches off-line and then go on-line to do the search. Searchbots work like meta-search engines – they submit a query to many different search engines – and have the same strengths and weaknesses. The advantage of a searchbot, though, is that the full results are then stored to your hard disk, and you can examine them at your leisure. It will also store the details of each search, making it easy to repeat.

There are dozens of searchbots, available as shareware or freeware from software archives such as Tucows (see <tucows.mirror.ac.uk/searchbot95. html> for Windows searchbots).

Both Internet Explorer and Netscape have built-in search facilities. Version 6 of Netscape allows you to choose one of a number of search engines, including Google and AltaVista, to submit your searches to. Internet Explorer 5.5 has Copernic Active Search, which is simply a built-in version of the freeware Copernic searchbot, one of the most popular searchbots for Windows, though not the most recent version.

Genealogy search tools

The search tools discussed so far have been general-purpose tools, but there are also many special-purpose tools. Some of these are discussed elsewhere in the text: there is a whole range of search engines dedicated to locating living people, by geographical location or e-mail address (see p. 80). Other useful dedicated tools are gazetteers, which allow you to locate places (see p. 100). Chapter 5 covers on-line catalogues to material which is itself not on-line. All of these are likely to be better for their particular purpose than the general search engines. However, there are also some search tools devoted solely to genealogy.

Probably the most useful search engine devoted to web sites with material on UK genealogy is the Genuki Search at <www.genuki.org.uk/search.html>, because it provides an index not only to Genuki itself, but also to the web sites of the Public Record Office, the Society of Genealogists, the Federation of Family History Societies and the Guild of One-Name Studies. Also indexed are the contents of all the family history society web sites and county surname interest lists to which Genuki provides links. Currently, it allows AND, OR and Boolean searches, though phrase searching is promised for the future.

For other genealogy search engines, Cyndi's List has a section at <www.CyndisList.com/search.htm#Genealogy>, but note that many of these are not sites with an index of the Web but searchable surname databases such as those discussed in Chapter 6. Others, such as I Found It! at <www.gensource.com/ifoundit/>, are actually directories of genealogy resources with a search facility.

Tutorials

Because of the importance of searching to serious use of the internet there are many sites with guides to search techniques and tutorials on searching. In addition to the sites listed under 'Choosing a search engine', the University of California at Berkeley has an on-line tutorial 'Finding Information on the Internet' at <www.lib.berkeley.edu/TeachingLib/Guides/Internet/FindInfo.html>, while Complete Planet has a 'Guide to Effective Searching of the Internet' at <www.completeplanet.com/Tutorials/Search/index.asp>, and provides links to dozens of other on-line tutorials at <www.completeplanet.com/resourcesites/resource_sites_tutorials.asp>. Rice University has a useful and concise guide to 'Internet Searching Strategies' at <www.rice.edu/Fondren/Netguides/strategies.html>. There is a guide to searching specifically for genealogy in 'Finding your ancestors on the Internet' at <genealogy.about.com/hobbies/genealogy/library/weekly/aa041700a.htm>.

12 Publishing Your Family History On-line

So far we have been concentrating on retrieving information and contacting others who share your interests. But you can also take a more active role in publicizing your own interests and publishing the results of your research for others to find.

Some of the ways of doing this have already been touched upon. You can post a message with details of your surname interests to a suitable mailing list or to one of the surnames newsgroups (see Chapter 10). Although such messages may be read by only a relatively small number of readers (compared to the total number of people on-line) such messages are archived, providing a permanent record. You can submit your surname interests to the surname lists for the counties your ancestors lived in (Chapter 6). This will be easier for others to find than material in mailing list archives, since anyone with ancestors from a county is likely to check the county. Both of these methods are quick and easy, but they have the limitation that they offer quite limited information, which may not be enough for someone else to spot a link with your family, and this is particularly the case with more common surnames. The alternative is to publish your family history on the Web.

Publishing options

There are two ways of putting your family history on-line: you can submit your family tree to a pedigree database such as those discussed in Chapter 6, or you can create your own web site. In fact, these are not mutually exclusive, and there are good reasons for doing both, as each approach has its own merits.

Pedigree databases
There are obvious advantages in submitting your family tree to one of the pedigree databases:

- It is a very quick way of getting your tree on-line.
- The fact that these sites have many visitors and are obvious places to

search for contacts means that you are getting your material to a large audience.

There are a couple of disadvantages:

- The material is held in a database, which means it can only be found by going to the site and using the built-in search facilities. It will not be found by anyone using a general Web search engine such as those discussed in Chapter 11.
- You can only submit material held in your genealogy database, and you will not be able to include any other textual or graphical material relating to your family tree.

Neither of these are reasons *not* to submit your pedigree to a database. They simply mean that you might want to consider having your own web site as well.

A personal web site

Creating your own web site may sound like much more work, but there are a number of reasons why it can be better than simply uploading your family tree to a database:

- You can put a family tree on your own site almost as easily as you can submit it to a database.
- You can include any other textual material you have collected which may be of interest: transcriptions of original documents, extracts from parish registers or General Register Office indexes for your chosen names.
- You can include images, whether they are scanned from old photographs in your collection or pictures you have taken of places where your ancestors lived.
- If you submit the address of your site to search engines, all the individuals in your tree and all the other information on your site will be indexed by them, so they can be found by the techniques discussed in Chapter 11.

The great thing about a personal web site is that it is not like publishing a book – you do not have to do all these things at once. You can start with a small amount of material, say a family tree or just a list of your surname interests, and add to it as and when you like.

But there are a couple of drawbacks to be aware of if you are going to create your own site:

- If you set it up in free web space provided by your ISP you will probably have to move the whole site if you subsequently switch to another provider. Search engines and everyone who has linked to your site will have to be informed.

- If your site is going to provide more than a basic family tree, you will need to learn how to create web pages.

Both of these issues are tackled later in this chapter.

It is worth pointing out that apart from the major on-line databases, much of the genealogical material on the Web is the result of the efforts of individuals making it available on personal sites. If you have any genealogical information that may be of interest to others, in addition to your personal pedigree, you should consider making at available on-line.

Whichever of these options you choose, you should avoid publishing information about living people, a topic that is discussed in more detail on p. 194.

Family trees for the Web

Probably the most important thing to put on the Web is your family tree. This will make it possible for other genealogists to discover shared interests and get in touch with you.

Whether you are going to submit your family tree to a pedigree database or create your own site, you are going to need to extract the data from your genealogy database software in a format ready for the Web. (If you are not yet using a genealogy database to keep a record of your ancestors and what you have discovered about them, look at 'Software' in Chapter 13, p. 184.) The alternative would be to type up the data from scratch, a method that would be both time consuming and prone to error.

GEDCOM

GEDCOM, which stands for **GE**nealogical **D**ata **COM**munication, is a standard file format for exchanging family trees between one computer and another, or one computer program and another. It was developed in the 1980s by the LDS Church as a format for users of Personal Ancestral File (see p. 185) to make submissions to Ancestral File (see p. 77). It has subsequently been adopted and supported by all major genealogy software producers to enable users to transfer data into or out of their programs. It can also be used to download records from the various LDS databases in a format that allows them to be imported into a genealogy program.

The reason you need to know about GEDCOM is that all the pedigree databases expect you to submit your family tree in the form of a GEDCOM file. Also, provided your genealogy software can save your pedigree information in GEDCOM format, there are many programs which can automatically create a set of web pages from that file. On the PC, GEDCOM files have the file extension .ged.

You do not need to know the technical details of GEDCOM in order to publish your family tree on the Web, but Cyndi's List has a page devoted to GEDCOM resources at **<www.CyndisList.com/gedcom.htm>** and David Hawgood's *GEDCOM Data Transfer, moving your family tree* is a useful printed guide (details at **<www.hawgood.co.uk/gedcom.htm>**).

Whatever genealogy software you are using for your family tree, you should be able to find an option to export data to a GEDCOM file. Typically, this option will be found under **Export** on the **File** menu but, if not, the manual or the on-line help for your program should contain information on GEDCOM export.

GEDCOM converters

When you submit your tree to an on-line pedigree database they will only need the GEDCOM file, and they will have software for indexing it and converting into the right format for the site.

However, if you are using a GEDCOM file because your genealogy software has not got any built-in facilities for creating web pages, you will need to use a special converter program to turn the file into an on-line pedigree. A large number of such programs are available. All are freeware or shareware and can be downloaded from the Web. For those that are shareware, you generally need to pay the registration fee (typically £10 to £20) if you continue to use the program after a trial period of 30 days. There are considerable differences in how these programs create web pages and what the results look like. In addition, there are important differences in the options available. There is not space here to list or discuss all the programs available, but there is a listing on the web site for my book *Web Publishing for Genealogy* at **<www.spub.co.uk/software.html>** and on Cyndi's List at **<www.cyndislist.com/construc.htm#plan>**.

Until recently, these converters were essential tools for genealogical web publishing. But now that recent versions of all the main genealogy database programs have got built-in facilities for creating a web pedigree, they are less significant. Indeed, even if you are using an older piece of software without web publishing features there is a very easy way to create a web pedigree without using a converter: just download Personal Ancestral File or Legacy 3.0 (free of charge, see Chapter 13, p. 185). These programs can import a GEDCOM file and turn it into a set of web pages.

Even so, it is well worth having a look at examples of the pages created by the converters, as you may find you prefer their appearance to the output of your genealogy database program. Mark Knight's web site at **<www.pinn.net/~knightma/>** shows sample output for most current converters, and the Surname Web has reviews of several GEDCOM converters at **<surnameweb.org/help/conversion.htm>**.

Web trees

All recent versions of the main genealogy database programs (certainly any version released in 2000 or later) have facilities to create a set of web pages, including the following:

- Ancestral Quest
- Family Matters
- Family Origins
- Family Tree Maker
- Generations
- Kinship Archivist
- Legacy
- The Master Genealogist
- Personal Ancestral File for Windows
- Relatively Yours
- Reunion (Macintosh)
- Ultimate Family Tree
- Win-Family

If you have one of these programs, it will be the easiest method of putting your pedigree on-line. (Family Tree Maker can only create pages for uploading to the manufacturer's web site – see **<familytreemaker. genealogy.com/ftm_uhp_home.html>**.)

The programs vary in what they actually produce for a web site, but at the very least all will give you a surname index, an index of individuals and a series of linked pages with either family groups or details of individuals. You should have a choice between an ancestor tree, a descendant tree or a full pedigree, and there are many options about which individuals, and what information about them, to include.

By way of example, Figure 12.1 shows a page created by Legacy 3.0. This is an 'individual report' but also provides links to parents and grandparents at the top of the screen, and to spouse and children in the box on the right of the screen. The superscript numbers link to descriptions of the sources.

Web publishing basics

If you are just going to upload a GEDCOM file to a pedigree database, you do not need to consider doing anything else. But if you are going to create your own web site you will need to familiarize yourself with what is involved in web publishing. While it is increasingly possible to create a web site without any technical knowledge, you still need to understand the basic process. There is not space here to deal with web publishing in detail, but this and the following sections cover the basics and there are suggested sources of further information at the end of this chapter.

What is a web site?
A web site is simply a collection of individual files stored on a web server, which is a computer with (usually) a permanent connection to the Web

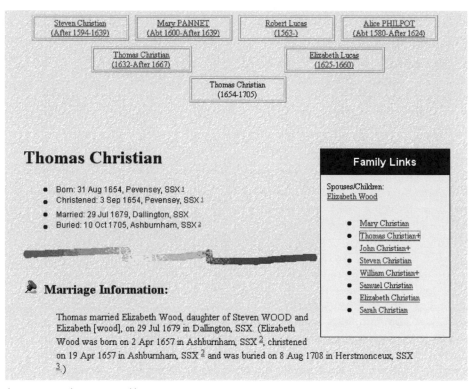

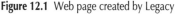

Figure 12.1 Web page created by Legacy

and the capacity to deal with lots of requests for web pages from all over the internet. While large companies have their own dedicated computers to act as web servers, smaller organizations and home users simply get a portion of the file space on the server belonging to their Internet Service Provider (this is called web hosting). When you create a web site, you first create all the pages on your own computer, then you connect to your ISP and upload the files to your space on the web server.

Assuming you already have internet access, what you need in order to create a web site is:

- Web space
- Software for creating web pages
- Software for uploading the pages to your web space

If you are going to have photographs or scanned images of documents on your site, you will also need graphics editing software.

One important aspect of web publishing is that it can be done with any computer and a wide range of software. You do not need a specially powerful computer, and you almost certainly have web publishing software on your computer already without knowing it (see p. 170). You will probably be able to use your browser for uploading pages, though there is dedicated freeware and shareware software which will make the process easier.

The other thing you need for a web site is time. Even though basic web publishing is not difficult, you will need to learn how it works and you will want to experiment before unleashing your site on the public. You will also need to give some thought to exactly what material you are going to publish, and how best to organize it so that your visitors can find the information they are looking for – just as you would for a book, in fact.

Web space

In order to have a web site you need to have space on a web server for the files which make up your web site. If you are paying your Internet Service Provider for your dial-up connection to the internet, you will almost certainly find that your subscription includes this facility at no extra cost. It is usual for ISPs to give their customers at least 10Mb of space, and 20Mb or more is not uncommon. Unless you are intending to include many high-quality graphics or a *very* large amount of primary data on-line this should be more than enough space for a personal genealogy site. It is even quite a respectable amount for a family history society.

While the free ISPs do not always give subscribers free web space, quite a number of them do. If yours does not, there are a number of companies that offer web space entirely free of charge regardless of who your ISP is. Tripod **<www.tripod.co.uk>**, for example, offers 12Mb with more available on application, while FortuneCity **<www.fortunecity.co.uk>** offers 100Mb. A good place for genealogy sites is RootsWeb **<www.rootsweb.com>** with its 'Freepages', free unlimited web space. Details will be found at **<accounts.rootsweb.com>**. (Other companies can be found by searching Yahoo for the phrase 'free web space'.) The disadvantage of such services is that they will include advertising on your pages, either as a banner ad at the top of a page or as adverts in a separate pop-up window. There may also be some restrictions on what you can put on your site, though this is unlikely to be of concern to genealogists creating personal sites.

The web address of your site will depend on who is providing your web space and what sort of account you have with them. There are a number of standard formats for URLs of personal web sites. The address of my personal genealogy page is **<homepages.gold.ac.uk/peter/>**, which is the name of the server the site is on, followed by my username on that system. Some providers actually combine the username with the server name directly, which gives you what appears to be your own web server. For example, free web-space provider Tripod gives user sites a name of the format **<user-id.tripod.com>**.

If you are planning a substantial web site with material of general interest rather than simply your own pedigree, or if you are going to set up a site for an organization or genealogy project, it is useful to have a permanent address rather than one that is dependent on your current ISP or web space provider. There is not space here to discuss the issues in any detail, but your options are to:

- Register your own domain name (see the Nominet site at **<www.nic.uk>** for information).
- Use a 'redirection service' such as V3 **<www.v3.com>** to be allocated a permanent free web address of the format **<go.to/user-id/>**, which redirects people to your actual web space, wherever it is.
- Get another organization to host your material. RootsWeb **<www. rootsweb.org>**, for example, provides domain names and web space for projects such as the Immigrant Ships Transcribers Guild **<istg.rootsweb. com>** and FreeBMD **<freebmd.rootsweb.com>**.

What is a web page?

When viewed on a web browser, web pages look like a form of desktop publishing and you might think that you need very complex and expensive software to produce a web site. In fact, web pages are in some ways very simple: each page is simply a text file with the text that is to appear on the page and instructions to the browser on how to display the text. The pictures that appear on a page are not strictly part of it, they are separate files and the page simply tells the browser where to download them from. This is why you can often see the individual images being downloaded after the text of a page has already appeared in the browser window. In a similar way, all the links on a web page are created by including instructions to the browser on what page to load when the user clicks on the links. (You can easily get a general idea of how this all works if you load a web page, ideally a fairly simple one, into your browser and use the **View Source** option in Netscape or Internet Explorer, on the **View** menu in both browsers.)

This means that a web page is not a completed and fixed design like the final output of a desktop publishing program on the printed page. It is a set of instructions which the browser carries out. And the reader has a certain amount of control over how the browser does this, telling it not to load images, what font or colour scheme to use, what size the text should be and, most obviously, controlling the size and shape of the browser window it all has to fit into. The reason for this flexibility is that those who view a web page will be using a wide variety of different computer equipment, with a range of screen sizes and resolutions and no guarantee that particular fonts will be available, or even that the reader has a full colour display. Also, readers will be using a range of different web browsers. The web page designer has to create a page that will look good, or at least be readable for all these users.

Figure 12.2 shows the text for a very simple web page:

```
<HTML>
<HEAD>
<TITLE>This appears at the top of the browser
window</TITLE>
</HEAD>
<BODY>
<H1>Here's the main heading</H1>
<P>Here's a very brief paragraph
of text with <B>bold</B> and <I>italics</I>.</P>
<P><IMG SRC="tree.gif">Here's another paragraph with
an image at the start of it.
</P>
<P>Here's a link to the
<A HREF="http://www.pro.gov.uk">PRO web site</A></P>
</BODY>
</HTML>
```

Figure 12.2 The text file for a simple web page

Figure 12.3 shows what this page looks like when displayed by Netscape.

The angled brackets mark the 'tags' which act as instructions to the browser, so the tag <IMG...> tells the browser to insert an image at this point. All the text that is not inside angled brackets appears on the page, but the tags themselves do not. Many of the tags work in pairs, for example the tags <B>...</B> tell the browser to use a bold font to display the text between them. Links to other web sites and other pages on your own site are created by putting the tag <A HREF="site-or-file-

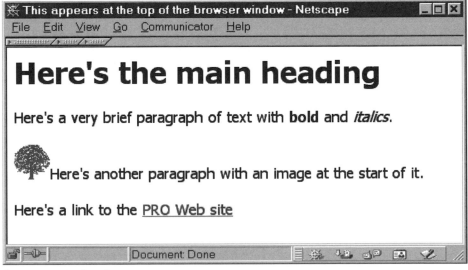

Figure 12.3 A simple web page

name">...</A> round the hotspot, i.e. the text you want the reader to click on, with the web address or file name between the inverted commas ('A' stands for 'Anchor').

You can get a good idea of how this works by saving a copy of the page shown in Figure 12.3 from **<www.spub.co.uk/protgi/dummypage.html>** and then editing it in Notepad (do not try it with a word processor!), to see what happens if you move or delete tags.

The set of tags that can be used to create web pages is specified in a standard called Hypertext Markup Language (HTML). The standard is controlled by the World Wide Web Consortium (W3C) **<w3c.org>** on the basis of extensive consultation with those who have an interest in the technology of the Web. HTML has been through several versions since its inception in 1991, and the latest is version 4, which came into use at the beginning of 1998. You may be accustomed to the fact that documents created by more recent programs often cannot be read by previous versions. With web pages, however an older browser, released before HTML 4.0, will simply ignore tags it does not understand, which is unlikely to cause any problems for web pages consisting mainly of text. There will not be another version of HTML, since the next development on the web is XML (eXtensible Markup Language), but HTML pages will remain readable and will not become obsolete.

Software

In order to create your web site you will need suitable software, and there is quite a range of possibilities. Which is best depends on what software you have already got, what your web site is to contain and how serious you are about your site. One thing to remember is that no matter what software you use, the output is always a plain text file. It is not a file in a proprietary format belonging to a single manufacturer which is what makes exchanging files between different word processors so problematic. This means you can use a variety of software programs to edit a single page.

Another important point is that you almost certainly do not need to buy additional software – it is very likely that you already have several web publishing tools installed on your computer. The following sections look at these different sorts of software.

There are three basic approaches to creating web pages:

- You can create them 'by hand', i.e. by typing in the tags yourself using a text editor.
- You can use a program which works like a word processor but automatically converts the page layout into the appropriate text and tags.
- You can use a program which automatically generates pages from a set of data.

Editors

In the early days of the Web there was no special-purpose software designed for web authoring, and commercial software did not take any account of web authoring. The only way to create pages was with a text editor, typing in both the text of the page and the HTML tags. The surprising thing is that, in spite of the many pieces of software that are now able to create web pages, many web authors still use text editors. The reason is that these give you complete control and do not make decisions for you. The disadvantage, of course, is that you will need to know what the relevant tags are and how to use them. But even if you mainly use another program to create your web pages, a text editor can still be useful. This is particularly the case where you have been using a program that is not designed specifically for web authoring, but has the facility to save files in HTML format as an add-on. All such programs have *some* failings in their web page output. If you need to correct these, it is easiest to use a text editor.

Although you can use a very basic text editor like the Windows Notepad, you will find it is hard work to create web pages with something so primitive and will be better off using a more sophisticated editor. Some, like TextPad **<www.textpad.com>**, even though designed as general-purpose editors, offer a number of features to make web authoring easier. TextPad, for example, allows you to have many documents open at once, and has a comprehensive search and replace function covering all open documents. It has a 'clip library' of the main HTML tags – just clicking on an entry in the library adds the tags to your page (see Figure 12.4).

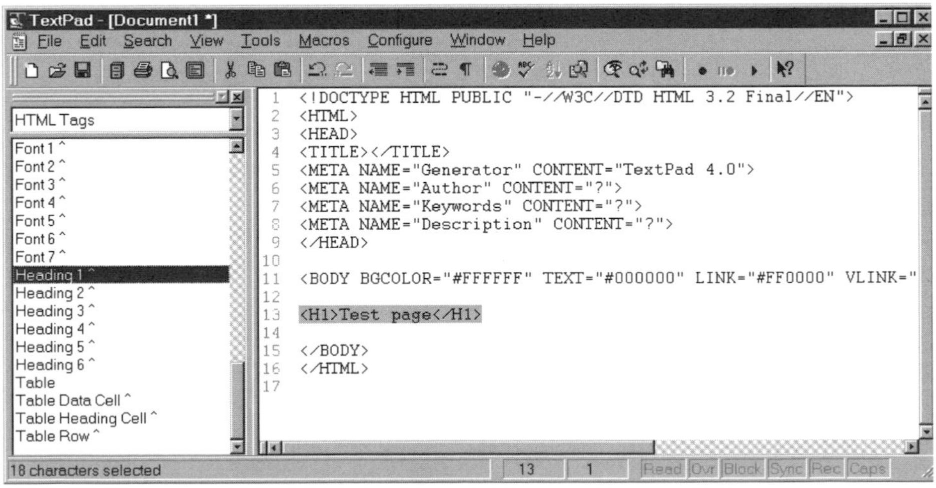

Figure 12.4 Web authoring with an editor: the <H1> tags in the main window were inserted around the text simply by selecting the text and then clicking on Heading 1 in the left-hand panel

Word processors

Assuming you have got a reasonably recent version of one of the main word processors, you will be able to use that to create web pages – see if there is a web or HTML option on the **File | Save As** menu, or on a **File | Export** menu. This way of creating pages is particularly useful if you already have material typed up, because you will be able to turn it into web pages very easily. But note that this will not create a web page for each *page* of your word-processed document, it will turn each *document* into a single page. Once you have saved a page (and thereby given it a file name) you will able to make links to it from other pages.

You might think that with this sort of facility there is no real need for other web authoring software but, unfortunately, word processors are not particularly good at producing web pages that will read well on the wide variety of set-ups internet users have. In particular, they often try to reproduce precisely every nuance of the word-processed document, which, since the layout facilities of HTML are strictly limited, can lead to very cumbersome web pages that may download slowly. However, for text-only pages with a straightforward layout, this is a very quick way to get material on to the Web.

Dedicated web authoring software

A better all-round option is a piece of dedicated web authoring software. This will provide *only* the layout facilities that are available in HTML. Many such packages offer both a design/layout mode, which looks like a word processor, and a text editing mode, allowing you to switch quickly between them. It is difficult to make long-term recommendations about individual packages as the software companies are constantly trying to outdo each other's products, but recent versions of Allaire's HomeSite and MacroMedia Dreamweaver have had consistently good reviews in the computer press. However, these are commercial products which you will need to buy, though a fully functional demo version of HomeSite can be downloaded from **<www.allaire.com>** and from software archives, and a trial version of Dreamweaver from **<www.macromedia.com>**. Demos of web authoring packages are frequently to be found on the cover CD-ROMs of computer magazines such as *Internet Magazine*. Many other commercial and shareware packages are available for downloading. The best place to look is Tucows **<tucows.mirror.ac.uk>**, which has a wide selection of web authoring software to download.

If you are only going to create a fairly simple site, you will not want to pay for a commercial web authoring package. In fact you almost certainly have some free web authoring software on your computer already. Netscape Communicator comes with a built-in web editor called Netscape Composer (to be found on the 'Communicator' menu). This does not have anything like the facilities of HomeSite or Dreamweaver, but has everything you need for doing straightforward pages. It works as a

WYSIWYG ('what you see is what you get') editor, with all the main HTML functions available from toolbars and menus. You can view the HTML code but you cannot edit at the text level within Composer, though there is nothing to stop you loading the text into NotePad and viewing both on the screen at once. If you have a full installation of Internet Explorer on your computer, you will also have a cut-down version of Microsoft's web authoring package FrontPage. Called FrontPage Express, this is considerably simpler to use than the full commercial version, but rather more sophisticated than Composer. It has both a WYSIWYG and text-editing mode.

There are other free web authoring packages available on the Web. A particularly good one for beginners, as long as you do not mind working with tags, is EvrSoft's FirstPage **<www.evrsoft.com>**, which has Easy, Normal, Expert and Hardcore modes, with more and more complex features available as you progress. Although there is no WYSIWYG editing, there is a preview window which can show you immediately the effect of adding to the page (see Figure 12.5).

On-line software

Some free web space providers have on-line tools for creating web sites directly on the site without having to upload it from your own computer. Obviously, this will not help you put your family tree on-line, but it is a quick way to get a web site up and running. Some of the providers offering this facility are: Freeservers **<www.freeservers.com>**, Homestead **<www.**

Figure 12.5 Editing with FirstPage. In some ways this is quite similar to an editor like TextPad, but note the preview panel which shows what the page looks like as well as the actual HTML below, and the colour palette at the right

homestead.co.uk> Tripod <www.tripod.co.uk> and Yahoo! GeoCities <geocities.yahoo.com>.

Databases and spreadsheets

If you are storing some of your genealogical information in a spreadsheet or database, there are several ways of creating web pages containing the data without having to retype it.

First, most recent databases can create web pages directly (probably via an Export menu or a Save As menu). Figure 12.6 and Figure 12.7 show data from my Microsoft Access database of Sussex births for the surname Christian extracted from the GRO indexes. The first shows the default export – just the data is output, in a table, using the browser's default font – while the second shows the output of the 'autoformatting' option in Access, with labels for each column, and the same font as the original data. Of course, since these have been output in HTML format, they can be opened in any web authoring package for further editing.

A second option, which may be useful if you have an older database with no HTML option, is to use your word processor's mailmerge function to create a document that extracts data from the database. You can then use your word processor's HTML output function.

Finally, if neither of these options are available, there is a last resort: plain text. Your database or spreadsheet will undoubtedly have a Save as text function, and all browsers can display plain text files. This will not

Sussex-births

B	1839	3	John	CHRISTIAN	Battle	7	154	
B	1839	3	Mary Ann	CHRISTIAN	Hastings	7	210	
B	1840	4	female	CHRISTIAN	Hastings	7	255	
B	1841	1	Sarah	CHRISTIAN	Brighton	7	198	
B	1847	3	Thomas	CHRISTIAN	Battle	7	183	
B	1850	1	Mary Ann	CHRISTIAN	Hastings	7	303	
B	1850	2	Mary Jane	CHRISTIAN	Hastings	7	242	
B	1851	1	Philly	CHRISTIAN	Battle	7	203	
B	1851	1	William	CHRISTIAN	Hastings	7	295	
B	1852	2	Elizabeth Emma	CHRISTIAN	Battle	2b	30	
B	1852	4	Emily	CHRISTIAN	Hastings	2b	0	page no unclear
B	1854	2	Emma Augusta	CHRISTIAN	Brighton	2b	187	
B	1854	3	Matilda	CHRISTIAN	Battle	2b	34	

Figure 12.6 A web page exported from a Microsoft Access database

GRO - Sussex Births

Event	District	Year	Quarter	Forename	Surname	Volume	Page	Notes
B	Battle	1839	3	John	CHRISTIAN	7	154	
B	Hastings	1839	3	Mary Ann	CHRISTIAN	7	210	
B	Hastings	1840	4	female	CHRISTIAN	7	255	
B	Brighton	1841	1	Sarah	CHRISTIAN	7	198	
B	Battle	1847	3	Thomas	CHRISTIAN	7	183	
B	Hastings	1850	1	Mary Ann	CHRISTIAN	7	303	
B	Hastings	1850	2	Mary Jane	CHRISTIAN	7	242	
B	Battle	1851	1	Philly	CHRISTIAN	7	203	
B	Hastings	1851	1	William	CHRISTIAN	7	295	
B	Battle	1852	2	Elizabeth Emma	CHRISTIAN	2b	30	
B	Hastings	1852	4	Emily	CHRISTIAN	2b	0	page no unclear
B	Brighton	1854	2	Emma Augusta	CHRISTIAN	2b	187	
B	Battle	1854	3	Matilda	CHRISTIAN	2b	34	

Figure 12.7 A web page exported from Microsoft Access with 'autoformatting'

```
B1839   3   John              CHRISTIAN        Battle
B1839   3   Mary Ann          CHRISTIAN        Hastings
B1840   4   female            CHRISTIAN        Hastings
B1841   1   Sarah             CHRISTIAN        Brighton
B1847   3   Thomas            CHRISTIAN        Battle
B1850   1   Mary Ann          CHRISTIAN        Hastings
B1850   2   Mary Jane         CHRISTIAN        Hastings
B1851   1   Philly            CHRISTIAN        Battle
B1851   1   William           CHRISTIAN        Hastings
B1852   2   Elizabeth Emma    CHRISTIAN        Battle
B1852   4   Emily             CHRISTIAN        Hastings
B1854   2   Emma Augusta      CHRISTIAN        Brighton
B1854   3   Matilda           CHRISTIAN        Battle
```

Figure 12.8 Plain text from a database

look as good as the examples above, but if someone finds an ancestor in your list, that will be the last thing they will be worried about. Figure 12.8 shows how this looks in a browser.

You can even take this text file and embed it in a proper web page. There is a special pair of tags, <PRE>... </PRE> (for *pre*formatted) which, when put round formatted text like this, will preserve all the line breaks and the multiple spaces, thus maintaining the original format.

In an ideal world, all of this would be unnecessary. You would simply put your database file on your web site and people could use their browser to search it just as you do on your desktop. There are in fact ways of doing this, but at present they are not easy for the novice to set up, and all require special software on the web server, which your ISP is not likely to provide for a non-corporate web site.

Web site design

Although there are many books on web site design, for someone publishing family history on the Web a few basic principles should suffice. What is important is to work out what the overall structure of your site will be (which pages is each page going to link to?), and to do so *before* you start creating actual pages. There are also a few technical matters, such as file-naming conventions and file formats for graphics (see below).

There is no single right way to design a web site. It depends on what it contains and who it is aimed at. For a personal genealogy site, your main visitors will be other genealogists looking for information on individuals and surnames that might be part of their own ancestry. If you have expertise in a particular area of genealogy, or have collected useful material on a particular topic, people may come looking for general background information. Your main job, then, is to make sure visitors to your site can see whether you have anything useful to them and can access it easily. While it is better, of course, if your site looks good, you should not be worrying about state-of-the-art graphic design, special effects, animation, background music, hit counters or any of the other things that many amateur web authors seem to find irresistible, but which irritate or distract readers and make pages slower to download.

Filenames

It is usual to give files for web pages names ending in .html. If you call a file *index.html* or *index.htm* it will be loaded by default. So when you go to Genuki's home page at **<www.genuki.org.uk>** you get exactly the same page as when you enter **<www.genuki.org.uk/index.html>** – the server delivers *index.html* because you have not asked for any specific file. (The filenames *default.html* or *default.htm* are used instead on some servers, such as the PRO's – try **<www.pro.gov.uk/default.htm>**). This means your home page should always be called *index.html* and be placed in the main folder in your web space.

On almost all web servers filenames are case sensitive: *index.html*, *Index.html* and *INDEX.HTML* are different files. To save confusion stick to lower case.

Graphics

Web browsers can display graphics in three of the many graphics formats: GIF, JPEG and PNG, of which the last is not widely used. For colour photographs, you need to use JPEG as it allows graphics with up to 16.7 million colours and is therefore capable of displaying subtle variations in tone. (JPEG files have the file extension .jpg on the PC). The GIF format, which allows a maximum of 256 colours, is poor for colour photographs but useful for black and white photographs and things like navigation buttons, logos or maps, which have simple colour schemes. You can compare the strengths and weaknesses of these two formats by looking at the examples at **<www.spub.co.uk/wpg/figures/figure10.html>**.

If you are going to use graphics extensively, you will need a graphics editing program such as Photoshop or PaintShop Pro. If you just need to crop images and covert them to GIF or JPEG format, there are freeware or inexpensive shareware tools that will do the job.

Each graphic is kept as an individual file on the web server, and any page which uses it has a tag which contains the file name. If you have downloaded *dummypage.html* to your own computer, it will not display the tree unless you also download the file *tree.gif* into the same folder, so that when the browser attempts to interpret the tag `<IMG SRC="tree.gif">` it can find the file.

You can use the same graphic on many different pages, so if you have a graphic such as a logo which appears on every page on your site, you only need to put one copy of the file on the server.

Adding your family tree

If you are designing your own site you will need to know how to include the pages showing the family tree you have created from your genealogy database software. Whatever software you use for your genealogy, it will almost certainly create a new folder on your hard disk and put all the created files in it, perhaps in a number of sub-folders.

You need to upload this new folder and all the files it contains on to your web site (see 'Uploading your web site', below), retaining the filenames and folder structure. If you change filenames or move files you will find that some parts of the tree do not link correctly.

From your home page you will need a link to the index file in the family tree folder. So suppose you have called the folder *johnson* because it contains your Johnson family tree, you would have a link

```
<A HREF="johnson">Johnson family tree</A>
```

on your home page. If you find this does not work, you may need to specify the exact filename of the index file (this should be fairly obvious if you look at the filenames in the family tree folder), for example:

```
<A HREF="johnson/default.htm">Johnson family tree</A>
```

When you are creating a web tree with your genealogy software, it is always worth checking for an option to make filenames lower case. There are other reasons for giving the exact filename, discussed on p. 179.

Design tips

There is plenty of advice about good design on the Web. Here are the most important points:

- Have a home page which tells visitors what they will find on the site, and provide links to the main areas of your site.
- Give each page a helpful title and heading, so that if someone bookmarks it, or comes to it directly via a link from another site (perhaps a search engine), they can immediately see what the page is about.
- Conversely, make sure that every page has a link back to the home page or some other higher level page, so that if someone comes to your site from a search engine they can get to other pages.
- Don't make your pages too long, and don't include large or unnecessary graphics, as this will only increase the time it takes your pages to download, and potential visitors will be put off.
- Don't use unusual colour schemes. They are unusual for a good reason – they make text unreadable.
- Don't put light text on a dark background – this can make it impossible to print out from some browsers.
- Put your e-mail address on the site so that people can contact you.

Uploading your web site

Once you have created a set of pages on your own computer, you need to go on-line and upload them to your web space. The standard way of doing this is to use a program called an FTP client. FTP stands for File Transfer Protocol, which is a long-established method for transferring files on the internet. There are many free and shareware FTP programs available from software archives like Tucows at **<tucows.mirror.ac.uk>**. CuteFTP and WS-FTP are among the most popular.

Before you connect to the internet to upload, you will want to set up an entry for your web site in your FTP client's list of sites. You need to enter:

- The address of the site. If you are not certain what it is, your ISP/web space provider will be able to tell you, and their help pages will probably provide detailed instructions for uploading files.
- Your username and password for that site.
- You should be able to enter the location of the folder containing your web site, though you will also be able to select a particular folder once you are connected.

Next connect to the internet. Once you are logged in, you should see something like Figure 12.9, where I am preparing to upload a family tree to the genealogy folder on my personal web site.

To upload your files, simply drag the icons for the files to be uploaded across to the right-hand panel. If you drag a folder icon, all the files in that folder will be included in the upload.

Finally, start your browser and type in the URL of your site to check it.

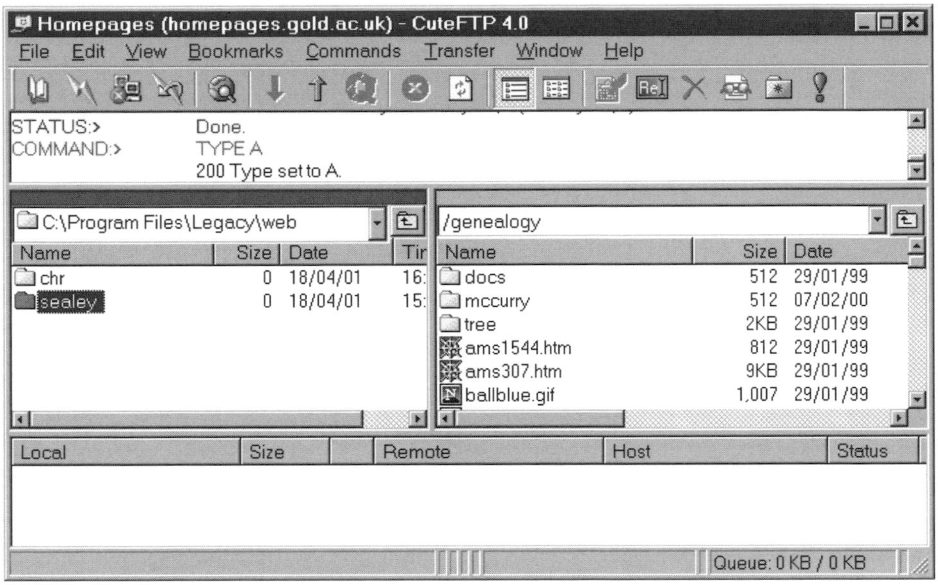

Figure 12.9 Using FTP to upload files to a web site

You can see the results of the upload in Figure 12.9 at **<homepages.gold. ac.uk/peter/genealogy/sealey/>**.

Modern web browsers can also be used to transfer files – see the on-line help for details of how to do this.

Publicity

Once you have created and uploaded your web pages, you will need to publicize the existence of your site. One simple way to do this is to put its URL in the signature attached to your e-mail messages. Apart from that, there are three main ways of approaching this:

- Submitting the site to search engines
- Notifying people via mailing lists and newsgroups
- Asking others to provide links to your site

Submitting to search engines

Making sure your site is known to the main search engines is probably the most effective way to publicize your web site. Since search engines index pages automatically, they have no way of knowing what the most important aspects of your site and your individual pages are unless you help them by organizing the material on each page. Among the things search engines look for when estimating the relevance of a page to a search done by a user are:

- Words appearing in the page title and between heading tags
- The initial section of text
- Words which appear frequently in the page

In addition, there are special tags you can add to a page to provide a list of keywords and a brief description of the page and the site. These are <META> tags, which are placed in the <HEAD> section of the page. They will not be visible to someone reading your page, but they are used by search engines.

```
<META NAME='description' CONTENT='The last will and
testament of Zebediah Poot, died 1687, Wombourn,
Staffordshire, England'>
<META NAME='keywords' CONTENT='genealogy, will,
testament, Poot, Wombourn, Stafford, Staffordshire,
STS'>
```

When a search engine lists this page in the results of a search, it will normally list its title (i.e. the text between the <TITLE> tags) and your description. If there is no description, it will take the first couple of lines of text from the <BODY> of the page.

Notifying mailing lists and newsgroups

A good way to draw attention to a new site is to post a message to appropriate mailing lists and newsgroups. You might think it is a good idea to post to every one you possibly can, to get maximum publicity, but there is little point in posting details of a Yorkshire web site to a Cornish list. Choose the county lists relevant to the material you are putting on the Web, and any special interest lists. It will be worth notifying the soc.genealogy.britain newsgroup (the GENBRIT mailing list). There is also a special mailing list, NEW-GEN-URL, for publicizing new web sites. If there is a mailing list relating to some social group your ancestors belonged to it will be worth notifying that list, so if you have information on coalmining ancestors on your site, for example, it would be worth posting to the COALMINERS list (see Chapter 10).

Requesting links

You can request other people to link to your pages, but you need to be realistic about expecting links from other personal sites. People will generally only do this if there is some connection in subject matter between your site and theirs, and if you are prepared to create a link to their site in return. Do not expect major institutions like the PRO or the SoG to link to a site with purely personal material, just because you have made a link to theirs.

If your site has material relating to a particular subject, it will be well worth contacting the maintainers of specialist web sites relating to that subject, such as those discussed in Chapters 7, 8 and 9.

If you have transcriptions of original source material of broader interest than extracts for individual surnames you should contact Genuki, who attempt to provide links to all UK source material on-line.

News

A number of genealogy newsletters will give a mention to personal web sites if you mail the editor (see Chapter 13, p. 183). If you have a web site which contains material of sufficiently general interest, i.e. not just your personal pedigree, you may also be able to get a mention in the news section of *Computers in Genealogy* (which will then provide a link from the web page for the relevant issue of the magazine), or in the 'Computer Intelligence' section of *Family Tree Magazine*. You can contact the relevant editors at **cig@sog.org.uk** and **EricDProbert@compuserve.com**, respectively.

Preserving your family history

While the Web is seen as a way of publishing your family history, in one important respect it is not like publishing it in print. A printed family history donated to a genealogy library will be preserved for ever, while your account with your web space provider is doomed to expire when you do, unless you can persuade your heirs otherwise.

But since a web site is just a collection of files there is no reason why all the information cannot be preserved, even if not on-line. If you copy all the files that constitute your site on to writable CDs, these can be sent to relatives and deposited in archives just like printed material. The advantage of distributing your material in this way is that people do not need special software (for example a particular word processor or the same genealogy database as you) in order to view the files, and everyone with a computer has access to a web browser.

If you are intending to do this you should make sure that every link gives a specific filename, as mentioned in 'Filenames' on p. 174. A web server knows to deliver a file called *index.html* if a link doesn't specify a filename; a stand-alone computer doesn't.

Further information

Obviously, this chapter has not been able to cover all you need to know about web authoring, but there is plenty of information available in books and on the Web.

A search on **<www.amazon.co.uk>** for 'HTML' or 'web publishing' will show you how many general books there are. But I know of only two books devoted specifically to publishing genealogical information on the Web:

Peter Christian, *Web Publishing for Genealogy*, 2nd edn, David Hawgood, 1999). There is also a US edition published by the Genealogical Publishing Co. (2000). The web site for the book, at **<www.spub.co.uk/ wpg/>**, has links to the web pages for web authoring software, genealogy software companies and GEDCOM converters, and to tutorial materials on the web.

Richard S. Wilson, *Publishing Your Family History on the internet* (Writers Digest Books, 1999) **<www.compuology.com/book2.htm>**.

An excellent overview of genealogical web publishing with links to relevant software and tutorial materials is Cyndi's 'Genealogy Home Page Construction Kit' at **<www.CyndisList.com/construc.htm>**.

Computers in Genealogy, Family Tree Magazine and *Genealogical Computing* are three print magazines which regularly carry articles on genealogical web publishing. In the case of *CiG* many of the articles are available on-line at **<www.sog.org.uk/cig/>**.

For links to some of the many on-line resources relating to web design in general, see **<www.spub.co.uk/wpg/reference.html>**.

13 The World of Family History

Previous chapters have looked at ways of using the internet in direct connection with your own pedigree. This chapter looks at the 'non-virtual' world of family history which exists off-line, and how you can use the internet to find out about it.

Societies and organizations

Every major organization involved in family history has a web site, and the same is also true of most of the smaller ones.

National bodies

There are a number of national genealogical bodies:

- The Society of Genealogists (SoG) <www.sog.org.uk>
- The Institute of Heraldic and Genealogical Studies (IHGS) <www.ihgs.ac.uk>
- Federation of Family History Societies (FFHS) <www.ffhs.org.uk>
- The Guild of One-Name Studies (GOONS) <www.one-name.org>
- Scottish Genealogy Society <www.scotsgenealogy.com>
- Scottish Association of Family History Societies (SAFHS) <www.safhs.org.uk>
- Association of Family History Societies of Wales <www.rootsweb.com/~wlsafhs/>

Family history societies

There are around 200 local family history societies in the UK and Ireland, the overwhelming majority of which have web sites. Most local societies are members of one or more of the three national federations/associations listed above, which are themselves umbrella organizations, not family history societies in their own right. The FFHS includes many member societies from Wales and Ireland, and most English societies are Federation members.

The definitive starting point for finding FHS web sites is Genuki's 'Family History and Genealogy Societies' page at <www.genuki.org.uk/Societies/>. This lists the national societies and has links to separate pages for the constituent nations of the British Isles, where details of local societies are to be found.

The individual FHS web sites vary greatly in what they offer, but all will have contact details and usually a list of publications, though many societies use GENfair (see p. 186) for their on-line sales. You will not generally find genealogical data on their sites, though some have members-only areas which may have material from the society's indexes. Helen Parsonage has a useful page at <www.geocities.com/Heartland/Plains/8555/fhspubs.html> which provides links to all the FHS publications catalogues that are available on-line.

Events

There is a wide range of genealogical meetings, lectures, conferences and fairs in the UK, from the individual meetings of family history societies to major national events such as the SOG's annual Family History Fair. One of the easiest ways to find out about such events is via the Web.

The major source for the whole of the UK is the Geneva page (the Genuki calendar of GENealogical EVents and Activities) at <users.ox.ac.uk/~malcolm/genuki/geneva/>, run by Malcolm Austen on behalf of Genuki and the FFHS. This lists events from the SoG's programme, any family history society events submitted and the regional family history fairs regularly held around the country. The 'Genuki UK Family History News' newsletter (see p. 184) also regularly lists forthcoming events. The PRO's programme of events, many of which are of interest to genealogists, can be found on-line at <www.pro.gov.uk/events/>.

Quite a few societies have computer groups which organize lectures on internet-related topics, details of which can be found on their web sites. The SoG offers a substantial programme of IT-related events, many of which cover the use of the internet for genealogy. It organizes an annual one-day genealogical computing conference in association with a local family history society, and in recent years has held a one-day event each summer devoted to internet genealogy. Details of all these will be found on the Society's web site at <www.sog.org.uk/events/calendar.html>.

Print magazines and journals

Many genealogical publications have a related web site, with at least a list of contents for the current issue and in some cases material from back issues.

The web site of *Family Tree Magazine* can be found at <www.family-tree.co.uk>, while its sister publication, *Practical Family History*, has a page on the same site at <www.family-tree.co.uk/sister.htm>. Each lists the contents of the current issue. There is an on-line list of contents for the IHGS' journal, *Family History,* at <www.ihgs.ac.uk/institute/fh_contents.html>.

The PRO's *Ancestors* magazine has a regular section on using the internet for genealogy. A web page at **<www.spub.co.uk/ancestors.html>** lists the internet topics covered in each issue. Details of the magazine will be found at **<www.pro.gov.uk/ancestorsmagazine>**.

The SoG's web site at **<www.sog.org.uk>** has a subject and name index to the *Genealogists' Magazine* and there are plans to put a collection of seminal articles on-line in the near future. The Society's computer magazine, *Computers in Genealogy*, has a web site at **<www.sog.org.uk/cig/>** with a list of contents for every issue since March 1994, a synopsis of every article and links to on-line versions of an increasing number of them. Notable among these are Eric Probert's lists of genealogy software at **<www.sog.org.uk/cig/software.html>**. In addition, there is a complete set of links for every on-line resource mentioned in the News section and in David Squire's regular 'Web Watch' column.

While *Computers in Genealogy* is the only UK computer genealogy journal, a number of others which cover on-line genealogy are published in English-speaking countries. Foremost among these is *Genealogical Computing*, a US journal published quarterly by Ancestry.com, which covers 'how to use your computer, the Net, and other tools like scanners, printers, digital cameras, palm pilots' in genealogy. It also carries reviews of software, data collections and new computer hardware of interest to the family historian. Details can be found in the Ancestry.com on-line bookshop at **<shops.ancestry.com>**. Copies are available at the SoG and other major genealogical libraries.

The bimonthly magazine *Local History* has a web site at **<www.local-history.co.uk>** with an index to the contents of past issues at **<www.local-history.co.uk/Issues/>**, as well as the usual listing for the latest issue. The site also provides links to other local history resources on the Web.

The most comprehensive on-line listing is the 'Magazines, Journals, Columns & Newsletters' page on Cyndi's List at **<www.CyndisList.com/magazine.htm>**. Subtitled 'Print & Electronic Publications for Genealogy', this page provides links to web sites for many print magazines, though many of course will be of interest only to those with North American ancestry.

PERSI, the Periodical Source Index, at **<www.ancestry.com/search/rectype/periodicals/persi/main.htm>** is a subscription database at Ancestry.com containing 'a comprehensive subject index to genealogy and local history periodicals written in English and French (Canada) since 1800.'

For sites relating to non-genealogical publications, see 'Newspapers' on p. 50.

On-line publications

As well as print publications there are, of course, on-line columns and newsletters for genealogists. Links to these will be found on Cyndi's List at **<www.CyndisList.com/magazine.htm>**. The majority of these are US-based, so are not of relevance to UK genealogists where they deal with genealogical records, but many have useful material on general genealogical topics, including using the internet.

For the UK, there is the 'Genuki UK Family History News' e-mail newsletter, edited by Rob Thompson and published three or four times a month. This carries details of new genealogy books and CD-ROMs, forthcoming events and new material on Genuki. It is the only on-line publication in the UK to carry regular web site reviews, and that alone makes it worth subscribing to. To subscribe send a message containing only the word **subscribe** to **<UK-FAMILYHISTORYNEWS-L-request@Rootsweb.com>**. Full details and links to past issues will be found at **<www.genuki.org.uk/news/>**. 'UK Genealogy News' is an on-line monthly newsletter with news items, reviews and brief articles published on the 'UK Genealogy' site (see p. 18) at **<www.ukgenealogy.co.uk>**.

It is impossible here to give an overview of all the US publications, but a good place to start is Ancestry.com, which hosts a number of weekly columns, all accessible from **<www.ancestry.com/learn/library/columnists/main.htm>**. Of these, Drew Smith's 'Digital genealogy' and Elizabeth Kelley Kerstens 'GC extra' are particularly recommended for material on the use of computers and the internet in genealogy.

Probably the best known of these columns to UK genealogists is Dick Eastman's Online Genealogy Newsletter, which originated on the Genealogy Forum in CompuServe, long before CompuServe was part of the internet. It carries details of new genealogy software and CD-ROMs, genealogical developments on the internet, new web sites and more. Although the main focus is on genealogy and IT, it is not exclusively so. Dick has many contacts in the UK, and regularly includes items of genealogy news from Britain. To subscribe to the e-mail version of the newsletter fill in the form at **<www.rootsforum.com/newsletter/>**. The current issues and several years of back issues can be read and searched at **<www.ancestry.com/library/view/columns/eastman/eastman.asp>**.

There are a few specialist mailing lists which are used to disseminate news. John Fuller's NEW-GENLIST mailing list will keep you up to date with new genealogy mailing lists, while NEW-GEN-URL allows people to publicize new genealogy web sites. Subscription details for all these lists will be found at **<www.rootsweb.com/~jfuller/gen_mail_computing.html>**. The CyndisList mailing list announces additions to Cyndi's List (see **<www.CyndisList.com/maillist.htm>**).

Software

The Web is an excellent source of information about genealogical software, since all the major software companies, and many individual software authors, have web sites providing details of their products.

Shareware products can be downloaded from the sites, and even for normal commercial products there will often be a demo version available for download.

It is not possible here to provide a guide to genealogy software, but there are a number of useful resources on the Web to point you in the right direction.

A very comprehensive listing is the one on Cyndi's List at <www.CyndisList.com/software.htm>. George Archer has a 'Guide to Online Searching for Genealogical Software' at <wdn.com/~garcher/gsguide.txt> and a listing of 'All Known Genealogy Software Programs in the World' downloadable from <wdn.com/~garcher/allgen.zip>.

The SoG's *Computers in Genealogy* publishes an annual overview of genealogy software in two parts (Windows and non-Windows software), usually in its March and June issues respectively. This gives the basic details of the programs, along with a list of UK suppliers and the web addresses of the software companies. The most recent lists are on the Society's web site at <www.sog.org.uk/cig/software.html>. See p. 183 for more information on *Computers in Genealogy*.

With so many software packages available, deciding which to buy can be very difficult. There is a useful comparative guide by Bill Mumford at <www.mumford.ab.ca/reportcard/> which scores all the main Windows genealogy programs on a dozen criteria, including data recording, reports, source documentation, multimedia and internet features, etc. The Genealogy Software Springboard at <www.gensoftsb.com> has comprehensive coverage of genealogy software, with a page devoted to each package outlining the main features and links to the producer's web site.

If you are just starting to use a computer for genealogy, it is probably worth downloading one of the two major freeware genealogy database programs. Personal Ancestral File (currently at version 5) can be downloaded free from the FamilySearch site at <www.familysearch.org>. It can be found by clicking on **Order/Download Products** on the opening screen. A manual can also be downloaded. The Millennia Corporation has made the basic version of its package Legacy 3.0 available as freeware, and this can be downloaded from <www.legacyfamilytree.com>. You need to be aware that these are very substantial downloads and could be lengthy if you have a slow connection.

Software retailers are included in the on-line shops discussed below.

On-line shops

There is an increasing number of on-line shops for genealogy books, data and software. Almost all use secure on-line ordering, though some are just on-line lists and orders must be sent by e-mail or post.

The SoG's on-line shop can be found at <www.sog.org.uk/bookshop/>.

This offers a huge range of genealogical books, microfiche and CD-ROMs, including a number of genealogy software packages.

The FFHS's on-line shop is at <**www.familyhistorybooks.co.uk**> and sells not only the Federation's own publications, both books and data, but also books from many other publishers. In order to make an on-line purchase your browser needs to download the shopping software, but you can browse the site without doing this.

On-line commerce is not something that it is very easy for individual family history societies to set up for themselves, but GENfair, 'The Online Family History Fair and Genealogy Bookshop' at <**www.genfair.com**> hosts a number of virtual shops for individual FHSs to sell their publications on-line. Currently over 50 societies have a presence on this site, including a number from Australia.

The PRO has an on-line bookshop at <**www.pro.gov.uk/bookshop/ Shop/**>, though it deals only with the PRO's own publications.

The Internet Genealogical Bookshop run by Stuart Raymond has a web site at <**www.soft.net.uk/samjraymond/igb.htm**>. Books must be ordered by e-mail and paid for on receipt of invoice. Many other bookshops are listed on Cyndi's List at <**www.CyndisList.com/books.htm**>. For a list of genealogy bookshops in the UK, North America and Australasia, consult Margaret Olson's 'Links to Genealogy Booksellers' at <**http://homepages. rootsweb.com/~socgen/Bookmjo.html**>.

If you are searching for second-hand books you will find many booksellers on-line. Yahoo UK has a substantial list at <**uk.dir.yahoo.com/ Regional/Countries/United_Kingdom/Business_and_Economy/Shopping_**

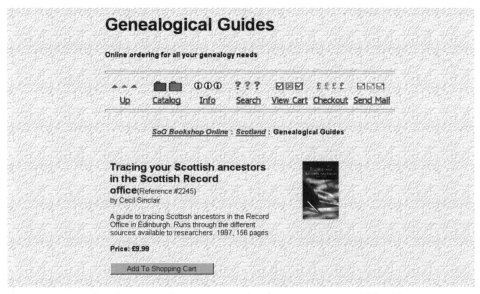

Figure 13.1 A page from the Society of Genealogists' on-line shop at <www.sog.org.uk/bookshop>

The Online Family History Fair and Genealogy Bookstore

GEN fair™

one-stop shopping for family history enthusiasts

now local history too

Add to Basket

Review Basket

Technical Help
Feedback
Information for Suppliers

Contact:
info@genfair.com

Enter

GENfair UK

UK Family History Societies and Suppliers

Enter

GENfair OZ

Australian Societies and Suppliers

We accept MasterCard and VISA credit card payments through our secure server facility

over 10,000 items for sale

more than 80 stands

GENfair belongs to the Which? Web Trader Scheme and follows its Code of Practice

VISA

MasterCard

Figure 13.2 GENfair at <www.genfair.co.uk>

and_Services/Books/Booksellers/Antique__Rare__and_Used/>. There are also sites, such as UKBookworld at <ukbookworld.com> or JustBooks at <www.justbooks.co.uk>, that will search the catalogues of many individual booksellers.

If you are looking for software, then the SoG's bookshop has a selection, while specialist suppliers S&N Genealogy and TWR Computing have wider ranges. S&N Genealogy at <www.genealogy.demon.co.uk> publishes many data CD-ROMs, including directories and parish registers. TWR Computing is at <www.twrcomputing.co.uk>. Most of the main genealogical software companies also have on-line ordering facilities.

Finally, the newsgroup soc.genealogy.marketplace carries postings by those selling genealogical products or individuals trying to find a taker for second-hand material.

Secure purchasing

Concern is often expressed about the security of on-line payments, but the reservations are out of all proportion to the actual risks. In fact, on-line transactions are much more secure than handing your credit card to a waiter in a restaurant or ordering over the phone. As long as your browser is using a secure connection, which means that anything you type in is encrypted before being sent across the internet to the supplier, your card details will be infinitely more secure than they are when sent unencrypted through the post on your monthly statement.

The only real dangers are that a supplier will subsequently store your credit card details unencrypted on a computer which is then stolen or hacked into (which is just as likely to happen with telephone orders), or that you have bought something from a bogus company. As long as you are dealing with an established supplier, such as those mentioned here, there is no reason to be suspicious of on-line transactions.

In fact a more significant problem with on-line suppliers is getting hold of them to deal with problems relating to your order or the product you have bought, particularly if the web site gives no phone number or postal address. However, on-line traders based in the UK are bound by the same consumer protection legislation as any other trader, and there is an organization called TrustUK <www.trustuk.org.uk> which has been set up to 'enable consumers to buy on-line with confidence' and is endorsed by the Government. The TrustUK web site has a page devoted to 'What to look out for when buying on-line', which offers advice on how to make trouble-free purchases on-line. TrustUK also approves other schemes for guaranteeing good practice and levels of service in on-line shopping. Of the three schemes endorsed so far, the only one of significance to genealogists shopping on-line is the Which? Web Trader Scheme <www.which.net/webtrader/>, run by the Consumers' Association. Companies which are part of the scheme, and display the logo on their web site, guarantee to adhere to a code of practice covering privacy, returns policy and the like. At the time of writing, both the SoG Bookshop and GENfair are part of this scheme. (You can see the Which? Web Trader and TrustUK logos in the screen shot of the GENfair home page in Figure 13.2.)

Before the advent of the internet, purchasing anything abroad from the comfort of the UK was far from straightforward. On-line shopping has made this much easier and, of course, those who live outside the UK can now easily order materials from British genealogy suppliers. Some practical difficulties remain: returning wrong or faulty products is not made easier by the internet. Also, you are less likely to be familiar with the reputations of overseas traders, which would be a source of concern in areas where UK consumer legislation does not apply – an impressive web site does not guarantee quality of service, let alone financial viability. However, one of the strengths of the internet is that it is a word-of-mouth medium, and it is very unlikely that there could be an unreliable company whose misdeeds have escaped being reported in the genealogy newsgroups or mailing lists. These are therefore good places to look for reports from other customers on their experiences with companies, or to place a query yourself. For software, the soc.genealogy.computing newsgroup is full of comments, positive and negative, on software products and service.

Professional researchers

There are many reasons, even with the internet, why you might want to employ a professional genealogist to undertake research for you: if you cannot get to the repository where original records are held, whether for reasons of time or distance; or if the records themselves are difficult for an amateur to use or interpret.

The SoG has a leaflet 'Employing a professional researcher: a practical guide' on its web site at **<www.sog.org.uk/leaflets/researcher.html>**, while Cyndi's List has a page on 'Professional Researchers, Volunteers & Other Research Services' at **<www.cyndislist.com/profess.htm>**.

The Association of Genealogists and Researchers in Archives (AGRA) is the professional body for genealogical researchers, with a web site at **<www.agra.org.uk>**. This provides a list of members, and an index to this by specialism, whether geographical or subject-based. The Association's code of practice is also available on the site. While many of the Association's members can be contacted by e-mail, this is by no means the majority as yet.

The PRO's web site also has a database of Independent Researchers who are prepared to undertake commissions for research in records at the PRO. The database is accessible from **<www.pro.gov.uk/readers/irlist/>** and can be searched only by subject matter.

For Scotland, the Association of Scottish Genealogists and Record Agents (ASGRA) is the professional association for researchers, and its site at **<www.asgra.co.uk>** has details of members and their specialisms.

If you have Irish ancestry, the Irish Family History Foundation's network of genealogy centres may be of use. There is a centre for each county, both in the Republic of Ireland and in Northern Ireland, and these hold copies of local material from many of the main sources for Irish genealogy (census, tithe applotments, etc.) as well as transcripts of many parish registers. The centres provide research services using these records. The Foundation's web site at **<www.irishroots.net>** has links to all the local centres as well as details of services available.

Individual researchers for Ireland can be found on the National Archives of Ireland web site at **<www.nationalarchives.ie/gen_researchers.html>** and the Association of Professional Genealogists in Ireland at **<indigo.ie/ ~apgi/>**.

Lookup services

If all you need is someone to check a particular reference for you, employing a professional researcher will be overkill. The internet makes it easy to find someone with access to particular printed publications, or records on CD-ROM, who will do a simple lookup for you. So-called 'lookup exchanges' give a list of publications and the e-mail address of someone prepared to do searches in each. Most are county-based and there are links to exchanges for most counties of the UK and Ireland from <www.geocities.com/Heartland/Plains/8555/lookup.html> and from the individual Genuki county pages. Since these services are provided entirely on a voluntary basis, requests should be as specific as possible, and may require a specific subject line – see the details at the top of each page before sending a request. And, of course, be reasonable in what you expect someone to do for you in their own time.

14 Issues for On-line Genealogists

While on-line genealogy is essentially about finding information and making use of it, it is important to be aware of some general issues involved in using internet resources and in using the Web as a publishing medium. Also important are the limitations on what is and is not likely to be on the internet. The aim of this chapter is to discuss some of these issues.

Good practice

Needless to say, technophobes, Luddites and other folk of a backward-looking disposition are happy to accuse the internet of dumbing down the noble art of genealogy – anything so easy surely cannot be sound research.

Loath as I am to agree with technophobes, there is actually some truth in this. Though the medium itself can hardly be blamed for its misuse, the internet does give scope to a sort of 'trainspotting' attitude to genealogy, where it is just a matter of filling out your family tree with plausible and preferably interesting ancestors, with little regard for accuracy or traditional standards of proof. Because more can (apparently) be done without consulting original records, it becomes easy to overlook the fact that a family tree constructed solely from on-line sources, unchecked against *any* original records, is sure to contain inaccuracies even if it is not entirely unsound. This is far from new, of course; today's is hardly the first generation in which some have been keener to construct an impressive family tree than an accurate one. The internet just makes it easier both to construct and to disseminate information of doubtful value.

But genealogy is a form of historical research, and you cannot really do it successfully without developing some understanding of the records from which a family history is constructed, and the principles for drawing reliable conclusions from them.

Some of the tutorial materials mentioned in Chapter 2 address these issues, but the most coherent set of principles and standards available on-line are those developed by the US National Genealogical Society, which can be found at **<www.ngsgenealogy.org/comstandards.htm>**:

● Standards for Sound Genealogical Research

- Standards for Using Records, Repositories, and Libraries
- Standards for Use of Technology in Genealogical Research
- Standards for Sharing Information with Others
- Guidelines for Publishing Web Pages on the internet

The first of these is essential reading for anyone new to genealogy. The third is important enough in the context of this book to bear reproducing in full:

Standards for Use of Technology In Genealogical Research
Recommended by the National Genealogical Society
Mindful that computers are tools, genealogists take full responsibility for their work, and therefore they –

- learn the capabilities and limits of their equipment and software, and use them only when they are the most appropriate tools for a purpose.
- refuse to let computer software automatically embellish their work.
- treat compiled information from on-line sources or digital databases like that from other published sources, useful primarily as a guide to locating original records, but not as evidence for a conclusion or assertion.
- accept digital images or enhancements of an original record as a satisfactory substitute for the original only when there is reasonable assurance that the image accurately reproduces the unaltered original.
- cite sources for data obtained on-line or from digital media with the same care that is appropriate for sources on paper and other traditional media, and enter data into a digital database only when its source can remain associated with it.
- always cite the sources for information or data posted on-line or sent to others, naming the author of a digital file as its immediate source, while crediting original sources cited within the file.
- preserve the integrity of their own databases by evaluating the reliability of downloaded data before incorporating it into their own files.
- provide, whenever they alter data received in digital form, a description of the change that will accompany the altered data whenever it is shared with others.
- actively oppose the proliferation of error, rumor and fraud by personally verifying or correcting information, or noting it as unverified, before passing it on to others.
- treat people on-line as courteously and civilly as they would treat them face-to-face, not separated by networks and anonymity.
- accept that technology has not changed the principles of genealogical research, only some of the procedures.

Using on-line information

The nature of the primary data on-line has an important implication for how you use information found on the internet: you need to be very cautious about inferences drawn from it. For a start, *all* transcriptions of any size contain errors – the only question is how many. Where information comes from parish registers, you need to be cautious about identifying an individual ancestor from a single record in an on-line database. The fact that you have found a baptism with the right name, at about the right date and in about the right place, does not mean you have found an ancestor. How do you know this child did not die two weeks later; how do you know there is not a very similar baptism in a neighbouring parish whose records are not on-line; how do you know there is not an error in the transcription? As more records are put on-line, particularly where images of the records accompany transcriptions, the last question may become less important, but no future internet development will allow you to ignore the other questions.

Unfortunately, the very ease of the internet can sometimes make beginners think that constructing a pedigree is easier than it is. It is not enough to find a plausible-looking baptism on-line. You have to be able to demonstrate that this must be (not just 'could be') the same individual who marries 20 years later or who is the parent of a particular child. The internet does not do this for you. It can only provide *some* of the material you need for that proof, and even then you will have to be more careful with on-line material than you would be with original records.

In particular, negative inferences (for example so and so wasn't born later than such and such a date) can be very important in constructing a family tree, but the original material on the internet will rarely allow you to make such inferences. Only where a particular set of public records has been put on-line in its entirety could you start to be confident in drawing a negative inference. For example, an ancestor apparently missing from the 1901 census was either not alive at the time, or was living abroad, or is in the census but has been mistranscribed in the index, or was in the census until the relevant enumeration book went missing. Of course, such problems relate to all indexes, not just those on-line, but you can never be *more* confident about on-line records.

Also, you need to be very cautious about drawing conclusions based not on primary sources but on compiled pedigrees put on-line by other genealogists. Some of these represent careful genealogical work and come with detailed documentation of sources, others may just have a name and possible birth date – insufficient detail to be of any value. You should regard such materials as helpful pointers to someone who might have useful information, or to particular sources you have not yet examined yourself. You should never simply incorporate the information in your own pedigree simply because it appears to refer to an individual you have already identified as an ancestor.

Copyright and privacy

The internet makes it very easy to disseminate information, but just because you *can* disseminate material it does not mean that you *should*. Both web sites and e-mail messages are treated by the law as publications. If you include material you did not create, you may be infringing someone's copyright by doing so. Of course, genealogical facts themselves are not subject to copyright, but the particular formulation in an original record will be and a compilation of facts in a database is also protected.

This means you should not put on your own web site, upload to a database, or post to a mailing list:

- Material you have extracted from on-line or CD-ROM databases
- Material scanned from books that are still in copyright
- Genealogical data you have received from others (unless they give their permission of course)

There is a exemption of 'fair use' which allows some copying, but this is for purposes of criticism or private study, not for republishing. Extracting a single record from a CD-ROM and e-mailing it to an individual is probably OK, but posting the same information to a mailing list, which means it will be permanently archived, is not. A number of people have been shocked to find their own genealogical databases submitted to an on-line pedigree database without their knowledge. Mark Howells covers these issues very thoroughly in 'Share and Beware – Sharing Genealogy in the Information Age' at <www.oz.net/~markhow/writing/share.htm>. Barbara A. Brown discusses the dissemination of 'dishonest research' in 'Restoring Ethics to Genealogy' at <www.iigs.org/newsletter/9904news/ethics.htm.en >.

The recently revised Crown Copyright rules, however, mean that you *can* include extracts from unpublished material held by the PRO (see 'Crown Copyright in the Information Age' at <www.hmso.gov.uk/document/cfuture.htm>). In general, you should have no qualms about the textual content of other historical material over 150 years old, but with images of documents you are on less firm ground, particularly if an image comes from a microfilm. If in doubt, consult the repository concerned.

David Hawgood's 'Copyright for Family Historians' at <www.genuki.org.uk/org/Copyright.html> offers some guidance tailored for genealogists, while for more general information, there is the official government-sponsored web site on copyright at <www.intellectual-property.gov.uk>.

Avoid publishing material about living people without their permission. It is probably not an infringement of the Data Protection Act if the information is drawn from public sources such as birth certificates, but many people still regard it as an invasion of privacy. Most genealogy databases have facilities for filtering out living people from a web family tree (if in doubt just exclude everyone born less than 100 years ago). The on-line pedigree databases either do this automatically or insist that you do so before submitting. Myra Vanderpool Gormley discusses the issues in 'Exposing Our Families To The Internet' at **<www.ancestry.com/home/ Myra_Vanderpool_Gormley/Shaking_Family_Tree06-19-97.htm>**.

Digitization

Quite apart from the obvious facts that more and more genealogists are getting on-line and more of the people who are on-line are getting interested in genealogy, a large number of major, well-funded projects are under way to put British records on the Web. As little as two years ago almost none of the material discussed in Chapter 4 was available on the internet. There is now the prospect that within a few years all General Register Office indexes and census records over 100 years old will be on-line.

What is more difficult to assess is whether, and when, other material will be put on-line. It is easy to see that there is a market for census records; and it is easy to see the rationale for projects like Access to Archives **<www.pro.gov.uk/archives/A2A/>** to make catalogues available on-line from Lottery funding. But it is more difficult to see how county record offices, say, could fund the digitization of material with a more limited appeal. The limitation on digitization is not technical; it is the amount of manpower required to transcribe handwritten documents. Barring a dramatic breakthrough in handwriting recognition, it would be optimistic to expect this situation to change, so it will be a matter of funding and potential income.

However, it is worth pointing out that genealogists make up a sizeable and growing constituency, and there is no reason why substantial Lottery grants should not be forthcoming to fund digitization projects if archives and genealogical organizations can draft the required proposals.

'Shy' data

There is an awful lot of genealogical data that *could* be on-line, material which has already been digitized – data held on a computer for lookups to be done or sold commercially on CD-ROM.

There are good reasons why data-owners should be reluctant to publish this material on-line. It is not yet straightforward for small organizations (whether charitable or commercial), who depend on such data for all or part of their income, to set up a pay-per-view or subscription system on the internet. Until such systems are available, or there are commercial sites which will host the data and pass on a royalty, it would be unreasonable to expect individual researchers or family history societies to make it available on-line. Particularly now that CD-ROM publication is so cheap and straightforward, it is understandable if people feel they have neither the time nor the expertise to explore on-line publication.

However, in the longer term it should be worth it. The benefits of drawing income from genealogists who might not be willing to buy a CD-ROM in the hope of finding one or two relevant records, but who would pay an on-line charge to retrieve them when located by a free index, should not be underestimated. Societies who make some of their material available on-line free to members could expect to see an increase in membership income.

Finding material

While every increase in the amount of genealogical material on the internet must be welcomed, information is not much use if you cannot find it. Search engines are already able to capture only a fraction of the material on the Web. As the amount of material increases the successfulness of search engines looks likely to decline further unless there is a significant breakthrough in searching technology. Web sites of individual genealogists, in particular, will become harder to find. In addition, the increasing amount of data held in on-line databases is not discoverable by search engines.

Another problem is the increasing number of sites with surname resources, making it impossible to check *everywhere* for others who share your interests. It is difficult to see how this situation can do anything but deteriorate.

The quality of indexing provided by search engines is limited by the poor facilities currently available for marking up text in HTML with semantic information. Search engines cannot tell that Kent is a surname in 'Clark Kent' but a place name in 'Maidstone, Kent' because web authors have no way of indicating this using HTML. As so many British surnames are the names of places or occupations, this is a significant problem for genealogists.

The situation could improve when XML starts to be used widely on the Web, since this would allow the development of a special markup language for genealogical information. However, such a development (and its retrospective application to material already published on the Web) is some way off and will require considerable work.[11]

---

[11] See Michael H. Kay's 'GedML: Genealogical Data in XML' at <users.iclway. co.uk/mhkay/gedml/>.

Looking ahead

Nothing that happens on the internet in the next decades is going to affect what genealogists need to do: consult records and share information. The internet is not going to 'automate' family history. What will change is its usefulness for these activities, the amount of data it holds and the number of people with shared interests who use it. Perhaps in 100 years, when the late 20th century's digital data is available *only* on-line, it will be impossible to do genealogy without the internet. The fact that the 1901 census is going to be available mainly via the internet is already a pointer in that direction. But there is nothing wrong with the traditional methods of genealogy. What the internet has revolutionized is not the process of genealogy, but the ease with which some aspects of it can be carried out.

Internet Glossary

Adobe Acrobat	A file format, popular for documents which need to be made available on-line with fixed formatting. Adobe distributes a free Acrobat reader (see <www.adobe.com>). Files have the extension .pdf, and so the term 'PDF' file is often used.
charter	The description of the aims and coverage of a newsgroup.
client	A piece of software on a user's computer which connects to a server to retrieve or submit data, e.g. your e-mail software is an e-mail client which connects to your provider's e-mail server; your browser is a 'web client'.
database	A collection of individual items of information ('records') which can be retrieved selectively via a search facility.
dataset	A collection of data, usually from a single source, held in a database.
directory	1. A collection of links to internet resources, arranged in a hierarchy of subject headings. 2. On some operating systems, a hierarchical folder containing individual computer files.
FAQ	Frequently Asked Questions; a document listing common questions in a particular area, along with answers.
flame	A rude or abusive message.
FTP	File Transfer Protocol; a method of transferring files across the internet.
gateway	1. A subject-specific directory. 2. A link between two different systems, e.g. newsgroups and mailing lists.
GIF	A graphics file format, mainly used on the Web for graphic design elements and not suitable for colour photographs.
hit	A matching item retrieved in response to a search.
HTML	HyperText Markup Language, in which web pages are written.

ISP	Internet Service Provider.
JPEG	A graphics file format, mainly used for photographs.
mailing list	A discussion forum which uses e-mail.
meta-search engine	A site which automatically submits a search to a number of different search engines.
netiquette	The informal, consensual rules of on-line communication.
newsgroup	Open discussion forums held on an internet-wide network of 'news servers'.
portal	A collection of internet resources for a particular audience – see the discussion on p. 11.
robot	A piece of software that trawls the internet looking for new resources, used by search engines to create their indexes.
search engine	Commonly, a site which has a searchable index of web pages, though more accurately *any* piece of software that searches an index.
searchbot	A piece of software that searches the Web for you (short for 'search robot').
server	A computer, usually with a permanent internet connection, that responds to requests from a client for data. There are different types of server according to the service offered, e.g. mail server, web server, list server.
spam	Unsolicited messages sent to many recipients.
subscribe	To join a mailing list.
URL	Uniform Resource Locator, a standard way of referring to internet resources so that each resource has a unique name. In the case of a web page, the URL is the same as the web address.
World Wide Web	A collection of linked pages of information retrieval via the internet.
XML	eXtensible Markup Language, a more sophisticated and flexible markup language than HTML (q.v.), likely to be increasingly used for web sites.

For a glossary of genealogy terms see the 'A-Z Of British Genealogical Research' at <www.genuki.org.uk/big/EmeryPaper.html>.

Bibliography

Anthony J. Camp, *First Steps in Family History*, 3rd edn (Society of Genealogists, 1998).

Peter Christian, *Web Publishing for Genealogy*, 2nd edn (David Hawgood, 1999).

David Hawgood, *Family Search on the Internet* (David Hawgood, 1998).

David Hawgood, *Genuki* (Federation of Family History Societies, 2000); full text on-line at <www.hawgood.co.uk/genuki/>.

Mark Herber, *Ancestral Trails* (Sutton, 1997).

Cyndi Howells, *Cyndi's List* (Genealogical Publishing Company, 1999; 2nd edn, 2 volumes, 2001).

Reader's Digest, *Explore Your Family's Past* (Reader's Digest, 2000).

Virginia Shea, *Netiquette* (Albion Books, 1994); full text on-line at <www.albion.com/netiquette.book/>.

Richard S. Wilson, *Publishing Your Family History on the Internet* (Writers Digest Books, 1999).

Subject Index

Web sites devoted to particular topics are not listed individually – consult the relevant subject heading.